# Public–Private Partnerships Po...  W9-BYW-949

## A Reference Guide

WITHDRAWN

Edited by

HK Yong

Commonwealth Secretariat
Marlborough House
Pall Mall
London SW1Y 5HX
United Kingdom

© Commonwealth Secretariat 2010

Published by the Commonwealth Secretariat
Edited by Wayzgoose
Designed by S.J.I. Services, New Delhi
Cover design by Tattersall Hammarling and Silk
Index by Indexing Specialists (UK) Ltd
Printed by Hobbs the Printers Ltd, Totton, Hampshire

The draft of this Reference Guide was prepared by Cambridge Economic Policy Associates Ltd (CEPA), a London-based economic and finance advisory firm (www.cepa.co.uk), for the Commonwealth Secretariat. Views and opinions expressed in this publication are the responsibility of the authors and should in no way be attributed to the institutions to which they are affiliated or to the Commonwealth Secretariat.

Wherever possible, the Commonwealth Secretariat uses paper sourced from sustainable forests or from sources that minimise a destructive impact on the environment.

Copies of this publication may be obtained from

Publications Section
Commonwealth Secretariat
Marlborough House
Pall Mall
London SW1Y 5HX
United Kingdom
Tel: +44 (0)20 7747 6534
Fax: +44 (0)20 7839 9081
Email: publications@commonwealth.int
Web: www.thecommonwealth.org/publications

A catalogue record for this publication is available from the British Library.

ISBN (paperback): 978-1-84929-020-3
ISBN (e-book): 978-1-84859-069-4

# Foreword

Historically, the public sector in Commonwealth countries has been the main provider of basic service delivery and infrastructure. However, large fiscal deficits have limited governments' capacity to meet growing infrastructure needs and have emerged as a major constraint to member countries' efforts to improve their investment climate. To augment limited public resources for infrastructure, private sector participation must be encouraged by creating an enabling environment for increased private sector involvement. Governments of most Commonwealth countries have been turning towards the private sector as a means of financing infrastructure development through Public–Private Partnerships (PPPs).

The Governance and Institutional Development Division of the Commonwealth Secretariat has responsibility for the Secretariat's mandate on public sector development. Its work covers the full spectrum of public sector administration and management. This book, *Public–Private Partnerships Policy and Practice: A Reference Guide*, augments our ongoing work on the Commonwealth PPP Network, an initiative to link senior public sector PPP policy-makers and practitioners from our member countries to each other, to PPP knowledge and resource centres, and to potential private sector investors.

It is recognised that PPP practices are ever evolving, and that there are already many excellent guides on some of these practices, many of which go into great detail. This book is structured with references and links to these guides and other external sources of current information and guidance to which readers can refer. It also offers practical lessons and emerging best practices from a range of case studies on successful and failed projects, and discusses recent experiences with PPPs in some Commonwealth developing countries.

The Secretariat is grateful to Cambridge Economic Policy Associates Limited for collaborating with us on this book. Thanks are also due to Guy Bentham of the Secretariat's Communications and Public Affairs Division for his support and co-ordination with HK Yong in bringing out this book.

**John Wilkins**
Acting Director and Head of Thematic Programme Group
Governance and Institutional Development Division
Commonwealth Secretariat

# Contents

# List of Tables

# List of Figures

# List of Boxes

# List of Abbreviations

| | |
|---|---|
| ADB | Asian Development Bank |
| ADR | Alternative Dispute Resolution |
| AfDB | African Development Bank |
| AICD | Africa Infrastructure Country Diagnostic |
| ALA | Asia and Latin America |
| BOO | Build-own-operate |
| BOT | Build-operate-transfer |
| BPDB | Bangladesh Power Development Board |
| CAPEX | Capital expenditure |
| CER | Certified emission reduction |
| CG | Comprehensive guarantee |
| DBB | Design-bid-build |
| DBFO | Design-build-finance-operate |
| DFI | Development Finance Institution |
| DFID | Department for International Development (UK) |
| EAIF | Emerging Africa Infrastructure Fund |
| EAP | East Asia and Pacific |
| EBRD | European Bank for Reconstruction and Development |
| ECA | Europe and Central Asia |
| ECG | Export credit guarantee |
| EIB | European Investment Bank |
| EPC | Engineering-procurement-construction |
| FEMIP | Euro-Mediterranean Investment and Partnership |
| FMO | Development Finance Company (The Netherlands) |
| GDP | Gross domestic product |
| GPOBA | Global Partnership for Output-Based Aid |
| GTZ | German Agency for Technical Cooperation |
| IBRD | International Bank for Reconstruction and Development |
| ICA | Infrastructure Consortium for Africa |
| ICF | Infrastructure Crisis Facility |
| IDA | International Development Association |
| IDB | Inter-American Development Bank |
| IFC | International Finance Corporation |
| IFI | International Financial Institution |

| | |
|---|---|
| IIFC | Infrastructure Investment Facilitation Centre (Bangladesh) |
| IPFF | Investment Promotion and Financing Facility (Bangladesh) |
| IPP | Independent power project |
| IRR | Internal rate of return |
| JEXIM | Export-Import Bank of Japan |
| KPI | Key performance indicator |
| kWh | Kilowatt hour |
| LAC | Latin America and Caribbean |
| LDC | Least developed country |
| MCA | Model concession agreement |
| MENA | Middle East and North Africa |
| MI | Micro-finance institution |
| MIGA | Multilateral Investment Guarantee Agency |
| MoF | Ministry of Finance |
| MW | Mega watt |
| NPV | Net present value |
| OBA | Output-based sid |
| OECD | Organisation for Economic Co-operation and Development |
| PFI | Private Finance Initiative |
| PFMA | Public Finance Management Act (South Africa) |
| PICOM | Private Infrastructure Committee (Bangladesh) |
| PIDG | Private Infrastructure Development Group |
| PPA | Power purchase agreement |
| PPIAF | Public–private Infrastructure Advisory Facility |
| PPP | Public–private partnership |
| PRC | Public–private Partnership Resource Centre |
| PRG | Political risk guarantee |
| PRG | Partial risk guarantee |
| PRI | Political risk insurance |
| PSC | Public sector comparator |
| PSIG | Private Sector Infrastructure Guidelines (Bangladesh) |
| SAR | South Asia region |
| SME | Small and medium-sized enterprise |
| SPV | Special purpose vehicle |
| SSIP | Small-scale infrastructure programme |
| SSA | Sub-Saharan Africa |
| TAF | Technical Assistance Facility |
| VfM | Value for money |
| VGF | Viability Gap Fund |

# 1

# Overview of the Reference Guide

*Public–Private Partnerships Policy and Practice* is a comprehensive reference manual on public–private partnership (PPP) theory and practice. It aims to be a practical and user-friendly handbook for senior policy-makers and other public sector officials in Commonwealth developing countries. The Reference Guide focuses on the key lessons learned – and emerging best practice – from successful and failed PPP transactions over the past 30 years (see Box 1.1 for a summary of the key lessons learned on best practice in infrastructure PPPs).

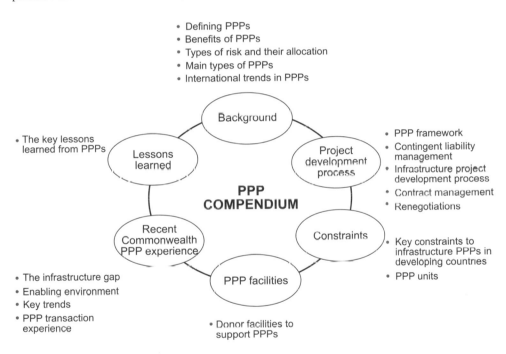

**Figure 1.1.** Overview of the PPP Reference Guide

The Reference Guide refrains from using the extensive 'jargon' on PPPs, but instead attempts to explain relevant concepts in terms suitable for the non-specialist. Key points are summarised at the beginning of each section and are useful for providing an overall high-level outline. References are provided throughout the text and at the end of each section which allow the reader to access further information on specific issues.

Box 1.1. Summary of key lessons learned on best practice on infrastructure PPPs

**Lesson 1: PPPs should be designed with sustainability and value for money (VfM) considerations in mind.**

- Robust feasibility analysis is essential for successful PPPs. Many projects have failed where governments and/or sponsors were over-optimistic about future revenues.

- Proper due diligence is required when selecting a private sector sponsor. Weak sponsors lacking relevant experience significantly increase the risk of project failure.

- Even in cases where private finance is available, a PPP approach may not be the optimal solution if sustainability and value for money cannot be assured. Particular attention needs to be paid to the affordability of user fees.

**Lesson 2: PPPs should be viewed as long-term commercial relationships between the public and private sectors, not one-off procurement exercises.**

- The public sector has an important ongoing role beyond the financing stage ('financial close') of a project to ensure that desired long-term outcomes are achieved.

- Establishing a flexible PPP framework helps establish the 'rules of the game' under which the public and private sectors can interact successfully over the lifetime of a contract.

- The public sector needs staff with appropriate business skills and experience in order to manage the relationship with the private sector effectively.

**Lesson 3: PPPs are inherently complex, costly and time-consuming to develop properly. A rushed project often becomes a failed project.**

- PPPs require high-level political support, especially during the project development stage to help overcome the typical obstacles that PPP projects encounter.

- It is important to manage political expectations about the time it takes to design and execute a PPP project properly (the project development phase from concept to financial close typically takes from three to four years).

- Expert legal, financial and technical advice is expensive, but essential to ensure proper project design. At the same time, governments should build in-house capacity to manage third-party advisers effectively.

Public–Private Partnerships Policy and Practice

# 2

# Introduction

.....................................................................................................................................................................

Over the past two decades, delivery of infrastructure services through the private sector, often referred to as PPP, has become an established means of providing essential services, such as power, transport and water supply, which were previously seen as the exclusive responsibility of governments. The fact that PPPs continue to spread around the world (for example, in states with socialist or communist governments, such as the Indian state of West Bengal or the People's Republic of Vietnam) and into new sectors (for example health and education) suggests that on balance they are seen as a successful way of raising capital and delivering better quality public services.

The debate about PPPs has moved beyond ideological arguments about the pros and cons of partnering with the private sector. It is now widely recognised that PPPs can be structured to achieve a range of public policy goals, including providing services to those who can least afford to pay for them (thus addressing one of the common misconceptions about PPPs, which is that they always involve increases in user charges). To fulfil their potential benefits, however, PPP projects must be designed to deliver specific performance improvements within a framework that shares costs and risks appropriately between the public and private sectors.

Three important themes run through this Reference Guide:

*   PPPs are long-term commercial partnerships between the public and private sectors. This definition of PPPs matters because it distinguishes PPPs from outsourcing arrangements and privatisations. Viewing PPPs as commercial partnerships, rather than as purely contractual relationships, has wide-ranging implications for how PPP programmes are designed and implemented.

*   The benefits of PPPs are much broader than accessing private capital. PPPs can help governments overcome short-term fiscal constraints; but their long-term benefits should be the delivery of improved infrastructure services at lower cost. Getting the early design of PPPs right is critical to ensure that these long-term 'value for money' benefits are realised.

*   PPPs can deliver significant benefits in terms of increased quality and quantity of infrastructure services, often at a lower overall cost compared to public sector provision. On the other hand, when PPPs fail, the financial, social and political costs can be very high. There are no short cuts to good project development; taking the time to get the early design of PPPs right is essential when there is so much at stake.

Three decades of global experience provides valuable lessons about what works and what does not, and points to some emerging best practices in infrastructure PPPs. Drawing on that experience, this Reference Guide aims to be a practical guide and information resource on PPPs, with particular relevance for developing countries. While the term 'best practice' is contentious – given that best practices evolve and change over time and may not be relevant in all circumstances – the Reference Guide aims to draw out the key lessons learned from successful and failed PPP transactions.

The Guide covers the following areas:

• A high-level review of theory and recent trends on PPPs;

• An identification of the main constraints to PPPs in developing countries and useful initiatives/measures adopted by different countries to deal with these constraints;

• A description of the growing number of international donor-funded project development and financing facilities that are available to help address specific constraints on PPPs in emerging markets; and

• Practical lessons and emerging best practices from a range of case studies on successful and failed projects.

As the title implies, another objective of the Guide is to be a trustworthy directory to the best resources on PPPs, allowing the reader to research specific topics in more depth. There are many excellent guides to PPPs available in print and on the internet, many of which go into more detail than space allows here. Boxes are provided throughout the text with references/links to external sources.

The rest of the Reference Guide is structured as follows:

• **Section 3** introduces the key definitions and concepts relevant to PPPs. The benefits of PPPs are discussed, together with an analysis of the evidence on value for money assessments of PPPs. The section also describes the evolution of PPP theory and practice over time from its origins in OECD countries, as well as current trends in developing countries.

• **Section 4** describes the overall PPP framework, including the policy, legal, regulatory and institutional framework, and the main lessons that can be learned from the experience of different countries. The section discusses the PPP project development process in detail, providing information on the different stages and the main activities, as well as an indication of the time and costs involved. Some issues for PPP portfolio management, including contingent liability management, contract management and monitoring, and renegotiations, are also discussed in this section.

• **Section 5** discusses the key issues and constraints faced by developing countries in structuring, developing, financing and operating PPPs. Experience in tackling some of these constraints through the establishment of PPP units and/or other types of government intervention is also discussed.

- **Section 6** describes donor-backed initiatives designed to address PPP constraints in developing countries, including project preparation facilities, financing facilities, guarantee facilities and project funding facilities.

- **Section 7** discusses recent experience with infrastructure PPPs in Commonwealth developing countries, and also provides a brief background to the infrastructure gap and state of the enabling environment for PPPs in those countries. Some specific PPP experience across the core infrastructure sectors as well as selected countries is discussed.

- Finally, **Section 8** summarises the key lessons learned on PPPs.

The main Reference Guide is supported by annexes that provide further data.

- **Annex 1** provides some frequently asked questions (FAQs) on infrastructure PPPs.

- **Annex 2** describes the overall trends in PPPs and private sector participation in infrastructure in general in low- and middle-income countries; trends are discussed by region, by country and by sector, as well as the overall trends in failed projects.

- **Annex 3** provides some useful published indicators for Commonwealth developing countries on the infrastructure gap and the enabling environment.

- **Annex 4** provides detailed tables on donor-backed PPP facilities for project preparation, infrastructure financing and guarantees.

- **Annex 5** describes some select case studies of infrastructure PPPs, deriving the key issues and lessons learned from their experience.

- **Annex 6** is a technical glossary.

# 3

# Background to PPPs: concepts and key trends

## Summarising the section

- A PPP is a long-term commercial arrangement for the delivery of public services, where there is a significant degree of risk-sharing between the public and private sectors. What distinguishes a PPP from other forms of private participation in infrastructure (e.g. outsourcing) is the greater degree of risk-sharing between the two parties.

- PPPs offer a number of benefits, including being a mechanism for financing infrastructure development despite government fiscal constraints. In addition, PPPs can help achieve value for money by transferring risks and costs to the private sector. Maximising VfM in a PPP arrangement depends on attracting the right quality partners, ensuring competitive pressure in the bidding process and designing a long-term contract with the right incentives for the private sector to deliver quality improvements and efficiency gains.

- The concept of 'risk' in a PPP is central. It relates to uncertainty regarding the occurrence of certain events and their consequent impact on the project. The cost of managing different project risks needs to be borne by someone, and one of the core elements of the design of a PPP is appropriate risk allocation.

- The essential principle for risk allocation in a PPP is to accord the risk to the party who can best manage it (usually the party that can do so at the lowest cost). The management of risks is a complex process and needs to be reviewed throughout the life of the project.

- PPP is not a new concept. Collaboration between the public and private sectors in the delivery of infrastructure services has been in existence in various forms for over 200 years. More recently, the trends in private participation in infrastructure in developing countries has exhibited a marked increase, both in terms of the number of projects and their diversity.

This section provides a definition of PPPs and summarises the potential benefits of PPP approaches, including an analysis of the evidence on whether or not PPPs have delivered value for money for taxpayers and consumers. The main types of PPP models are described, followed by a discussion of the different types of risks involved in PPPs and how they should be allocated to the public or private sector. Finally, the section explains how PPP theory and practice have evolved over time, including how PPP approaches are increasingly being adopted in developing countries in the Commonwealth. The analysis is supported by a broader consideration of trends in Annex 2.

## 3.1. Defining PPPs

PPPs are long-term contractual arrangements between the public and private sectors for the delivery of public services. The defining feature of PPPs, as against other forms of private participation in infrastructure, is that there is a significant degree of risk sharing between the two parties. Put simply, risk sharing means that both the government and the investors will suffer financially if the contract fails. The benefits of PPPs, discussed in more detail below, come about because both parties are incentivised to ensure that the contract is a success over the full project life. The *degree* of benefits largely depends on how well risks are allocated between the public and private sector and how strongly the incentives are built into the contract.

A PPP is a long-term contractual arrangement for the delivery of public services where there is a *significant degree of risk sharing between the public and private sectors.*

The main features of a PPP include:

- **Risk transfer:** The key element of a PPP contract is the transfer of risk from the public to the private sector. The principle behind this risk transfer is that risk should be allocated to the party that can best manage it. Within the suite of PPP contracts, certain risks relating to the design, construction and operation of the infrastructure are transferred to the private sector, where it has a greater capacity (e.g. financial resources) and ability (e.g. skills and expertise) to mitigate the losses arising from the risks. Section 3.3 provides a detailed discussion on the types of risks and their allocation.

- **Long-term contract:** A PPP usually follows a 'whole-of-life' approach to the development of the infrastructure, thus requiring the contract to be long term in nature. A PPP is typically for a period of 10 to 20 years – although there are some PPPs that may be of a shorter duration of, say, three to five years.

- **Partnership agreement:** Key to this long-term contract between the public and private sectors is that it is viewed as a 'partnership', in that both parties have a mutual interest and a unified commitment. PPPs represent co-operation between the public and private sectors, drawing on the relative strengths of each party, in order to establish a complementary relationship between them.

Many types of private sector participation in the delivery of public services are not 'true' PPPs. For example, governments outsource basic services such as rubbish collection or street cleaning to private sector providers, often on a relatively short-term basis (e.g. two to three years). In these cases the government retains almost 100 per cent of the risk involved in delivering services to the public, so the commercial arrangement cannot really be described as a PPP. At the other end of the spectrum are privatisations and divestitures where governments transfer responsibility for asset construction and ownership, service delivery and revenue collection to private owners (there are many examples of this in the telecoms sector). In these cases, the private sector bears most, if not all, the risks involved.

The approaches and expertise needed to see a PPP project through from design to successful implementation are very different from those appropriate for outsourcing contracts or privatisations. Indeed, a key lesson from the case studies presented in the Reference Guide is that governments need to view PPPs as an ongoing commercial relationship with a private sector partner, not as a one-off procurement or sales transaction. This has implications for how governments design the institutional framework for PPPs and what type of technical capacity is needed, an issue discussed in Section 4.

It is important to note that the use of the term PPP differs widely across countries and organisations. Box 3.1 provides some examples of definitions of PPPs used around the world. As can be seen, many organisations adopt a broad definition of PPPs. A form of PPP that has been widely used in the UK context is the private finance initiative (PFI). Box 3.2 discusses the concept of PFI as a form of PPP.

---

**Box 3.1. Definitions of PPPs worldwide**

There is no universally accepted definition of a PPP; its exact meaning differs between countries and organisations, and over time. Below are some definitions that are used in practice, many of which are broader than the definition used in this Reference Guide.

**Infrastructure Australia – National PPP Guidelines**

' ... defined as being where:

- the private sector provides public infrastructure and any related services; and
- there is private investment or financing.

'PPPs as a procurement method are part of a broader spectrum of contractual relationships between the public and private sectors to produce an asset and/or deliver a service. They are distinct from early contractor involvement, alliancing, managing contractor, traditional procurement (design and construct) and other procurement methods.

'Compared with other infrastructure delivery methods that are focused on design and construction, PPPs are typically complex given their lengthy contract periods involving long-term obligations and a sharing of risks and rewards between the private and public sectors.'

*Infrastructure Australia, 'National PPP Guidelines: Policy Framework' (2008).*

*http://www.infrastructureaustralia.gov.au/files/National_PPP_Policy_Framework_Dec_08.pdf*

**Government of India, Department of Economic Affairs**

'Partnership between a public sector entity (Sponsoring Authority) and a private sector entity (a legal entity in which 51% or more of equity is with the private partner/s) for the creation and/or management of infrastructure for public purpose for a specified period of time (concession period) on commercial terms and in which the private partner has been procured through a transparent and open procurement system.'

*Department of Economic Affairs, Ministry of Finance, Government of India, 'Public Private Partnerships: Creating an Enabling Environment for State Projects' (2007).*

*http://assamppp.gov.in/adb-dea.pdf*

---

**National Treasury PPP Unit (South Africa) – Treasury Regulation 16 of Public Finance Management Act**

' ... public–private partnership means a commercial transaction between an institution and a private party in terms of which the private party –

(a) performs an institutional function on behalf of the institution; and/or

(b) acquires the use of state property for its own commercial purposes; and

(c) assumes substantial financial, technical and operational risks in connection with the performance of the institutional function and/or use of state property; and

(d) receives a benefit for performing the institutional function or from utilizing the state property ... '

*South Africa National Treasury, Public Private Partnership Manual (2001).*
*http://www.ppp.gov.za/Documents/Manual/Module%2001.pdf*

**Public–private Infrastructure Advisory Facility (PPIAF)**

'A public–private partnership (PPP) involves the private sector in aspects of the provision of infrastructure assets or of new or existing infrastructure services that have traditionally been provided by the government.'

*PPIAF, 'What are Public–private Partnerships' webpage, http://www.ppiaf.org/content/view/118/153/*

**HM Treasury, UK**

'Public private partnerships (PPPs) are arrangements typified by joint working between the public and private sector. In the broadest sense, PPPs can cover all types of collaboration across the interface between the public and private sectors to deliver policies, services and infrastructure. Where delivery of public services involves private sector investment in infrastructure, the most common form of PPP is the Private finance initiative.'

*HM Treasury, Public private partnerships homepage, http://www.hm-treasury.gov.uk/ppp_index.htm*

---

**Box 3.2. The difference between PPPs and PFIs**

The private finance initiative relates to a UK government initiative on PPPs. A PFI contract is a form of PPP where, in its most common form, the private sector designs, builds, finances and operates (DBFO) facilities based on 'output' specifications decided by the public sector. Under a PFI contract, the public sector does not own the asset, but pays the PFI contractor a stream of committed revenue payments for the use of the facilities during the contract period. Once the contract has expired, the ownership of the assets either remains with the private sector contractor or is returned to the public sector, as per the original terms of the contract.

The term PFI has also sometimes been used in a misleading manner to refer to all PPPs in the UK. It should actually refer only to those PPP contracts where the private sector performs the DBFO functions and in return receives a fixed payment stream from the government.

The PFI-type model has mainly been applied to social infrastructure projects such as schools and hospitals in the UK. Its applicability bears direct relevance to the UK government policy on these social infrastructure services being regarded as merit goods.

There is a question as to the direct applicability of the PFI model to developing countries, stemming from two key issues: (i) the capacity of developing country governments to provide a regular payment stream to the PFI contractor; and (ii) the poor creditworthiness of some governments for private investors and therefore the higher cost of capital and concomitant impact on the value for money of the potential contract.

## 3.2. Benefits of PPPs

Governments around the word have embraced PPPs because they offer three main types of benefits:

- The ability to **develop new infrastructure services** despite short-term fiscal constraints;

- **Value for money** through efficiencies in procurement, construction and operation; and

- Improved **service quality and innovation** through use of private sector expertise and performance incentives.

### Accelerated infrastructure development

Many governments around the world are constrained in terms of how much they can borrow to invest in infrastructure projects. This is especially true for greenfield developments, such as a new power station or major toll road, which typically involve hundreds of millions of dollars of upfront capital expenditure. The problem is most acute in poorer countries, where infrastructure needs are large relative to the size of economies and where fiscal capacity is often severely limited, with many competing demands for scarce resources.

In these situations, PPPs offer a way of bringing forward a programme of infrastructure investments, since projects can be financed from private capital markets with the cost repaid over the lifetime of the assets. For example, a toll road might be financed by a consortium of private debt and equity investors who are repaid over a period of 20 to 30 years through a combination of user charges and annual payments from the government. As a result, governments can avoid directly accumulating excessive debt burdens which could crowd out private sector investment in other areas of the economy.

Access to capital is often the primary reason cited by policy-makers for wanting to encourage PPPs. But it would be wrong to see PPPs as no more than a sophisticated financing mechanism. In fact, as discussed further below, VfM and improved service quality are likely to prove more important benefits in the long run, as evidenced by the fact that even governments that are not fiscally constrained (e.g. Singapore) choose to implement PPPs. A common mistake when designing PPPs is for policy-makers to focus too much attention on raising finance, while ignoring other essential design issues that can influence whether or not VfM is achieved.

### Value for money

PPPs allow the government to transfer certain types of costs and risks of infrastructure projects to the private sector. This can help achieve VfM because in theory the private sector brings specialist expertise and a commercial approach that helps drive down project costs over the whole life of the contract. Many studies have shown, for example, that the private sector outperforms governments in delivering large construction projects without major delays or cost over-runs. If the PPP is properly designed at the outset, these efficiency gains are passed on to the end-consumer. A related benefit is that governments and the taxpayer are given increased certainty about the total cost of infrastructure projects, because risks of cost over-runs are either reduced or passed on to private investors.

Of course, the level of efficiency gains achieved by involving the private sector must be weighed against the costs of developing a PPP project (a typical large infrastructure development might involve third-party legal and advisory fees in the region of US$5 million or more) and the requirement to pay investors a financial return that will generally exceed the government's own cost of borrowing.[1] Maximising VfM in a PPP arrangement depends on attracting the right quality partners, ensuring competitive pressure in the bidding process and designing a long-term contract with the right incentives for the private sector to deliver the required efficiency gains (see Box 3.3). In some cases, the judgement may be that public provision remains the best option.

A final point to emphasise is that VfM is about more than driving costs down to the lowest possible level. It involves the reliable delivery of quality services over the life-time of the contract. There is a risk that focusing exclusively on cost considerations could lead governments to select bidders who lack the necessary experience to success-fully deliver against the contract, a lesson that is highlighted in Section 8. A focus on cost to the exclusion of other considerations is one of the main criticisms of using a public sector comparator (see Box 3.4). In some cases, the private sector may be able to deliver a service more quickly and to a higher standard, even though the public sector could in theory provide a basic service at lower cost.

---

**Box 3.3. Collapse of the East Coast rail franchise in the UK**

The collapse of the East Cost rail franchise in the UK in 2009 highlights the importance of getting the incentives right for the private sector to ensure maximum benefits and efficiency gains from a PPP. Lower than anticipated revenues, due to poor revenue forecasts and the impact of recession, meant that National Express could not pay the agreed £1.4 billion in concessions fees to the government. It also appears that National Express assumed the govern-ment would guarantee any losses. As Sir Alan Beith MP said, 'Quite unrealistic expectations were built into the franchise because GNER (Great North Eastern Railway) were so desperate to win the franchise'.[2] However, some argue that the contract was flawed from the outset and the government allowed its judgement to be clouded by the attractiveness of the private sector payments.[3] The UK Government has been strongly against a renegotiation and the contract has been cancelled. Commentators suggest the government's transport budget could suffer a £700 million hit as a result, impeding the progress of other vital projects.

---

**Box 3.4. Value for money assessment and key lessons**

Value for money is a holistic concept that considers the whole package of benefits, costs and risk over the life cycle of a project. Grimsey and Lewis (2004) define it as: '*The optimum combination of whole-of-life cycle costs, risks, completion time and quality in order to meet public requirements*'.[4]

### Methods for VfM assessment

Assessing whether PPP is likely to deliver greater VfM than traditional procurement is controversial, as the comparison process is fraught with difficulty. Several methods can be used, the most detailed of which is full cost-benefit analysis. However, most countries that perform systematic VfM investigations (including the UK, Australia, Ireland, Canada, Japan and the Netherlands) use variations of a Public Sector Comparator (PSC) test, first developed to assess UK PFI projects in the 1990s. The PSC test is a two-stage process where a hypothetical benchmark (risk-adjusted) cost of providing the specified service is calculated, as if it were to be provided by the public sector. The same calculation is made for PPP provision. The respective costs are then compared, with the lowest cost option providing the greatest VfM and judged to be the preferred procurement option. Figure 3.1 shows the key elements of a PSC test.[5]

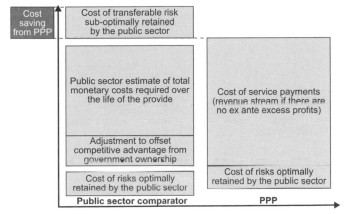

**Figure 3.1.** Illustrative public sector comparator test

Criticisms of the PSC test, as illustrated in Figure 3.1, have grown over time, reducing its credibility as a practical tool. Concerns focus on omissions, arbitrariness, room for discretion and costliness of execution. Takim *et al.* (2009)[6] and Leighland and Shugart (2006)[7] provide critiques of PSC practice in the UK, Australia and Japan. Failures in the UK have led to it being considered as a supporting instrument for VfM assessment, rather than the centrepiece.

### Evidence of VfM

Despite the methodological problems with PSC tests, they can provide some useful information. The results from a sample of analyses are provided in Table 3.1.

**Table 3.1.** Evidence from public sector comparator tests

| Project/meta-study | Saving vs. PSC |
|---|---|
| Fazakerley and Bridgend prisons, UK[8] | 10% |
| Berwick Hospital, Australia[9] | 9% |
| Surrey Outpatient Hospital, Canada[10] | 8.8% |
| LSE and Arthur Anderson (2000) 29 PFIs[11] | 17% |
| National Audit Office, UK (2001) 15 projects[12] | 20% |

Risk adjusted whole-of-life savings compared to the PSC vary between projects and within meta-studies. Although some projects that have gone ahead would have been scored higher if they had been publicly provided, these figures show the scale of benefits that can be achieved when PPP is properly applied. These figures show the benefits that governments can reap if they carefully consider their PPP programme.

Instead of focusing on abstract and flawed concepts of VfM, it can be useful to consider concrete and observable measures of improvements that indicate VfM. Table 3.2 shows the improvement in delivery and cost containment that PPPs have brought in the UK.

Table 3.2 shows that PPPs were both more likely to be ahead of (or on) time and within (or on) budget compared to public projects. These results show how PPP can boost at least two key drivers of VfM. These figures do not show the distribution of outcomes and focus only on upfront costs, but they do provide encouraging evidence, at least in the UK.

**Table 3.2.** National Audit Office results on construction performance of PFI and conventional government procurement projects[13]

|  | PFI projects 2002 NAO census | Government procurement 1999 survey |
| --- | --- | --- |
| On budget | 76% | 30% |
| On time | 78% | 27% |

Surveys of perceptions of VfM can also be useful. In a CEPA (2005)[14] study of PPPs in Scotland, more than half of the public authorities surveyed found that their contracts offered 'good or excellent VfM'. Figure 3.2 shows the public sector perception of VfM at contract letting and then at the point of survey. Despite a reduction in perceptions of VfM over time, only one authority out of 36 found its project to be poor value.

Most of the relevant projects had PSC tests, with an average saving of 13 per cent, reflecting very high savings in some projects.

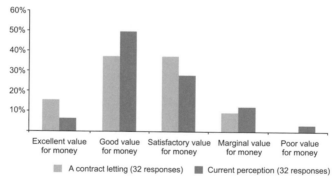

**Figure 3.2.** Public sector perceptions of value for money
*Source: CEPA, 2005*

### Lessons

Considering VfM should be a central part of any procurement process. However, it is important to realise that the benefit of formal VfM analysis is highly contextual. It is telling that the role of PSC analysis has been scaled down in the UK. Formal VfM analysis is rarely used in developing countries. However, this is often inappropriate, as the relevant counterfactual is no service rather than public provision. The most important lesson from VfM assessment is that governments must carefully consider the rationale behind their procurement methods, rather than focusing on potentially spurious analyses.

*Improved service quality*

Linked to the concept of VfM is the potential for innovation and higher service quality. This is partly about the specialist skills brought in by the private sector – for example, a specialist energy company is likely to be able to operate a gas-fired power station more efficiently that a state-owned enterprise. But more importantly, it is about having the right commercial incentives in place to deliver improved performance over the full life of the contract, for example by ensuring proper maintenance of the underlying assets. These are incentives that are typically lacking for the public sector. For example, the Meghnaghat independent power project (IPP) in Bangladesh, a 450-megawatt, combined-cycle, gas-fired power station, has increased power reliability at a reasonable cost in a country where just over 30 per cent of the population have access to electricity.[15]

### 3.2.1. The impact of PPPs on employment

The shift towards cost-reflective prices that occurs under PPP arrangements typically leads to a more sustainable level of employment than under public provision of infrastructure. However, the impact on absolute levels of employment is not completely clear.

In the case of greenfield PPP projects, the impact on employment is clearly positive. For example, the Emerging Africa Infrastructure Fund (EAIF) provides financing for a number of greenfield energy projects in Africa, including in Kenya and Uganda, that will lead to an increase in employment in both the short and long term.[16] What may be contentious is the *relative* positive impact when compared to a public sector counterfactual. Had the government developed and financed the project, it is possible that employment levels would have been higher, but this would need to be weighed against efficiency and sustainability considerations.

The impact of PPPs on employment is less certain when the PPP is based on existing infrastructure assets. For example, in the case of the Manila water concessions, some of the existing staff in the public utility were absorbed by the new private sector contractor, while a large number of staff were transferred from the water utility to the regulator. Hence there was no or minimal negative impact on employment. In addition, with the experience of the Manila water PPP, the private water company is now also bidding on other projects in the region, which could have a further positive impact on employment. However, there are other examples where the introduction of the private sector has led to a reduction in employment, such as the Kenya-Uganda rail concession.

## 3.3. Types of risk and their allocation

Risks in a PPP arise due to uncertainty regarding the occurrence of certain events and their consequent impact on the project. Given the long term nature of the contract, there is a possibility of a number of different events occurring such as changes in government policy, delays in accessing land, decline in demand for the infrastructure service, etc, which can raise costs or reduce revenues, impacting on the effective delivery of the infrastructure service. One of the core elements of the design of a PPP is the appropriate allocation of these risks to the party that is most able (typically at the lowest cost) to mitigate and/or bear the risks should they occur.

Box 3.5 describes the main types of risk in a PPP structure. Different risks may be relevant at different stages of the project, while some risks may be prevalent throughout the life of the project. For example, risks associated with the construction of the infrastructure are relevant only during the construction period; political risks, however, can be relevant throughout the life of the project.

---

**Box 3.5. Risks underlying a PPP structure**

At the highest level, risks for a PPP project can be classified into the following:

- **Market risks:** Market risks refer to risks that arise due to uncertainties about the market demand for the infrastructure service. These include, for example, volume risks – which relate to uncertainties arising from the number of users and their frequency and intensity of use of the infrastructure service – and price risks, which arise due to uncertainties in the tariff that can be charged for the use of the infrastructure service. Thus market risks are closely linked to the users' willingness and ability to pay.

- **Development/planning risks:** Development or planning risks are the risks arising from planning or preparing projects for private sector participation. Governments or the private sector may invest substantial amounts of money to develop a project (through payment for several scoping, feasibility and structuring studies), but bear the risk of the project being infeasible.

- **Project risks:** Project risks relate to uncertainties in relation to project construction, completion and operation (i.e. activities post award of contract and which occur while implementing the PPP project) and financing, and can be split into start-up risks, such as capital cost over-run, completion delays and ongoing risks, such as operating performance, operating costs and life cycle costs.

- **Political risks:** Political risks are risks that arise from wars, civil disturbances, terrorism, etc., and include currency transfer restrictions, expropriation, war and civil disturbance, and breach of contract. Political risks are more serious in certain regions of the world than in others.

- **Regulatory risks:** Risks that arise from the lack of a suitably developed regulatory system which, for example, ensures regulatory independence from the government, regulations for the participation of the private sector in infrastructure or appropriate periodic review of tariffs can cause considerable uncertainties for lenders and investors in any infrastructure sector.

- **Financial risks:** Infrastructure projects are impacted by financial risks such as exchange rate appreciation/depreciation and changes in interest rates, which can have a substantial impact on costs and revenues. The ability to hedge financial risks depends on the level of development of capital markets and/or access to specialist hedging facilities (see Section 6).

---

Key to the design of a PPP is the allocation of these risks between the public and private sectors, so as to ensure that the PPP delivers VfM. The essential principle for risk allocation in a PPP is to accord the risk to the party who can best manage it. This needs to be determined by assessing each party's ability to influence the risk factor, and correspondingly mitigate/absorb the risk to the greatest extent possible.

Table 3.3 presents an adapted excerpt from a risk matrix prepared by Partnerships Victoria,[17] describing the nature of the risk, relevant mitigation strategy and consequently the preferred allocation between the private and public sectors.

**Table 3.3.** Sample extract of a risk matrix[13]

| Risk category | Description | Consequence | Mitigation | Preferred Allocation |
|---|---|---|---|---|
| Native title | Costs and delays in negotiating indigenous land use agreements where project site may be subject to native title | Delay and cost | Search of registers and enquiry, if appropriate, and taking expert advice | Public sector (as it generally has a better understanding of procedures and has special powers in relation to the acquisition and use of native title land) |
| Changes in law/policy | Change in law/policy which could not be anticipated at contract signing | Requirement of the private party to fund and carry out capital works, etc. | Government mitigates by excluding changes such as tax changes; also, mechanisms could be used to minimise and manage the financial impact on government and, where appropriate, a regulatory regime to allow pass-through to end users | Public sector (although the parties may share the financial consequences) |
| Construction | Events occur during construction which prevent the facility being delivered on time and on cost | Delay and cost | Private party will generally enter into a fixed term, fixed price building contract to pass the risk to a builder | Private party will generally be liable |
| Financing unavailable | When debt and/or equity is required for the project, it is not available then, and in the amounts and on the conditions anticipated | No funding to progress or complete construction | Government requires all bids to have fully documented financial commitments with minimal and easily achievable conditionality | Private party |
| Competition | In a 'user pays' model the risk of alternative suppliers of the contracted service competing for customers | Revenue shortfall competition for service and barriers to entry | Private party to review likely competition for services and barriers to entry | Private party (except to the extent that government has committed to an availability payment element or agreed to provide redress for the impact of government-subsidised competition) |

As the matrix demonstrates, it is often the case that a private sector operator is able to control, and is therefore best placed to manage, certain types of project and financial risks, whereas the public sector is better equipped to deal with political and regulatory risks. Market risks are often shared between the public and private sector because of uncertainty about the level of likely demand for certain services. For example, in the Kenya-Uganda rail concession (discussed in detail in Annex 5), concession companies and lenders have assumed the commercial risks associated with the project, including the investment and operation risks, as well as the traffic (market) risks. The political and government-related risks are covered by an IDA partial risk guarantee.[19]

However, it should also be noted that the context for each project will be different and hence the risks need to be accorded appropriately. For example, in the case of the Panagarh-Palsit highway project in India (see Annex 5), the market risk was allocated to the government through fixed payments to the private operator ('the annuity based model'). Thus, the optimal allocation of risk is a technical issue that varies between projects, countries and over time, and must be considered carefully when considering or structuring PPPs.

The management of risks is a complex process and needs to be reviewed throughout the life of the project. The nature and level of risks may change during the course of the project, and new risks may also be identified. Box 3.6 describes a typical process for risk management and review that should be undertaken as part of any project development.

---

**Box 3.6. Risk management and review process**

A typical process for risk management entails the following five steps, as shown in Figure 3.3.

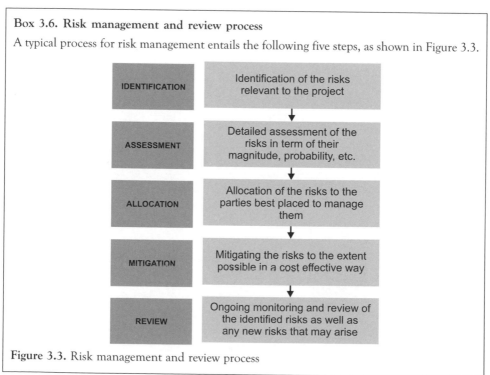

**Figure 3.3.** Risk management and review process

---

## 3.4. Main types of PPPs

There are a number of models of private sector participation in infrastructure, primarily distinguished by two key factors: (i) the degree of risk allocation between the public and private sectors; and (ii) the length of the contract period.

Table 3.4 provides some details of the various models for private participation in infrastructure, highlighting which models are considered to be PPPs and which are not.

**Table 3.4.** Models for private participation in infrastructure and their key features

| | Type of model | Description | Level of risk assumed by the private sector | Length of contract (number of years) | Capital investment | Asset ownership | Most common sector in developing countries |
|---|---|---|---|---|---|---|---|
| **Core PPPs** / **Broad definition of PPPs** | Service contract | Contract for infrastructure support services such as billing | Low | 1–3 | Public | Public | • Water utilities<br>• Railways services |
| | Management contract | Contract for management of a part/ whole of the operations | Low/medium | 2–5 | Public | Public | • Water utilities |
| | Lease contract | Contract for management of operations and specific renewals | Medium | 10–15 | Public | Public | • Water sector |
| | Build-operate-transfer contract | Contract for investment in and operation of a specific component of the infrastructure service | High | Varies | Private | Public/private | • Energy sector IPPs<br>• Highways<br>• Sanitation/desalination plants |
| | Concession | Contract for financing and operations and execution of specific investments | High | 25–30 | Private | Public/private | • Airports/ports/rail<br>• Energy networks |
| | Divestiture/privatisation | Contract of transfer of ownership of public infrastructure to the private sector | Complete | Indefinite | Private | Private | • Telecoms |

As highlighted in the table, 'core PPPs' are models in which a significant degree of risk is transferred to the private sector, such as concession contracts and build-operate-transfer projects (BOTs).[20] These contracts are usually long term in nature and involve substantial investment by the private sector, and therefore concomitant risk transfer, and are consequently viewed as core PPPs.

Other models of private participation, such as service, management and lease contracts, are not classified as core PPPs, as the degree of risk transfer is low. There are, however, examples of management contracts where the risk transfer to the private sector is significant (for example, where the remuneration to the private sector is materially linked to performance), and these can be included in the 'broad' definition of PPPs. However, for the most part, management contracts do not involve substantial risk transfer to the private sector and hence are not considered as PPPs.

## 3.5. International trends in PPPs: theory and practice

Private sector participation in infrastructure in general, and PPPs in particular, has become increasingly important in developed and developing countries over the years. The development of the UK private finance initiative in 1992 was a landmark in this regard, and its experience offers many lessons to other OECD and developing countries. However, as Box 3.7 discusses, PPPs are not a new invention. In fact they have existed in various forms in Europe for over 200 years. Concession agreements were a particularly common feature of nineteenth and early twentieth century infrastructure projects in the USA.

---

**Box 3.7. Early forms of PPPs**

Infrastructure development in Europe was often achieved through early forms of PPP. For example, from the early 1700s turnpike trusts increasingly took responsibility for either improving and maintaining existing roads or developing new ones – through the charging of tolls to road users and an initial 21-year 'concession'. Canals, and then railways, were developed through Acts of Parliament that gave rights to private companies to develop the necessary infrastructure and then charge users. Finally, electricity, gas and water infrastructure was also developed by private companies, again usually through a specific Act of Parliament – often with forms of incentive-based regulation built into the Act.

---

### 3.5.1. Development of thinking on PPPs

The overall rationale for PPPs has evolved over the years. While initially viewed as a way of avoiding government budget constraints, PPPs are increasingly being recognised as a VfM option. Thus the key question facing governments now is how can they effectively provide infrastructure services in the most efficient and suitable manner, deriving maximum benefits for the resources put in by both the public and/or private sectors. This has also been discussed above in Section 3.2.

Another issue that has been explicitly recognised over time is the important role of governments in PPPs beyond financial close of the project. Governments remain ultimately accountable to the public for the delivery of infrastructure services; hence contract management and monitoring by the government is crucial to the success of the PPP. A further discussion of this is also provided in Section 4.3.

A closely linked issue is the role of an independent regulator in monitoring the operations of private and public players in the infrastructure sectors. Most developing countries have initially tended to include suitable regulatory mechanisms within individual PPP contracts due to the lack of development of an appropriate enabling environment, including the establishment of sector-specific or multi-sector regulators. However, the need and role of an independent regulatory body over time cannot be overemphasised. This is also discussed in more detail in Section 4.1 on the PPP framework.

Finally, the importance of renegotiation of contracts has been increasingly recognised. Given changing economic circumstances, both globally and nationally, as well as the difficulty of forecasting demand and therefore financial returns for an infrastructure project, renegotiation may play an important role, preventing failure or cancellation of the contract. It is important to recognise that renegotiation does not imply failure and that good contract design explicitly includes rules and procedures for renegotiation. This is discussed in Section 4.4.

### 3.5.2. Trends in infrastructure PPPs in developing countries

The overall growth in private sector participation in infrastructure in developing countries has been remarkable – a proof in point being the increase from 58 projects reaching financial close in only eight countries in 1990 to 288 projects achieving financial close across 64 countries in 2007. However, the trend has been far from uniform, with macroeconomic shocks, global events, growth/decline of major private players, etc. determining the overall and regional based trends. This is illustrated in Figure 3.4.

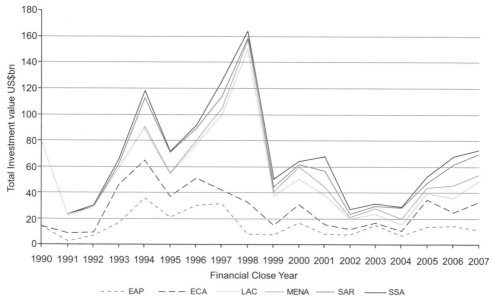

**Figure 3.4.** Investment commitments from infrastructure projects with private sector participation in low- and middle-income countries, 1990–2007[21]

There have been changes in both the number of projects reaching financial close – while the number of projects achieving financial close pre-2000 was higher than that in the post-2000 years, there has also been a greater degree of instability in the former period – and average size of projects – the median project size was high in the early 1990s (above US$200 million), and declined thereafter (to around US$100 million), with a steep decline in 2002 (around US$30 million). There has, however, been a slow rise in recent years.

Some of the key aspects of trends in private participation in infrastructure in developing countries over the period 1990–2007 are presented below.

- The **regional trend** is dominated by Latin America and the Caribbean (LAC) and the east Asia and Pacific (EAP) regions, with sub-Saharan Africa (SSA) traditionally lagging behind the other regions.[22]

- The overall regional trend, however, masks considerable **country level** diversity, with some countries dominating over half of the share of investment commitments in the region and others having only a marginal number of projects. For example, China dominates EAP region projects, having 63.1 per cent of all projects from 1990 to 2007.

- In terms of **sector**, private participation in the telecoms sector has dominated since 1990, with water and sanitation projects attracting the lowest investment commitments.[23] While a number of OECD countries have moved beyond private sector participation in 'hard' infrastructure sectors only (i.e. a number of social infrastructure services for education and health are being provided through private partnership models), this experience remains limited in developing countries.

- In terms of **type** of private involvement in infrastructure, there has been a relatively steady growth in concessions, and management and lease contracts since 1990 (see Figure 3.5). The number of divestitures and greenfield projects grew rapidly in the first half of the 1990s, but then declined to lower levels soon after reaching their peaks. Greenfield projects have been the largest type of projects since the late 1990s. The number of PPP projects has been much larger than other forms of private participation in infrastructure, with a slight upward trend in the post-2000 years.

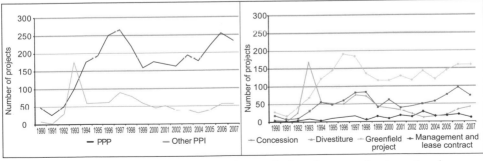

**Figure 3.5.** Number of projects reaching financial close by type of private involvement, 1990–2007[24]

**Box 3.8. The International Finance Corporation Infrastructure Crisis Facility**

The International Finance Corporation (IFC) announced the creation of the Infrastructure Crisis Facility (ICF) on 11 November 2008 as part of a wider suite of initiatives devised in response to the financial crisis. The IFC projected that financing across its crisis initiatives would exceed US$31 billion over the following three years.

The role of the ICF is to address the impact of the economic downturn on private infrastructure financing in developing countries. In particular, the increased scarcity of equity funding, shortening of tenors on project loans and higher interest rates have meant that previously viable projects under development are being delayed or cancelled, while fully structured projects are struggling to achieve refinancing. Research by the IFC and World Bank has indicated that over US$110 billion of new and pipeline projects risk delay or postponement and a further US$70 billion face heightened financing or refinancing risk.

In light of these problems, the ICF was established to:

- Stabilise viable infrastructure projects facing temporary liquidity problems; and
- Support the continuation of new project development in private infrastructure.

To achieve these goals, the ICF has adopted a three-part structure, as shown in Figure 3.6.

The ICF loan and equity components are designed to provide roll-over financing and substitute temporarily for commercial financing of new projects. They should be sufficient to support approximately 100 viable privately funded projects with three- to six-year funding. The advisory facility is designed to ensure the continuation of the project preparation cycle. By 1 December 2009, the ICF had mobilised over US$4 billion of funds from IFIs and other sources.

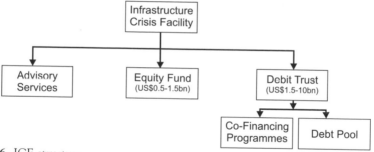

**Figure 3.6.** ICF structure

*Loan financing trust*

The ICF Debt Trust is a vehicle designed to provide loans for existing and new infrastructure projects. Total commitments to the Trust will be up to US$10 billion, split into the following two streams:

- the Debt Pool, a limited-life collective investment vehicle; and
- parallel co-financing programmes.

Commitments to the ICF include a €700 million interest subsidy and US$11 million equity participation from the German government, a €500 million contribution to the debt pool from KfW Entwicklungsbank and €200 million from Proparco, the French investment company for economic co-operation (established under the Private Infrastructure Development Group (PIDG) umbrella). Co-financing opportunities have earmarked US$400 million from DEG, €800 million from Proparco and €1 billion from the European Investment Bank. Depending on demand, the facility may seek additional rounds of financing from governments.

Finally, it is also useful to examine the trends in failed projects. Between 1990 and 2007, 194 private infrastructure deals were cancelled, representing 4.76 per cent of the total number of projects (4,078). Projects were cancelled on an average 6.9 years after financial close. In terms of trends in failures by sector, region and type of private sector involvement, the highest rates of cancellation occurred in the water and sanitation sector, the SSA region, and management and lease contracts. The greatest absolute number of failures occurred in the energy sector, the LAC region and across greenfield projects. Failure of PPP projects is the outcome of a number of constraints in developing countries, discussed at length in Section 5.

## Notes

1. However, there has been significant debate on whether governments misrepresent their own cost of funding for a project and it has been argued that the difference between public and private funds is much less than is often claimed. For example, Klein (1996) argues that the 'apparent cheapness of sovereign funds stems from taxpayers not being remunerated for the contingent liability they effectively assume'.

2. http://www.journallive.co.uk/north-east-news/environment-news/2009/07/02/crisis-after-1-4bn-east-coast-rail-franchise-collapse-61634-24054142/

3. http://blogs.telegraph.co.uk/news/alexsingleton/100001905/government-greed-caused-collapse-of-the-east-coast-rail-franchise/

4. Grimsey and Lewis (2004), p. 1.

5. For details on the PSC test, see Grimsey and Lewis (2004), pp. 136–138.

6. http://www.ccsenet.org/journal/index.php/ass/article/viewFile/237/218

7. http://www.ppiaf.org/documents/gridlines/4africa.pdf

8. NAO, UK, 'The PFI Contracts for Bridgend and Fazakerley Prisons', HC253 Session 1997–98, HMSO (1997).

9. Fitzgerald, P, 'Review of Partnerships Victoria Provided Infrastructure', Review of Partnerships, Victoria (2004).

10. Partnerships BC, 'Project Report: Achieving Value for Money Surrey Outpatient Hospital' (2009), http://www.partnershipsbc.ca/files/documents/sof_vfm_final_web_20090603.pdf

11. Arthur Andersen and Enterprise LSE, 'Value for money drivers in the Private Finance Initiative' (2000).

12. Grimsey and Lewis (2004), pp. 136–138.

13. NAO, UK, 'Managing the Relationship to Secure a Successful Partnership in PFI Projects', HC HMSO (1997).

14. CEPA, 'Public Private Partnerships in Scotland: Evaluation of Performance' (2005). http://www.scotland.gov.uk/Resource/Doc/917/0011854.pdf

15. A detailed case study of the Meghnaghat IPP is provided in Annex 5.

16. Private Infrastructure Development Group (PIDG), *Annual Report* (2008).

17. Partnerships Victoria, *Risk Allocation and Contractual Issues – A Guide* (2001). http://www.partnerships.vic.gov.au/CA25708500035EB6/WebObj/RiskAllocation and ContractualIssues1-Entire/$File/Risk%20Allocation%20and%20Contractual%20Issues1%20-%20Entire.pdf

18. Partnerships Victoria (2001)

19. Matsukawa *et al.*, 'Review of Risk Mitigation Instruments for Infrastructure Financing and Recent Trends in Development' (2007).

20. There are a number of variants to the BOT contract for project delivery, such as DBB (design-bid-build), DBFO (design-build-finance-operate) and BOO (build-own-operate). These variants should be considered alongside standard BOTs.

21. http://ppi.worldbank.org

22. An important point to note, however, is that with the majority of the countries in sub-Saharan Africa being low-income countries, the region has been more resilient to external shocks (global financial and economic crises). Projects in the south Asia region (SAR) have increased considerably since 2000, with total investment commitments of only US$1.7 billion in 2003, rising to US$16.0 billion in 2007.

23. Divestitures have dominated the telecoms sector, with most projects being for mobile access. Energy sector projects have mainly been greenfield projects, nearly 75 per cent of which are in electricity generation.

24. In the graph, PPP refers to the sum of concession and greenfield projects, while 'other private' refers to divestitures and management and lease contracts. Note that while some management contracts can be PPPs as well, it has not been possible to split the data. http://ppi.worldbank.org

## Key references

### Introduction to PPPs

Grimsey, D and Lewis, MK, *Public Private Partnerships: The Worldwide Revolution in Infrastructure Provision and Project Finance*, Edward Elgar Publishing Ltd (2004). ISBN: 9781840647112

A wide-ranging book covering major PPP issues, drawing on detailed project cases.

Yescombe, ER, *Public Private Partnerships: Principles of Policy and Finance*, Butterworth-Heinemann (2007). ISBN: 9780750680547

An excellently balanced book serving as a valuable introduction to PPPs, while providing a level of detail useful to those already familiar with the basic concepts.

### PPP definitions and classification

ADB, *Public–private Partnership (PPP) Handbook* (2008). http://www.adb.org/Documents/Handbooks/Public-private-Partnership/default.asp

Section 4, 'Structuring a PPP: Available PPP Options', discusses the main options and how they should be selected against reform objectives.

The World Bank, ICA and PPIAF, *Attracting Investors to African Public–private Partnerships: A Project Preparation Guide* (2009). http://www.partnershipsuk.org.uk/uploads/documents/Attracting%20Investors%20to %20African%20Public-private%20Partnerships.pdf

Chapter 2 clearly articulates the key issues on the definition and classification of PPPs.

World Bank/PPIAF, *PPP Unit Guide – Public–private Partnership Units: Lessons for their Design and Use in Infrastructure* (2007). http://www.ppiaf.org/documents/other_publications/PPP_units_paper.pdf

Chapter 2 highlights important distinctions between what a PPP is and what it is not.

## Benefits of PPPs

Yescombe, ER, *Public Private Partnerships: Principles of Policy and Finance*, Butterworth-Heinemann (2007). ISBN: 9780750680547

Chapter 2, 'PPPs – For and Against', balances a range of benefits and costs of PPPs.

Deloitte, *Closing the Infrastructure Gap: The Role of Public–private Partnerships* (2006). http://www.deloitte.com/assets/Dcom-UnitedStates/Local%20Assets/Documents/us_ps_ClosingInfrastructureGap2006(1).pdf

Includes a section on 'The Case for Public–private Partnerships'.

City of London, *Developing India's Infrastructure through Public Private Partnerships: A Resource Guide*, prepared by Research Republic LLP and International Financial Services London (2008). http://www.muidcl.com/downloads/pppinitiatives.pdf

Includes sections on the strengths and weaknesses, and misconceptions surrounding PPPs.

HM Treasury (UK), *Value for Money Assessment Guidance*, HM Treasury (2007). http://www.hm-treasury.gov.uk/ppp_vfm_index.htm

PFI value for money guide, accompanied by quantitative evaluation spreadsheet.

National Audit Office (UK), *A Framework for Evaluating the Implementation of Private Finance Initiative Projects* (2006). http://www.nao.org.uk/publications/0506/pfi_framework.aspx?alreadysearchfor=yes

A two-volume report setting out issues to be considered in the evaluation of PFI projects central to assessing value for money.

Shugart, C, *PPPs, the Public Sector Comparator, and Discount Rates: Key Issues for Developing Countries* (forthcoming). http://jdi-legacy.econ.queensu.ca/Files/Conferences/PPPpapers/Shugart%20Sept%2015%20version.pdf

A detailed analysis of the Public Sector Comparator approach to VfM assessment, focusing on the choice of an appropriate discount rate and practical steps forward for developing countries.

Klein, M, 'Risk, Taxpayers, and the Role of Government in Project Finance', Policy Research Working Paper 1688, World Bank (1996). http://www-wds.worldbank.org/external/default/WDSContentServer/IW3P/IB/1999/08/15/000009265_3970311115003/Rendered/PDF/multi_page.pdf

An important paper in which Klein argues that the apparent cheapness of sovereign funds stems from taxpayers not being remunerated for the contingent liability they effectively assume.

## Types of risks and their allocation

Partnerships Victoria, *Risk Allocation and Contractual Issues – A Guide* (2001). http://www.partnerships.vic.gov.au/CA25708500035EB6/WebObj/RiskAllocationandContractualIssues1-Entire/$File/Risk%20Allocation%20and%20Contractual%20Issues1%20-%20Entire.pdf

New South Wales Government, *Working with Government: Risk Allocation and Commercial Principles* (2007). http://www.treasury.nsw.gov.au/__data/assets/pdf_file/0012/3135/risk_allocation.pdf

A detailed guide covering the state's preferred risk allocation for privately financed projects.

Dewatripont, M and Legros, P, 'Public–private partnerships: contract design and risk transfer', EIB Papers, Vol. 10, No. 1 (2005).
http://www.eib.org/attachments/efs/eibpapers/eibpapers_2005_v10_n01/eibpapers_2005_v10_n01_a05_en.pdf

An assessment of implications of contracting and risk transfer in PPPs, arguing that the premium required to transfer risk can outweigh its benefits.

De Palma, A, Leruth, L and Prunier, G, 'Towards a Principal-Agent Based Typology of Risks in Public–private Partnerships', IMF Working Paper No. 09/177 (2009).
http://www.imf.org/external/pubs/cat/longres.cfm?sk=23190.0

Using incentives and principal-agent theory, the authors examine the implications in terms of optimal risk sharing between the public and private sectors.

### Trends in private sector participation in infrastructure

World Bank and PPIAF Private Participation in Infrastructure Database, http://ppi.worldbank.org/

Information on over 4,100 infrastructure projects across low- and middle-income countries. The database covers projects involving private sector participation from 1983 to 2007, but not all are PPPs. The website also publishes data updates and sectoral 'snapshot' notes analysing trends emerging in the data.

### Assessment of the impact of the crisis on new private participation in infrastructure projects

http://ppi.worldbank.org/features/march2009/200903PPIFinancialCrisisImpact.pdf

http://www.ppiaf.org/documents/Impact_of_the_crisis_note_June09.pdf

A note analysing the short-term impact of the financial crisis drawing on emerging data from the new 'Impact of the Financial Crisis on PPI' database, covering 522 infrastructure projects with private participation in low-income countries, August 2008–March 2009.

PPIAF Gridlines Series http://www.ppiaf.org/content/view/260/429/

This series of papers provides concise and accessible reviews of emerging trends and issues in private participation in infrastructure. Important articles include Marin and Izaguirre, 'Private Participation in Water: Toward a New Generation of Projects?' (2006) and Gassner et al., 'Does the Private Sector Deliver on its Promises? Evidence from a Global Study in Water and Electricity' (2008).

World Bank Public Policy for the Private Sector Journal Series
http://rru.worldbank.org/PublicPolicyJournal/

A long-running series of short articles reviewing public policy innovations for private sector/market solutions for development. Many articles provide useful insights for PPPs, including Harris et al., 'Infrastructure Projects: A Review of Cancelled Private Projects' (2003) and Kerf et al., 'Concessions for Infrastructure: A Guide to Their Design and Award' (1998).

# 4

# The infrastructure PPP project development process

........................................................................................................................................

## Summarising the section

- A PPP framework comprising policy, legal, regulatory and institutional aspects is a key building block for PPP projects in a country. A supportive and flexible PPP framework facilitates deal flow and helps ensure the smooth development and operation of PPP projects.

- The infrastructure project development process is a complex and resource intensive (in both time and costs) process, typically lasting three to four years. It comprises six broad phases: (i) development of the supportive enabling environment; (ii) definition of the project; (iii) feasibility assessment; (iv) project structuring; (v) transactions; and (vi) post- implementation support in terms of contract management/monitoring.

- Contract management and monitoring is a process that takes place throughout the life of the contract. Appropriate monitoring frameworks and tools need to be developed to ensure that a credible performance evaluation process exists, public policy objectives are being met and the PPP project is value for money for the government.

- The public sector should have a transparent mechanism for the allocation, valuation and management of contingent liabilities that may arise from PPP arrangements.

- Contract renegotiations are costly and involve considerable time and effort. Hence, renegotiations should only be carried out if they enhance value for money and/or prevent the collapse of the contract. It is important to understand that a renegotiation does not imply failure of the contract.

This section covers the following topics:

- The framework for infrastructure PPPs, in terms of the enabling environment, comprising policy, legal, regulatory and institutional structures as well as a discussion on contingent liability management;

- The infrastructure project development process, including a detailed discussion of the various elements involved in the different stages of project development; and

- Post-project implementation issues such as contract management and monitoring, as well as renegotiations.

## 4.1. The PPP framework

This section describes the key elements of the PPP framework, including policy, legal and regulatory aspects, which are important for facilitating PPPs. A description of the key issues to be covered under each aspect is provided, followed by a summary discussion of the main conclusions from the experience of developing countries. The issue of contingent liability management is also discussed.

### 4.1.1. Overall policy framework

A clear policy framework is the foundation for a PPP programme for a country. The policy framework needs to set out at least the following:

- The objectives and rationale for the use of PPPs;
- How the government plans to take forward its PPP programme;
- Overall guidelines in terms of how the government will assess PPPs;
- The institutional structures and processes involved, including the role of different government departments for project selection, preparation, procurement and approvals.

The policy framework needs to be clear and transparent and is extremely important, as it reflects the government's commitment to implementing a PPP programme in the country.

Building on the policy framework, the government needs to develop a well-structured investment framework that delineates the planned infrastructure projects and the level of investment required, covering both public and private sector projects (i.e. beyond simply a list of PPP projects). This will help the private sector to gauge the links between various infrastructure projects which might impact upon their feasibility, among other considerations. The investment framework needs to be developed for the different infrastructure sectors of the economy.

Box 4.1 discusses the different elements of the PPP policy framework in India and the supporting institutional structures.

---

**Box 4.1. The Indian policy and institutional framework for PPPs**

The Government of India (GoI) has launched several institutional initiatives for PPPs in India including:

- A Committee on Infrastructure, chaired by the Prime Minister, that initiates policies, develops structures for PPPs and oversees the progress of key infrastructure projects.

- A Viability Gap Fund (VGF) and the India Infrastructure Finance Company Limited (IIFCL) that provides long-term capital to help finance PPPs, as well as capacity building and other forms of assistance. An initial Rs2 billion (US$40 million)[1] was set aside by the GoI for VGF. IIFCL has been incorporated as a wholly government-owned company, with authorised capital of Rs20 billion (US$400 million), of which paid-up capital is currently Rs10 billion (US$200 million).[2]

- An India Infrastructure Project Development Fund (IIPDF) within the Department of Economic Affairs (Ministry of Finance) that promotes the development of credible and bankable projects. IIPDF has been established with an initial GoI contribution of Rs1 billion (US$20 million).[3]

- Institutional structures such as the PPP cell within the Finance Ministry for organising activities to promote PPPs and administer proposals; PPP cells at state level to promote state-level PPPs; an interministerial Public Private Partnership Appraisal Committee (PPPAC) charged with determining the requalification of bidders under PPP and preparing toolkits and model concession agreements, among others.

---

## 4.1.2. Legal framework

The legal framework for PPPs is at three different levels:

- The general legal framework for the country, covering issues such as property rights and land acquisition;

- The legal framework for infrastructure PPPs that looks at specific issues relating to PPPs, such as procurement;

- Finally, the legal framework at the contract level, which includes specific issues relevant to the contract, drawing on the legal framework for PPPs as a whole (if available).

A well-developed legal framework is crucial to the success of a PPP programme. It saves time and effort and allows for some flexibility in contract issues, as they can be referred back to the overall legal framework.

The various elements of a legal framework essentially need to ensure contract enforcement and effectiveness, and provide both the public and private sectors with the assurance that their interests will be protected. Some of the issues to be covered under the legal framework include:

- The rights of the private sector, including those of the investors (in terms of how their investment will be protected) and the lenders (including how their debt/loan provided for the infrastructure project will be protected).

- Appropriate rules and procedures for the resolution of contract disputes, including the rights and obligations of the parties involved. A country may develop internal procedures for contract dispute resolution or this may be facilitated through international courts or agencies.

- Rules for repatriation of profits for overseas investors and the use of expatriate personnel.

- Laws for licences and permits for the different issues, such as land use and environmental impact.

- Rules and procedures for handling renegotiation of contracts and appropriate compensation mechanisms, as may be required.

- Whether unsolicited proposals are acceptable and, if so, the process and system for managing them.

Most of the above legal issues are dealt with in a 'PPP Act' or a 'Concession law' (see Box 4.2 for core principles for modern concession law), but can also be included in separate laws to deal with individual issues such as procurement law, dispute resolution law, expropriation law, foreign ownership legislation, labour law, foreign exchange law, tax laws and laws on public disclosure. While some countries may have specific procurement legislation, an overarching PPP Act is also important as it covers a wider set of issues as highlighted above. Needless to say, all these laws need to be compatible with each other. Some countries have also developed model concession agreements (MCAs), structured legal documents that facilitate PPPs (see Box 4.3).

However, it should be noted that an overly onerous legal system can imply considerable transaction costs and may work to the detriment of both the public and private sectors. The legal framework, therefore, needs to be carefully balanced and rationalised to effectively promote the PPP programme. It is important that the legal framework is clear, consistent and non-conflicting, and especially important that it is stable and fair.

**Box 4.2. Core principles for a modern concession law**

The European Bank for Reconstruction and Development (EBRD) has prepared a list of core principles for a modern concession law.[4] According to the EBRD, a modern concession law should:

- Be based on a clear policy for private sector participation;
- Create a sound legislative foundation for concession;
- Provide clarity of rules (including a clear definition of the scope and boundaries of application of the concession legal framework);
- Provide a stable and predictable concession legal framework;
- Promote fairness, transparency and accessibility of concession rules and procedures, including providing for transparent and competitive selection of the concessionaire (with limited exceptions allowing direct negotiations), rights of foreign and domestic investors and regulatory instruments relevant to the concession;
- Be consistent with the country's legal system and particular laws;
- Allow for negotiability of concession agreements;
- Allow for enforceable court or arbitral determinations;
- Allow for state undertakings and guarantees;
- Accommodate security interests (i.e. provide for the availability of reliable security instruments on the assets and cash flow of the concessionaire in favour of lenders, including 'step-in' rights).

---

**Box 4.3. Model concession agreements**

MCAs are structured legal documents employed by some governments, including India, South Africa and the UK, to facilitate concession PPPs. Standardisation can help streamline the procurement process and enhance the stability of the regulatory and policy framework. Each contract initiated under standard conditions involves limited tailoring and minimal scope for negotiation, thereby also supporting governments with weak capacity and experience in PPPs.

MCAs have been viewed as particularly successful when used for a number of similar projects in a country (for example, toll roads in India), but have also been criticised for rigidity and not being suitably adapted to changing circumstances in different types of projects. MCAs are useful where there are a number of planned projects that can benefit from the standardised document – in the case of only one or a few projects the transactions costs may be too high.

**Examples of MCAs in practice**

- MCAs for roads and ports in India: http://infrastructure.gov.in/mca.htm
- PPP provisions in South Africa: http://www.ppp.gov.za/StandPPPProv.htm
- UK PFI contracts: http://www.hm-treasury.gov.uk/ppp_standardised_contracts.htm

### 4.1.3. Regulatory framework

Along with the overall policy and legal framework, a regulatory framework forms an integral part of the overall PPP framework for a country. In most countries, regulatory offices have been set up to support the introduction of private sector participation. A regulatory framework aims to promote infrastructure investments by protecting investors from political opportunism/arbitrary actions, provide improved or maintained quality of infrastructure services for the consumers and protect them from abuse of market power, promote economic efficiency and help ensure stability. Some of the issues addressed by a regulatory framework include:

- The market structure and the impact on the infrastructure service delivery, particularly in terms of the price of the service;

- Ensuring acceptable service quality – operators with market power may be incentivised to reduce costs at the expense of decreasing the quality of the service and the regulatory framework can include several schemes such as quality standards, monitoring schemes and penalties for non-compliance to ensure quality;

- Environmental protection – in the same way that it should ensure the quality of the service, the regulatory framework can also cover schemes and incentives to ensure protection of the environment.

The degree to which the regulatory system in a country can meet its objectives is based to a large extent on its credibility and commitment. An approach to strengthening the commitment of the regulatory system is to establish rules that limit the regulator's discretion, i.e. constrain the regulator's decision-making powers by setting out rules that must be followed. There are various forms that these rules can take, which reflect increasing levels of commitment, but concomitantly lower levels of flexibility, as illustrated in Figure 4.1 below.

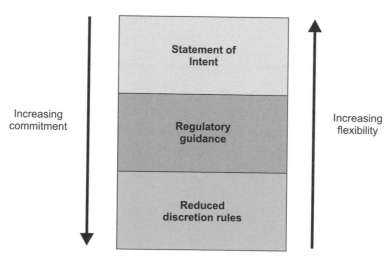

**Figure 4.1.** Options for creating regulatory commitment[5]

As presented in the figure, a 'Statement of Intent', which sets out only the broad principles as to how the regulator will approach a decision, may provide some level of comfort to investors, as it provides some insight into the regulatory approach to be undertaken. However, this is limited, in that a Statement of Intent is not binding on the regulator (except inasmuch as it may be enshrined in primary legislation). 'Regulatory guidance', on the other hand, represents a higher level of commitment, as the regulator goes beyond broad principles/mission and sets out the regulator's expected behaviour, although the regulator is still not legally bound to follow this. 'Reduced discretion rules' provide the highest level of commitment, as the regulator is legally bound to follow the rules. As a result, however, this approach reduces the degree of flexibility and discretion of the regulator.

These approaches are particularly suited to different contexts, given their trade-offs between commitment and flexibility. Thus, for example, where the legal and institutional environment is strong, a more flexible approach to regulation (through a Statement of Intent or Regulatory Guidance) may be employed, as against an environment where a high degree of commitment is required to encourage investments (as is the case in a number of developing countries at present). As Alexander (2008) recommends, 'it is good regulatory practice to provide some form of statement of intent and also regulatory guidance. The real question is whether it is necessary to go beyond this and provide reduced discretion rules.' The use of different approaches will also vary according to the issue being addressed. For example, for appeals and dispute resolution under PPP contracts, investors would prefer reduced discretion rules outlining the process for dispute resolution and how disputes will be resolved where they do arise (alternative dispute resolution (ADR) systems).

A mechanism for incorporating reduced discretion rules is through the PPP contract ('regulation by contract') – an approach that is often employed by a number of developing countries due to the lack of a suitable overall regulatory framework (see Box 4.4 for a description of the type of regulatory models in practice). While this may be useful, it is only a second-best solution, especially for long-term projects where there is much uncertainty with regards to the investments and operations. Contracts may, however, work for short-term projects (where uncertainty is low) or for one-off projects (there will be lower transactions costs for regulation by contract as against creating an entire framework for a one-off project) or even for large capital expenditure (CAPEX) projects such as IPPs, where there is a single large investment. Establishment of an overall framework also prevents duplication of efforts or any contradictory procedures between projects.

## Box 4.4. Type of institutional arrangements for infrastructure regulation

Utility regulation in developing countries has been shaped by two broad legal traditions – former British colonies have established independent regulatory agencies, whereas former European, for example French, colonies have tended to rely on regulation by contract. However, hybrids of these systems are increasingly being implemented, for example Mali, a Francophone African country, has entered into water and electricity concessions and also subsequently established an independent regulatory agency.

International experience indicates that there are four broad types of institutional arrangements for infrastructure regulation:

- **Regulation by government or self-regulation:** This refers to a regulatory system in which the utility is supervised by its own board of directors. This model is generally encountered where the infrastructure service is provided by the public sector, for example a municipality, ministerial department or state-owned body. There are water sector examples in France, India and South Africa, among others. The key challenge of this approach relates to potential conflicts of interest when government regulators seek to regulate state-owned utilities.

- **Independent regulation:** Independent regulation refers to regulation by an independent body, in terms of decision-making, institutional and management structure, and source of funding. For example, Zambia and Kenya have independent regulators in the water sector. The effectiveness of independent regulatory agencies depends on the degree of independence enjoyed by the agency and the strength of professional regulatory competence. Weak political commitment may compromise the effectiveness of the independent regulator.

- **Regulation by contract:** Under this system, regulatory provisions are enshrined in the contract between the asset owner and the service provider. Highly specified contracts may provide comfort to investors, but may then have to be renegotiated at a later date. This approach is often used in developing countries where a regulator/regulatory framework does not exist, but is not suited to long-term projects where there is much uncertainty as regards investments and operations.

- **Outsourcing of regulatory functions:** Outsourcing or contracting out of regulatory functions involves the use of external experts to perform certain functions, such as tariff reviews, monitoring and benchmarking. This may be a useful approach when the legitimacy or independence of the regulator is in question or when regulatory contracts require additional support. For example, under the water concession in Bucharest, tariff setting was contracted out to an expert panel. Under this system, strategic decisions need to be made with regards to the appropriate functions that should be outsourced; these may change over time, with, for example, an improvement in the capacity of the regulator.

The list of institutional arrangements described above is by no means exhaustive. In practice, many countries have adopted hybrid models with varying elements of the different regulatory models. The key lesson (as also described in Section 4.1.4) is that there are no hard and fast rules for the adoption of regulatory models – instead a country needs to tailor the regulatory model to suit its own particular circumstances and local context.

Key references

- Eberhard, A, 'Infrastructure Regulation in Developing Countries: An Exploration of Hybrid and Transitional Models', PPIAF Working Paper No. 4 (2007).
  http://www.ppiaf.org/documents/working_papers/AFURhybridmodels4.pdf

- Trémolet, S and Hunt, C, 'Taking Account of the Poor in Water Sector Regulation', Water Supply and Sanitation Working Notes, Note No. 11 (2006).
  http://siteresources.worldbank.org/INTWSS/Resources/WN11.pdf

- Brown, AC et al., *Handbook for Evaluating Infrastructure Regulatory Systems*, World Bank (2006).
  http://siteresources.worldbank.org/EXTENERGY/Resources/336805-115697 1270190/HandbookForEvaluatingInfrastructureRegulation062706.pdf

## 4.1.4. Experience of countries with the PPP framework and lessons learned

As discussed in Section 5.1 below, one of the most important constraints in putting together successful PPPs in developing countries is the lack of a suitable PPP framework. Many countries lack an overall PPP policy, as well as the related legislative and regulatory frameworks. The importance of the PPP framework cannot be overemphasised. However, it must also be recognised that in many countries PPPs have progressed in spite of the absence of some, or all, aspects of this framework. For example, a number of countries have followed the 'regulation by contract' route, as against establishing separate national sectoral regulators (for example the Manila water concessions discussed in more detail in Annex 5). However, as discussed in Section 4.1.3 above, the growing consensus is that a suitable regulatory framework should be put in place, instead of re-inventing the wheel for each contract. Thus experience shows that while PPPs can be developed and implemented in the absence of a well-developed PPP framework, this is more difficult and time-consuming than in situations where a PPP framework is in place. This is also discussed in the next section on the project development process.

Second, the concept of 'best practice', with regards in particular to the PPP framework, needs to be viewed with caution, as there is no 'one size fits all' solution to developing a supportive PPP framework. What works in one country may not work in another, let alone be transferred to or replicated in another sector or region within the same country. For example, as discussed in Box 4.3 above, there are many different types of regulatory models. In practice, however, the exact scope, remit and institutional arrangements need to be assessed in the light of a particular county's needs and the local context – often resulting in hybrid regulatory models being implemented.

These lessons are also elaborated on in Section 8.

## 4.1.5. Contingent liability management

Contingent liabilities refer to liabilities that may arise due to the occurrence of specific events in the future. Government contingent liabilities under a PPP programme include:

- **Explicit contingent liabilities:** These include a wide range of *formal* government guarantees provided to both private sector entities involved with PPPs, such as banks and project vehicles (for example exchange rate and interest rate guarantees) and arms-length public sector bodies such as parastatals. A key feature of these liabilities is that they involve a legal obligation on the part of government in the event that a specified event occurs.

- **Implicit contingent liabilities:** These potential liabilities arise where the PPP relates to infrastructure or infrastructure-related services that are strategically important – and where it is unlikely that the government will let the PPP counterparty fail. These include obligations conditional upon certain events, such as ensuring systematic solvency of the banking system and bailing out strategically important private firms that get into financial difficulties.

Both explicit and implicit liabilities need to be appropriately managed to prevent an over-commitment on the part of the government that it may not be suited to honour. The nature of the costs of guarantees are uncertain and could have major fiscal consequences – particularly if a large number of the risks that are guaranteed are correlated. Thus contingent liability management forms an integral part of the PPP policy of a country – although many Commonwealth countries have not yet instituted a formal policy to this effect.

Irwin (2006) recommends that governments should have an integrated policy towards guarantees, comprising allocation, valuation and management.[6]

- As discussed in Section 3.3 above, risks under a PPP project should be *allocated* to those best placed to manage them. This is based on the ability of the party to influence the particular risk factor, influence the sensitivity of the total project value to the particular risk factor and absorb the risk.

- In addition, guarantees need to be *valued* so as to provide a quantitative estimate of the guarantee and its impact on the total project value. If the guarantee does not substantially increase the total value of the project, its use may be questionable.

- Finally, guarantees need to be appropriately *managed* through suitable budgeting rules, suitable disclosure of guarantees or the creation of special funds for payment of the guarantee (if called upon).

The topic of accounting principles for contingent liabilities has received much attention. Some countries do not include their contingent liabilities from PPPs on their balance sheets and hence run the risk of overcommitment and shortage of funds in the event that the guarantee is called upon. Efficient management of contingent liabilities requires their appropriate disclosure in the government's financial accounts. Incorporation of the potential future costs into medium-term budgetary projections and into an assessment of medium-term debt sustainability is important.

Box 4.5 provides some information on international experiences with contingent liabilities and their management.

**Box 4.5. International experience with contingent liabilities and their management**

**Provisioning for contingent liabilities**

**Brazil**[7] established the FGP (Fundo Garantidor de Parcerias Público-Privadas), a Guarantee Fund which provides cover for financial obligations of federal government entities under PPP contracts. The Fund's assets, which include shares in state-owned enterprises, have an upper limit of R$6 billion (approximately US$3.1 billion),[8] which are held as the guarantee of repayment for obligations under PPP contracts.

In **Colombia**,[9] each government entity providing a guarantee must include the estimated cost in its budget using valuation methodologies established by the Contingent Liabilities Division in the Ministry of Finance. Contributions to the centralised Contingency Fund for State Entities (FCCEE) are made at a level to cover costs arising with 95 per cent probability. Potential risks are reviewed annually to ensure that all reasonable eventualities are appropriately covered. Each entity has a separate account in the Fund for each project and each risk. If the contingent liability becomes an actual liability and the guarantee is called, the Fund will pay out up to the value of the specific account. The state entity bears any remaining costs directly. Once a risk account is no longer relevant, funds are transferred into other risk accounts for the same project. When the project concludes, funds are transferred to the entities' other projects. Full funds are only reimbursed to the entity when is has no further projects.

In **Canada**,[10] the present value of expected fiscal cost is transferred from the sectoral budget allocation to a central reserve fund.

**Management of guarantees**

**Canada** has developed a management framework for loan guarantees that requires, among other things, that:[11]

• Lenders must bear a minimum of 15 per cent of the net loss arising from a default;

• Where the government bears substantial downside risks, consideration is also given to allow parallel sharing of upside potential; and

• Parliament sets a maximum limit on new loans and guarantees.

Similarly, in **Chile** minimum revenue guarantees (and exchange rate guarantees) to operators of highways and other concessions are partially offset by revenue sharing with the government when toll revenue is above a certain level.[12]

**Reporting and disclosure of guarantees**

**Chile** reports estimates of the probability-weighted present value of guarantees for toll roads and airports in its annual budget documentation.[13]

In **Colombia**, an estimate of contingent liabilities has begun to be reported annually to the Congress as part of the medium-term fiscal framework.[14]

In **South Africa**, official medium-term fiscal projections reflect expected outlays on contingent liabilities.[15]

## 4.2. The infrastructure project development process

The infrastructure project development process refers to the development and structuring of a PPP project, right from the initial stages of establishing the feasibility of the project through to detailed structuring and securing private sector finance, as well as the subsequent management and monitoring of the project.

The key activities in the project development process can be classified into six broad phases as depicted in Figure 4.2.[16] Each phase is also described in detail below. The description is also supplemented by Box 4.6, which summarises the key activities undertaken by InfraCo, an infrastructure project development company, in the development of a wind power project in Cape Verde in West Africa. The box provides useful information of the various phases of the project development process in practice. In particular, the information highlights the work done by InfraCo in supporting the government to develop an enabling environment for the project.

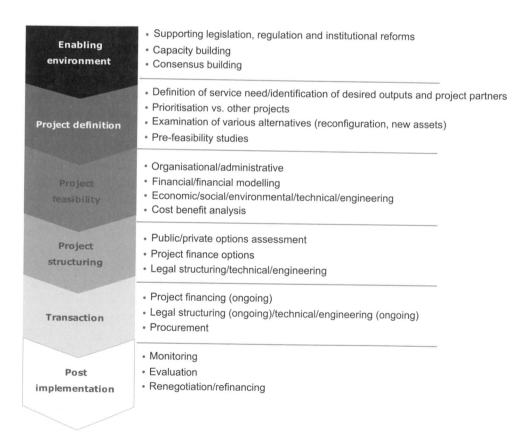

**Figure 4.2.** The infrastructure project development process

## Phase 1: Enabling environment

The enabling environment refers to the relevant policies, laws, regulations and institutions which allow and support the development of infrastructure projects, as well as overall government support, capacity and commitment for PPPs in the country. Examples of activities in this phase include:

- Designing enabling legislation (e.g. laws governing BOT or concession agreements and legislation enabling the restructuring of state-owned utilities in infrastructure sectors);

- Designing, reviewing or changing regulatory approaches if they appear to be insufficient to support sustainable infrastructure development;

- Resolving project-related institutional reform, e.g. solving inconsistencies in the mandate of regional and national authorities;

- Capacity building of the different stakeholders involved in the project; and

- Consensus building within government and the wider stakeholder community for project acceptance.

Development of a supportive enabling environment may be a time-consuming and expensive exercise, but it needs to be in place to ensure more effective PPPs. However, if the enabling environment is already in place, the project development process can commence from phase 2 (project definition) directly. As highlighted in the example of the Cape Verde project development process (Box 4.6), some aspects of the supporting legislation, regulation and institutional reforms were not in place and hence had to be facilitated by the developer at the start of the project development process. Capacity and consensus building also formed a core activity during the early stages of the project development process.

## Phase 2: Project definition

This phase includes early stage concept design work and is needed before the full feasibility phase, as it defines the project's parameters. Activities in this phase include:

- Definition of the need for the infrastructure service;

- Identification and scoping of desired outputs and their wider economic benefit;

- Prioritisation of the project in relation to other national/regional demands on resources;

- Examination of the various alternatives in hand such as reconfiguration of existing infrastructure;

- Identification of project partners (e.g. completely public or a PPP);

- Planning and prioritising the complex tasks associated with project development; and

- Commissioning of early stage pre-feasibility studies.

### Phase 3: Project feasibility

If the pre-feasibility study reaches a positive conclusion, then more detailed feasibility studies need to be undertaken covering organisational, financial, technical, social, environmental and other aspects of the project. A detailed cost-benefit analysis is also crucial to establishing the feasibility of the project.[17]

### Phase 4: Project structuring

This phase involves creating the appropriate commercial and technical structure for the project and is crucial not only for attracting finance, but also for attracting the right mix of finance. This involves:

- Assessing the options for public and/or private participation and the development of a preferred option;

- Development of project finance options;

- Development of an overall commercial structure and preliminary legal structuring; and

- Ongoing support to assess the technical and engineering aspects of the project structure which might impinge on project financing.

### Phase 5: Transactions

This phase entails moving the project on from the planning to the implementation stage. Detailed work is undertaken to translate plans into tangible agreements and to procure goods and services. Activities in this phase involve the further development of activities in the project-structuring phase, including developing project financing, legal structuring, and documentation for all major commercial and finance agreements, technical and engineering support and, finally, procurement. At the end of this phase, the project reaches financial close.

Figure 4.3 presents the structure of a PPP and an example of the various agreements and contracts that need to be in place at the end of the transactions phase and achievement of financial close.

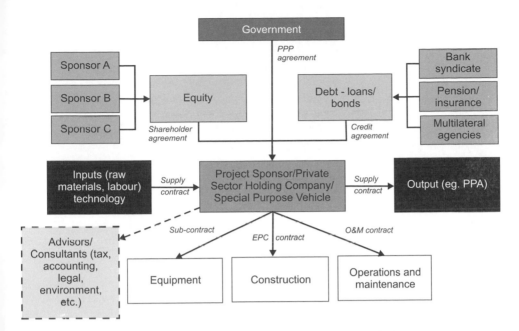

**Figure 4.3.** PPP structure and agreements/contracts at financial close

### Phase 6: Post-implementation

Once the project is in the implementation stage, monitoring of outcomes and progress is crucial – for both the private and public sectors. Typically, monitoring and evaluation plans are produced during the project structuring and transacting phases. Contract management and monitoring by the public sector are discussed further in Section 4.3. In addition, as elaborated in Box 4.6, the private project developer InfraCo has an ongoing interest in providing advisory support and training as appropriate.

Post-implementation support will be necessary to deal with any unexpected circumstances which may lead to renegotiation of procurement agreements, or financing terms and conditions. Renegotiations are also discussed in Section 4.4.

**Box 4.6. The project development process for the Cape Verde wind power project[18]**

InfraCo, a project development company active in Africa, is currently supporting the government in developing a wind power project on four sites in the islands of Santiago, Sal and Boa Vista in Cape Verde, aimed at increasing power supply to meet the rapidly increasing demand in the country in an environmentally friendly and cost-efficient manner. The project will displace a minimum of 20,000 tons of diesel power per year, thereby reducing greenhouse gas emissions and avoiding expensive fuel imports.[19]

The project development process entailed the following activities:

**Enabling environment**

Supporting legislation, regulation and institutional reforms

1. Passing legislation approving the Joint Development Agreement (JDA) for the wind project and the establishment of a PPP joint venture company to execute the project.

2. The establishment of a Designated National Authority (DNA) for the registration and approval of certified emission reductions (CERs).

**Capacity building**

1. Training of staff in the Ministry of Environment in DNA procedures.

2. Training of students at the University of Cape Verde Renewables Department in: (i) wind analysis from the met towers installed by the project; (ii) analysis of lizards' habits and how to mitigate the impact of the construction (the construction area formed the local habitat for a local species of lizards); (iii) general support for the Renewables Department within the university.

**Consensus building**

1. Familiarisation and training of local utility and government staff in the role and capacities of a PPP structure to deliver a successfully financed project.

2. Training of staff in the Ministry of Environment in DNA procedures.

3. Building consensus on the necessity for project finance structures with Ministry of Finance.

4. Building consensus within the local utility on the size and design of the project.

**Project definition**

1. Defining the optimal size of a project that would reduce, to the maximum extent possible, expenditures on imported fossil fuels.

2. Defining the optimal size of the project, given wind resources in Cape Verde.

3. Expanding the project concept to include strengthening the national grid to enable higher absorption of wind energy.

**Project feasibility**

1. Commission full market study for each island to assess the overall demand for power.

2. Engage technical experts to update wind studies prepared over the past ten years

3. Engage environmental experts to conduct a full environmental assessment of the project.

4. Discuss and agree with local officials the outcome of the market and technical studies.

5. Develop a financial model of potential project viability.

6. Develop full technical specifications for the conducting of a full international procurement exercise for plant and equipment.

**Project structuring**

1. Conceptual development of all the major project contractual structures, including power purchase agreements (PPAs), support agreements and site acquisitions.
2. Develop a proposed shareholding structure attractive to incoming investors.
3. Develop a debt and security structure acceptable to potential equity and debt investors.

**Transactions**

1. Engage legal, technical and financial advisory support to undertake simultaneous negotiations with bidding parties for the engineering, procurement and construction (EPC) contracts.
2. Engage and manage a competitive process for equity sale that includes development and negotiation of a shareholders agreement, support agreement and associated project agreements.
3. Conduct a full competitive tender for provision of an EPC contract.
4. Conduct a full competitive tender for incoming equity investors.

**Post-implementation**

Post-implementation support for the project is yet to be determined, but is likely to include:

1. An ongoing advisory role and shareholding role for InfraCo and its affiliates.
2. Ongoing training of Electra as the system operator.

---

As has been illustrated through the range of activities discussed above, the development of a PPP project is a complex and time-consuming process (Box 4.7 also provides an indication of the timing and costs involved during a typical project development cycle). The experience of different countries has shown that the role of the public sector in project development varies considerably between countries. Where there is considerable government capacity (both in terms of specialist knowledge and expertise for project development and resources), governments have been involved in project development, right from the initial stages of managing the feasibility of the project and structuring it appropriately for private participation, through to tendering the opportunity and selecting the preferred bidder (see Box 4.8 for a description of the stages involved in the competitive selection of the preferred bidder). However, in countries where government capacity is weak, most of these activities have been carried out by the private sector itself, leading to 'unsolicited proposals'; correspondingly, this may involve direct negotiation with the developer or competitive negotiation with a smaller group of private players. (Box 5.1 in Section 5 discusses unsolicited proposals and their management.)

**Box 4.7. Indicative costs and timelines for the project development process**

Figure 4.4 presents indicative project development costs and timeframes for a medium-sized project (US$50–250 million). It is important to note that this is an indicative presentation only and in practice may vary substantially between projects. In reality, project development costs may range from US$3 million to US$5 million, especially contributed by the transactions phase, which is particularly complex. For example, it may take considerable additional resources to achieve financial close when there are few bidders. The key message, however, is that the project development process is time-consuming and can involve substantial costs for the developer.

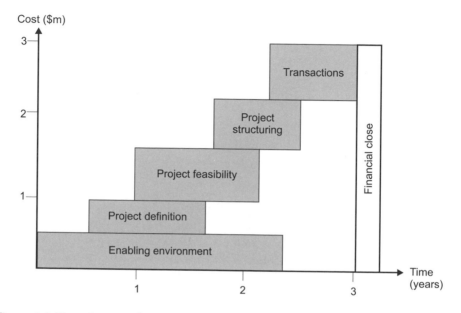

**Figure 4.4.** Typical time and cost of project development process for a project developer for a medium-sized infrastructure project

**Box 4.8. The competitive procurement process**

A competitive procurement process is important for achieving VfM for the government, because it incentivises private bidders to find innovative ways of delivering the infrastructure service at the lowest possible cost.

In order to solicit a reasonable number of bids from the private sector, it is important that the government markets the project opportunity well. Thereafter, most procurement processes follow at least a two-stage process of an initial pre-qualification of a shortlist of bidders, followed by a subsequent evaluation for the selection of the preferred bidder. Governments must undertake a comprehensive due diligence of the bidders in order to arrive at a decision on which is the most suitable bidder. Negotiation with the preferred bidder is also a key step before contract is signed.

The different stages in the competitive procurement process are described in Figure 4.5.

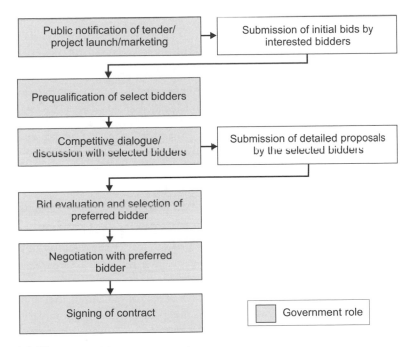

**Figure 4.5.** The competitive procurement process

In practice, each of these phases may take about one to two months to complete, implying that the entire competitive procurement process typically lasts for six months to a year. However, there have been many examples where the procurement process has been delayed or stalled for a number of reasons (see Section 5 for constraints on infrastructure PPPs), resulting in a longer timescale for the selection of the preferred bidder and signing of the contract. The negotiation stage is particularly difficult and time-consuming and may be delayed, sometimes even resulting in a restart of the procurement process if agreement cannot be reached. Competitive procurement has, however, been observed to be a faster process than sole sourced/direct negotiation transactions.[20]

A number of countries have developed detailed guidelines for competitive procurement, including indicative timelines. For example, the South African PPP Manual notes an indicative timeline ranging from 41 to 103 weeks for the process, based on the particular project circumstances. The World Bank procurement guidelines also note that 'not less than six weeks from the date of the invitation to bid or the date of availability of bidding documents, whichever is later, shall be allowed for International Competitive Bidding. Where large works or complex items of equipment are involved, this period shall generally be not less than twelve weeks to enable prospective bidders to conduct investigations before submitting their bids.'

Useful references include:

South Africa PPP Unit, 'National Treasury PPP Manual – Module 5 PPP procurement'.
   http://www.ppp.gov.za/Documents/Manual/Module%2005.pdf

Ministry of Finance, Singapore, *Public Private Partnership Handbook* (2004).
   http://app.mof.gov.sg/data/cmsresource/PPP/Public%20Private%20Partnership
   %20Handbook%20.pdf

Infrastructure Australia, *National PPP Guidelines: Policy Framework* (2008).
   http://www.infrastructureaustralia.gov.au/public_private_partnership_policy_
   guidelines_pdf.aspx

HM Treasury, UK, 'Operational Taskforce Note 1: Benchmarking and Market Testing Guidance' (2006). http://www.hm-treasury.gov.uk/d/operational_taskforce_note_1.pdf

World Bank, *Guidelines Procurement Under IBRD Loans And IDA Credits* (2004, updated 2006).
   http://siteresources.worldbank.org/INTPROCUREMENT/Resources/ProcGuid-10-06-
   ev1.doc

## 4.3. Contract management and monitoring

After the award of the PPP contract and financial close of the project, the construction of the infrastructure commences. It can take a number of years before the infrastructure is operational and can deliver services. In the interim, governments need to manage the PPP contract and monitor the progress made on the development of the infrastructure. Even after the infrastructure service is operational, the PPP contract needs to be monitored for performance, especially if the asset will ultimately be handed back to the government (i.e. the government is the ultimate owner of the asset). Thus contract management and monitoring is a process that takes place throughout the life of the PPP contract.

Contract management/monitoring can be of two different types:

1. Ensuring that the private operator is in line with the regulatory and legal provisions of the sector and country;

2. Technical monitoring of the project – including in terms of the key performance indicators (KPIs) identified in the contract.

Several institutional mechanisms for contract management and monitoring are available. Box 4.9 provides some examples of institutional structures for contract management and monitoring.

**Box 4.9. Institutional arrangements for contract management and monitoring**

While the management of a PPP contract usually lies with the relevant line ministry/public office, the monitoring function can be supported by the regulatory office. For example, in the **Philippines**, in the case of the Manila water concession (see Annex 5), a regulatory office was established under the contract to monitor and enforce the PPP agreement. In **Jamaica**,[21] the licence for the telecoms industry was negotiated and awarded by the Government of Jamaica, and monitored and enforced by the Jamaican Office of Utility Regulation (OUR), a multi-sector regulatory authority also responsible for electricity, water and some transport industries.

The City of Johannesburg in **South Africa**[22] has established a specialised Contract Management Unit (CMU) to provide ongoing support and advice to Johannesburg's 12 utilities, agencies and corporatised entities (collectively referred to by the City as UACs) and to monitor and evaluate their performance. The CMU manages the contractual arrangements and obligations with the UACs and is also responsible for ensuring that services are rendered to the City and its residents.

In the **UK**,[23] the Office of the PPP Arbiter (OPPPA) was established under the Greater London Authority Act 1999, principally to deal with disputes about the financial terms of the PPP agreements for the London Underground. OPPPA documents directions and guidance, instructs external advisers, monitors performance of the PPP agreements and commissions research on relevant and emerging issues.

In establishing suitable contract management and monitoring frameworks for PPPs in developing countries, the institutional location and independence, capacity and expertise and exact remit of a monitoring body need to be carefully examined. For example, it may not make sense to set up a separate unit or organisation for this function when the number of PPP transactions is small. Ultimately, an important monitoring and enforcement role is also played by the customers of the infrastructure service being delivered through the PPP.

Appropriate monitoring frameworks and tools need to be developed and implemented to ensure that a credible performance evaluation process exists, public policy objectives are being met and the PPP project is delivering VfM. Efficient contract monitoring requires that the contract contains explicit targets, an acceptable procedure for measuring and evaluating performance against those targets, clear penalties for failing to meet targets and a well laid-out reporting regime.

The PPP contract should require that the private partner provides regular information on the performance of the project. In addition, an 'independent' engineer or other specialists may also be employed to inspect and monitor the development of the project. Detailed contract performance data need to be fed back to the public sector authority to enable determination of performance-based payments (or deductions as the case may be). However, the contract also needs to be flexible enough to handle change (i.e. renegotiations as discussed in the next sub-section) or failure in the case of adverse events.

Ensuring a smooth transition of assets and operations at contract maturity is an important part of contract management and a procedure for this should be clearly laid out at the start. Options or alternatives may be specified that the public authority may have to choose between. For example, some PPP arrangements include an option for the public authority to purchase the asset at the end of the contract. Other contracts may specify that the ongoing operation should be retendered to competitive bids, a process which must be carefully managed. The contract managers must aid a smooth transition between parties or even prepare to return operations to the public sector.

## 4.4. Renegotiations

Renegotiation of a contract may arise from lack of compliance with agreed terms and/ or departures from expected promises of sector improvements. It can arise for various reasons: the political environment (for example, when the political costs of failure are too high or the government does not honour contract clauses); the design of the PPP contract (for example, if the criterion for selecting a bidder is low tariffs, this may encourage aggressive bidding); the nature, type, existence and autonomy of the regulatory framework; or other issues, such as asymmetry on cost information between the operator and the government. Renegotiation only takes place when there are substantial departures from the original contract (as against, for example, tariff adjustments arising from inflation or period reviews).

Renegotiation of concessions and other PPP contracts is commonplace across infrastructure sectors. For example, excluding telecoms, more than 41 per cent of concessions in the LAC region have been renegotiated. A large number of renegotiations in a country can suggest opportunistic behaviour on the part of the private players or the government in an attempt to secure additional benefits, rather than a lack of completeness in the contract. For example, if private operators believe that renegotiation is feasible, this may undermine the competitive bidding process and they may either underbid or overbid in view of renegotiation at a later date. Renegotiation is costly and involves considerable time and effort. It should therefore be carried out only if it enhances welfare by addressing a failure in the PPP contract.

More generally, renegotiation can be avoided to the extent that the PPP contract is well designed and properly implemented. Elements of good contract design and implementation that can reduce the likelihood of renegotiation are set out in Box 4.10.

**Good contract design**

- As far as possible, contracts should be designed to avoid ambiguities.
- Contracts should include clauses committing government to no renegotiation except in the case of well-defined triggers.
- There should be some system of compensation to operators for unilateral changes to a contract by the government.

**Good implementation**

- Avoid hurried, quickly organised PPP programmes.
- Use a competitive bidding process to award contracts.
- Put in place an appropriate regulatory framework and agency prior to awarding contracts.
- Make appropriate choice of the type of regulation, and understand the allocation of risk in each type and the implications of this for renegotiation.
- Proper regulatory accounting should be put in place to avoid ambiguity.

## Notes

1. Current exchange rate of US$1.Rs50 has been used in all calculations in this section.

2. http://www.iifcl.org/

3. http://finmin.nic.in/the_ministry/dept_eco_affairs/ppp/guideline_scheme_IIPDF.pdf

4. http://www.ebrd.com/country/sector/law/concess/core/coreprin.pdf

5. Alexander, I (2008), 'Regulatory Certainty Through Committing To Explicit Rules – What, Why and How?', Fifth Annual African Forum of Utility Regulators (AFUR) conference.

6. Irwin, T (2006), 'Public risk in private infrastructure', Paper presented at the high-level seminar on 'Realising the Potential for Profitable Investment in Africa', organised by the IMF Institute and the Joint Africa Institute, Tunis, Tunisia, 28 February–1 March 2006.

7. Castalia (2007), 'Advice on Fiscal Management of Infrastructure PPPs in Pakistan', Draft Final Report to World Bank. http://www.ipdf.gov.pk/tmpnew/PDF/Pakistan%20FM%20Final%20Report%20(Final)%20-%20December%2015%202007.pdf

8. Article 16 of Federal Act 11.079/04.

9. International Monetary Fund (2005), 'Government Guarantees and Fiscal Risk', prepared by the Fiscal Affairs Department. http://www.imf.org/external/np/pp/eng/2005/040105c.pdf

10. Brixi, HP (2000), 'The Challenge of Dealing with Contingent Liabilities'. http://www1.worldbank.org/publicsector/pe/PEM%20Course%202004%202000.PPT

11. International Monetary Fund (2005), op. cit.

12. Ibid.

13. Ibid.

14. Ibid.

15. Brixi, HP (2000), 'The Challenge of Dealing with Contingent Liabilities'. http://www1.worldbank.org/publicsector/pe/PEM%20Course%2004%202000.PPT

16. Different organisations and resource books classify the project development process in a number of different stages. The objectives and key activities are the same as presented here, but the classification adopted may differ from other sources. Some countries, for example the UK and Australia, employ specific quality assurance mechanisms such as the 'Gateway Review Process' to ensure that necessary actions have been taken at important decision-making points (such as establishing the case for the project, readiness for the market and procurement) in the project development process. The 'Gateway' process essentially involves a review at key decision-making points to provide assurances that the project can progress successfully to the next stage. More information is available at http://www.ogc.gov.uk/what_is_ogc_gateway_review.asp and http://www.gatewayreview.dtf.vic.gov.au/

17. Although, of course, the standard problem that arises with cost-benefit analysis means that attributing a single definitive value will be problematic. But it should be possible to determine the likely direction of impact.

18. InfraCo, http://www.infraco.com/

19. Private Infrastructure Development Group (PIDG), *Annual Report 2007*.

20. http://www.ppiaf.org/documents/working_papers/Unsolicited_Proposals_Experience_Review_Report_FINAL_2006.pdf

21. Brown, AC *et al.* (2006), *Handbook for Evaluating Infrastructure Regulatory Systems*, World Bank. http://siteresources.worldbank.org/EXTENERGY/Resources/336805-1156971270190/HandbookForEvaluatingInfrastructureRegulation062706.pdf

22. http://www.dwaf.gov.za/dir_ws/WSDP/docs/WSDP/GT/JHBwsdpDraft_12May05_64.pdf

23. http://www.ppparbiter.org.uk

## Key references

### *PPP framework*

Alexander, I, 'Regulatory Certainty Through Committing to Explicit Rules – What, Why and How?' (2008).
http://www.cepa.co.uk/documents/RegulatoryCertaintypaperdraftforcomment.pdf

Focuses on the establishment of predetermined rules committing regulators to future actions.

Alexander, I, 'Appeals and Dispute Resolution – Using Detailed Rules and Processes to Prevent and/or Resolve Disputes' (2008). http://www.cepa.co.uk/documents/RDR AppealsandDisputeResolutionpaperdraftforcomment.pdf

Examines methods of reducing the uncertainty surrounding dispute resolution, with a particular focus on setting rules that pre-empt disputes by removing the discretion of the regulator.

Alexander, I, 'Improving the Balance Between Regulatory Independence, Accountability, Decision-making and Performance', Paper prepared for Fourth Annual Meeting and Conference, African Forum for Utility Regulation (AFUR) (2007). http://www.cepa.co.uk/documents/FinalPaperIanAlexanderAFUR19June2007clean.pdf

Covers the causes and context of regulatory distrust, potential remedies and its relevance to state-owned companies.

Eberhard, A, 'Infrastructure Regulation in Developing Countries: An Exploration of Hybrid and Transitional Models', PPIAF Working Paper No. 4 (2007).
http://www.ppiaf.org/documents/working_papers/AFURhybridmodels4.pdf

Examines regulatory frameworks based on common or civil law legacies of colonial administrations.

World Bank, ICA and PPIAF, 'Attracting Investors to African Public–private Partnerships: A Project Preparation Guide' (2008).
http://www.ppiaf.org/documents/trends_and_policy/Attracting_Investors_to_African_PPP.pdf

Chapter 3 provides a good overview of the rationale behind establishing a framework and of key aspects of its structure.

## Contingent liability management

Irwin, T, 'Public Risk in Private Infrastructure' (2006).
http://imf.org/external/np/seminars/eng/2006/rppia/pdf/irwin.pdf

Discusses guarantees and the risks they pose for governments.

Irwin, T, 'Government Guarantees: Allocating and Valuing Risk in Privately Financed Infrastructure Projects' (2007).
http://siteresources.worldbank.org/INTSDNETWORK/Resources/Government_Guarantees.pdf

Comprehensive review of issues related to the use of government guarantees, including their history, risk allocation principles and techniques for valuation.

IMF, 'Government Guarantees and Fiscal Risk', Prepared by the IMF Fiscal Affairs Department (2005). http://www.imf.org/external/np/pp/eng/2005/040105c.pdf

Covers issues surrounding the fiscal risks resulting from the use of government guarantees.

Brixi, HP, 'Addressing Contingent Liabilities and Fiscal Risk', in *Fiscal Management*, World Bank (2005). http://siteresources.worldbank.org/PSGLP/Resources/FiscalManagement.pdf

Includes a useful section on 'Public Risk in Private Infrastructure'.

## Project preparation

ICA and PPIAF, 'Infrastructure Project Preparation Facilities: Africa User's Guide' (2006).
http://www.ppiaf.org/documents/recent_publications/InfrastructureProjectPreparationFacilitiesUserGuideEnglish.pdf

An introduction to the phases of project preparation and examination of individual facilities.

World Bank, ICA and PPIAF, 'Attracting Investors to African Public–private Partnerships: A Project Preparation Guide' (2008).
http://www.ppiaf.org/documents/trends_and_policy/Attracting_Investors_to_African_PPP.pdf

Assesses the relevant issues for selecting a project for PPP, actions for preparing projects for the market and the management process. The Guide is intended for hiring and managing expert advisers and explains how the public sector should interact with the private sector during the project selection and preparation phases to ensure that decisions made during these phases are realistic. It also provides an analysis of the issues involved in engaging with the private sector during the tender and after a contract has been signed.

PPP Unit, 'PPP Manual' (2004). http://www.ppp.gov.za/PPPManual.htm

Systematic guide to PPP project cycle phases for national and provincial governments, produced by South Africa's PPP Unit.

## Guidance on contract management and monitoring

Partnerships Victoria, 'Contract Management Guide' (2003).
http://www.partnerships.vic.gov.au/CA25708500035EB6/WebObj/ContractManagement
Guide2-PartOne/$File/Contract%20ManagementGuide2%20-%20Part%20One.pdf

Covers the principles and tools used in contract management in Canada.

Public Private Partnerships Programme, 'A Guide to Contract Management for PFI and PPP Projects' (2007).
http://www.partnershipsuk.org.uk/uploads/documents/OTF4ps_ContractManagers_guide.pdf

PFI/PPP contract management guide for local authorities and other stakeholders.

## Renegotiation

Guasch JL, 'Granting and Renegotiating Infrastructure Concessions – Doing It Right' (2004).
http://www-wds.worldbank.org/servlet/WDSContentServer/WDSP/IB/2004/05/06/
000090       341_20040506150118/Rendered/PDF/288160PAPER0Granting010
renegotiating.pdf

Focuses on the impact of concession design and implementation on contract renegotiation in Latin American countries.

# 5

# Constraints to infrastructure PPPs and measures to alleviate them

................................................................................................................................

## Summarising the section

- There are a number of constraints to infrastructure PPPs in developing countries. They include the lack of political acceptability of PPPs; weak capacity of the public sector; an inappropriate enabling environment; the high costs and risks of project development; lack of private sector players; absence of long-term debt; inability of users to afford service fees; and the small size of the economy/sector.

- Governments can address these constraints in a number of ways, including improving the enabling environment and setting up dedicated PPP units, project development facilities and financing vehicles.

- Important lessons can be learned from the experience of PPP units worldwide, including the need for strong political support and for access to high calibre advisers and staff with appropriate commercial experience.

This section discusses the key issues and constraints faced by developing countries in structuring, developing, financing and operating PPPs. The constraints are described in detail, supplemented by examples of practical experience in different countries and a discussion of the implications of each constraint. Relevant mitigation strategies by the public and private sectors are also discussed.

A number of government and donor-supported initiatives have been developed to address some of these constraints. The establishment of specialist PPP units is increasingly being recognised as a useful approach to support PPPs. This section provides examples of government measures to support PPPs, including the experience of specialist PPP units in various countries. Donor initiatives to support PPPs through all stages of the project cycle are discussed separately in Section 6.

## 5.1. Constraints to infrastructure PPPs in developing countries

While infrastructure PPPs have been employed on a considerable scale in developed countries, they have been slow to take off in least developed countries (LDCs). This stems from a number of constraints, including:

- Lack of political acceptability of PPPs;
- Lack of a clear policy statement;

- Weak capacity of the public sector;
- An inappropriate enabling environment in terms of legal, regulatory and institutional frameworks;
- The high costs and risks of project development facing the private sector;
- Lack of private sector players;
- Absence of long-term debt;
- Inability of users to afford service fees;
- The small size of the economy/sector.

These constraints impact on the government, as well as on private sector players (developers, sponsors, investors, etc.), impeding the development of PPPs. These constraints are discussed below.

## 5.1.1. Lack of political acceptability of PPPs

Involving the private sector in the provision of infrastructure services remains politically sensitive in some countries. The main reasons for this include objections that private participation in infrastructure entails higher tariffs and will lead to labour retrenchment; these are issues that can become highly politicised.[1]

The implication of this is that a PPP programme may not get off the ground and that projects may be stalled, delayed or even cancelled. For example, a number of water and sanitation projects have been cancelled due to opposition from consumers and politicians to price increases and higher collection rates. The Cochabamba water concession in Bolivia is an example where increased tariffs created widespread opposition and ultimately caused the cancellation of the project in 2000.[2, 3]

In contrast, strong political support has been regarded as one of the most important factors driving the development and smooth functioning of PPPs. The experience of India is a case in point. The Government of India remains committed to the development of infrastructure PPPs and has put in place supportive initiatives for PPPs.[4] The Prime Minister chairs the Committee on Infrastructure and PPPs receive considerable support. Of course, political support does not guarantee success – there are examples where PPP units have fallen under the aegis of the Prime Minister's Office, but have not been successful, as PPPs were not viewed as a high enough priority. Notional political support is not helpful – there needs to be a high-level political champion for the promotion of PPPs in the country.

Both public and private sectors can work towards improving the political acceptability of PPPs by creating awareness of their benefits through public relations campaigns and/or organising stakeholder consultations to build consensus. It is interesting to note the strategy of the Karnataka Urban Infrastructure Development and Finance Corporation (KUIDFC) in India, whereby a management contract has been let out to facilitate uninterrupted water supply in certain districts. The KUIDFC and the private operators are now exploring a step-by-step mechanism to 'buy in' the public to pay for water tariffs by first introducing dummy water bills to initiate consumers to the concept of paying for water and then slowly introducing proper bills.

## 5.1.2. Lack of a clear policy statement

The success of a PPP programme requires formal support in terms of a clear policy statement on the government's strategy for the development of infrastructure PPPs, including a definition of PPPs and objectives for their use. The lack of a clear policy statement will imply uncertainty and ambiguity, and projects may therefore never get off the ground. This is an important constraint for private investors, as their view of the risks involved in a project will be extremely high.

Governments need to develop explicit PPP policies and include the use of PPPs in their planning documents. For example, in 2009 the Government of Pakistan released a draft policy on PPPs which summarises their objectives and implementation structure, and provides guidelines on key issues such as viability gap funding, the project life cycle and unsolicited proposals.[5] Other countries have also developed detailed guidelines and useful reference handbooks and manuals on PPPs, including Australia[6] and Singapore.[7]

## 5.1.3. Weak public sector capacity

Lack of appropriate skills and experience in infrastructure PPPs can lead to delays, inefficiencies and sometimes the failure of infrastructure projects. Poor project development skills in the public sector can lead to the preparation of 'unbankable' projects, a issue common to many countries, where the project design and structure is unattractive to private investors. Moreover, weak capacity in the public sector reduces the government's ability to negotiate and communicate effectively with private companies.

Lack of project development capacity and resources on the government side has also led to the rise of unsolicited proposals from the private sector. While governments are not obliged to consider such proposals, their limited project development capacity may mean that this is the only route to facilitate PPPs. However, unsolicited proposals must be managed carefully to avoid corruption, as well as uncompetitive and non-transparent behaviour (see Box 5.1).

In order to strengthen public sector capacity in relation to infrastructure PPPs, some countries are now establishing PPP units to provide a centre of excellence within government. A discussion on PPP units is provided in Section 5.2. Governments can also hire external advisers to support them during the PPP project development process; for example, external legal, technical and financial advisers are usually hired by governments to support them during the transaction phase of the project development process.

Standardisation of documents can also help mitigate poor capacity; for example, some countries have adopted model concession agreements to facilitate PPPs (see Box 4.3).

## Box 5.1. Unsolicited infrastructure proposals and their management

Public authorities may receive 'unsolicited proposals', or proposals from private sector consortia, made without the issue of any formal tender request. The government has no obligation to accept or even look at these proposals. However, a lack of project development capacity or finance, or political pressure may lead them to look at these proposals closely. The private sector may generate innovative plans for feasible projects that fit into the country's strategic infrastructure plan and the government may wish to take them forward.

Approved unsolicited proposals can harness the benefits of private sector creativity. However, if the consortia putting forward the proposals have too strong an advantage in being awarded the contract to implement their plans, the result can be a non-transparent, potentially corrupt or uncompetitive tender process that generates projects that are poor value for money.

### Options for managing unsolicited proposals

Authorities need a clear framework in place to deal with the ad hoc nature of unsolicited proposals. There is no one-size-fits-all policy and each authority must find its own balance of incentives to develop projects and mechanisms to ensure a transparent and competitive process for the award of the final contract.

*Total ban*

In circumstances where it is unlikely that there will be a transparent and competitive bidding process – for example when the government is particularly close to business – the best policy may be to ban unsolicited proposals outright. If they are likely to result in poor projects, it may be best not to encourage or consider them at all. In India, for example, government capacity to develop projects is relatively strong and is backed by private sector consultants, with the result that the government does not consider unsolicited proposals.

*Proposal cost reimbursement*

If governments wish to consider unsolicited proposals, they must accept that developing them is a costly and time-consuming activity that the proposers will expect to be paid for one way or another. One way of doing this is to award them the contract, but this will not always be efficient. Another is to purchase the proposal or concept from the proposer and then tender it out competitively, ensuring equality among bidders. This guarantees some payment for the effort made, and the company that has made the proposal does not lose out completely if a competitor is awarded the contract. This strategy encourages bids from small companies, as well as from large ones that can afford to play the odds. However, it is difficult to set the level of reimbursement for each project, and to achieve a balance between the risk of having to pay for numerous poor proposals and ensuring the generation of high quality projects.

*Advantages of an open bidding process*

Rather than paying the proposer at the concept stage, it may be sensible to give them an advantage at the competitive bidding stage. There are three main ways in which this has been done:

- *Bonus system (used in Chile and South Korea)*

  The original proposer may be awarded a defined advantage in the bidding process. This can take various forms, including bonus technical or financial proposal points or a financial advantage (for example, the proposer will win an auction so long as their bid is not more than x per cent or $x higher than other bids). The key disadvantage of this system is that the bonus may scare away other bidders from the auction, leading to fewer competitive bids.

- *Modified Swiss challenge (used in the Philippines, Italy, Taiwan, Guam and India)*

  Other parties may be given the opportunity to make better offers than the original, with no allowance for bonuses. The original firm then has the opportunity to counter the new offers. The main disadvantage of this system is that the window for counter offers is often necessarily short, giving very little time to generate a counter-proposal. This discourages firms from competing if they consider they will have insufficient time to fully prepare. In addition, this approach encourages overly aggressive bidding to deter the original proponent and an expectation of renegotiation. Further problems arise when competing offers have different specifications.

- *Best and final offer system (used in South Africa and Argentina)*

  This system is a hybrid of the previous two, developed in response to each of their failings, and involves multiple rounds of tendering. Unless the proposer has already won the contract, it is always given access to a final bidding round (even if it has not submitted the most competitive bid up to that point), and all bids are then assessed on equal terms without bonuses or predetermined advantages.

**Key references**

- Hodges, J, 'Unsolicited Proposals – Competitive Solutions for Private Infrastructure', Public Policy for the Private Sector, Note No. 258, World Bank (March 2003).

- Hodges, J and Dellacha, G, 'Unsolicited Infrastructure Proposals: How Some Countries Introduce Competition and Transparency', Gridlines Note No. 19, PPIAF (March 2007).

## 5.1.4. Inappropriate enabling environment

Private sector participation in infrastructure requires an enabling legal, regulatory and institutional framework that will guide and support transactions. Section 4.1 describes the various elements of a country framework necessary to support PPPs. Box 4.1 also elaborates on some of the initiatives and institutional structures developed by India to support the growth of PPPs.

However, many countries do not have legislation to regulate infrastructure PPPs or a regulator that monitors performance and ensures compliance. For example, one of the reasons cited for the problems with the Kenya-Uganda rail concession is the absence of a suitable regulator in Uganda (see Annex 5 for a detailed case study). The concession of Metro Manila's Metropolitan Waterworks and Sewerage System (MWSS) also took place in the absence of a regulatory body, with implications for the efficiency of the transaction (see Annex 5).

In a number of cases, the absence of legislation or regulation for an infrastructure PPP transaction has required that parts of the enabling framework are built into the specific project contract – an important option, but one which can introduce additional difficulties, costs and delays. This was the case in the Manila water concession, where it was decided that a regulatory office would be established within MWSS as part of the concession agreement; this also raised questions about the independence of the regulatory office.

An inappropriate enabling environment is likely to reduce confidence among private investors. For example, in the absence of suitable dispute resolution mechanisms or enforceable property and intellectual property laws, private investors are likely to be deterred from investing.[8] While this can be overcome through the inclusion of international dispute resolution and other measures, it may create political problems, as national governments have to comply with international rulings on domestic matters.

### 5.1.5. High costs and risks of project development for the private sector

Early stage project development involves a significant investment of resources (in developing feasibility studies, negotiating licence agreements with government, securing land rights, etc.) that are only recoverable if the project is ultimately successful. In many cases, the assessment by commercial developers, especially for smaller projects or those in more difficult sectors (e.g. water and sanitation), is that the attractiveness of the opportunity and its likelihood of success are insufficient to justify the upfront investment. In addition, in many developing countries, the private sector is at an early stage of development and lacks the knowledge to develop, prepare and structure projects. As a result, infrastructure projects are not fully defined or, if they are, they may be developed to such a low standard that competent private sponsors or investors will not be interested.

In response to this constraint, some countries are attempting to develop their project development capabilities by setting up dedicated project development funds. As described in Box 4.1, India has set up the India Infrastructure Project Development Fund, with the objective of structuring and developing bankable projects that can then be offered to the private sector on a PPP basis. The IIPDF funds the PPP project development expenses, including the costs of engaging consultants and transaction advisers. Pakistan is also currently considering developing a Project Development Fund (PDF) to support the development of infrastructure PPPs.

A number of donor-funded project preparation facilities, discussed in Section 6 below, provide a range of different types of support, including financial support for the public and private sectors for project development, and advisory and capacity building support.

### 5.1.6. Lack of private sector players

Lack of private sector players implies non-competitive bidding, as well as poor performance during the project due to insufficient experience and skills. The experience among Commonwealth countries has differed in this regard. In some countries, such as India, the government is able to develop projects to the extent that at the bidding stage there are generally enough bidders to facilitate competition; in many African countries (with the possible exception of South Africa), there may be few, and sometimes no, private bidders.[9] For example, City Water was the sole bidder for the Tanzanian water distribution contract, having qualified for the final proposal stage together with two other bidders. However, these bidders did not submit final proposals and hence the Tanzanian government awarded the contract to City Water.

The international private sector may not be interested in bidding for projects in smaller developing countries, especially when the size of the project is below the minimum efficient size (discussed in detail in Section 5.1.9 below); the risks may be too high for the project to be attractive.

International bidders can be encouraged to participate by structuring a consortium to include both international and domestic sponsors, with a minimum equity contribution from the international sponsor. This consortium structure has been employed in a number of water sector PPPs, in particular, where the service/management contract is with the international sponsor and the domestic sponsors provide most of the equity.

Suitable contract design, for example structuring a larger contract instead of many smaller contracts, can also attract international private sector participation.

### 5.1.7. Absence of long-term debt

A 20-year life cycle (sometimes longer) for an infrastructure project implies a considerable time lag between the raising of finance and the ability to pay back through project-generated revenues, especially when utilisation of the service is expected to grow over the life of the asset. Thus infrastructure development requires debt that can be of sufficiently long tenor to match cash flows. In most developing countries, it is not possible to raise finance of sufficiently long tenor for infrastructure development. This not only constrains the development of infrastructure due to increased uncertainty, but also makes the infrastructure services more expensive in the short term because of the front-end loaded prices and other factors.

Long-term debt for infrastructure projects can be denominated either in foreign or local currency. Foreign currency denominated debt is useful when the project involves considerable imports for the construction of the infrastructure (and involves foreign exchange rate risk). Local currency debt is useful as the debt is in the same currency as the revenues that will be received through consumption of the infrastructure services, and hence does not involve exchange rate risk. But local currency finance is often unavailable because of a lack of liquidity and/or the underdevelopment of local capital markets.

In response to this constraint, some governments have set up project financing facilities.[10, 11] The aim of most of these facilities is to help crowd-in private sector finance by taking up greater risks in the project, for example the facility may provide subordinated debt as a means of attracting senior debt from the private sector. The Government of India has established the India Infrastructure Finance Company Ltd., a dedicated institution for infrastructure financing.[12] The Government of Bangladesh has set up the Infrastructure Development Company Limited (IDCOL) (see Box 5.2). Some countries have also set up sector-specific funds, such as the Long Term Credit Fund (LTCF) in Pakistan, which focuses on the energy sector; while the fund is now essentially non-operational, there are important lessons to be learned from its experience (see Box 5.3).

---

**Box 5.2. Infrastructure Development Company Limited, Bangladesh**

IDCOL was established in 1997 by the Government of Bangladesh to promote private sector participation in infrastructure. It has had a significant impact in supporting commercially viable mid- to large-scale infrastructure and smaller-scale renewable energy projects throughout the country. Its most high profile project to date has been the US$80 million financing of the 450MW Meghnaghat Power project (see Annex 5 for a detailed case study).

IDCOL is a government-owned non-bank financial institution. It administers World Bank funds from the International Development Agency (IDA) Private Sector Infrastructure Development Project on behalf of the government. It has access to resources from a number of donors to support projects by providing competitive long-term senior and subordinated loans. IDCOL funding acts as a catalyst for mobilising additional external support and is provided alongside commercial sources of finance. It only supports viable private projects in a limited number of core infrastructure sectors. However, it also provides grants and concessional loans for rural energy and infrastructure projects.

IDCOL employs a number of specialist technical experts covering economics, law, finance and engineering. This enables it to perform various functions in addition to financing, including technical assistance and skills development roles. Its independent board of directors includes representatives from both the public and private sectors.

---

## Box 5.3. Long Term Credit Fund, Pakistan

The LTCF (originally the Private Sector Energy Development Fund) was established by the Government of Pakistan in 1985 in partnership with the World Bank and USAID as part of the Private Energy Division of the National Development Finance Corporation. The Fund was designed to overcome the barrier of the country's poor credit rating and to mobilise investment in the industry by taking a catalytic lead investment role and setting up an institutional framework.

By 1994, the LTCF had total commitments close to US$1 billion, including US$400 million from both the World Bank and the Export-Import Bank of Japan (JEXIM). Between 1989 and 1994, it provided subordinated loans to energy projects with nominal interest rates below market levels, eight-year grace periods and generous exchange rate insurance, covering up to 30 per cent of project costs. Modifications in 1994 included the introduction of fixed rate instruments.

Over its active life, the LTCF provided US$840 million to five projects in loans with a total value of US$2.9 billion. The largest two projects (the US$1.5 billion HUB power project and the US$600 million Uch power project) consumed nearly two-thirds of the Fund's resources.

The LTCF is now essentially non-operational and faces an uncertain future. Following bankruptcy in 2002, it was transferred to a commercial institution, the National Bank of Pakistan. The Fund was meant to be a temporary support that would kick-start investor interest. However, it was never able to replenish its capital through loan repayments and thus establish a sustainable footing.

Klingebiel and Ruster (2000) draw several lessons from this experience:

- An adequate policy framework is crucial to attract private financing, as well as a good credit rating;
- Direct funding increased commercial risk exposure for the government without adequate control or recompense, leading to damaging renegotiation;
- The ability of subsidised funds to attract investments discouraged the government from pursuing the more sustainable solution of regulatory reform; and
- Although the fund was established to tackle the lack of long-term finance for the power sector, it is not clear that this was the main obstacle.

### Key references

Klingebiel, D and Ruster, J, 'Why Infrastructure Financing Facilities Often Fall Short of Their Objectives', World Bank Policy Research Working Paper No. 2358 (2000). http://www-wds.worldbank.org/external/default/WDSContentServer/IW3P/IB/2000/07/07/000094946_00062305373440/Rendered/PDF/multi_page.pdf

USAID, 'Private Sector Power Project: End of Contract Report' (1994). http://pdf.usaid.gov/pdf_docs/PDABL094.pdf

## 5.1.8. Affordability issues

Lack of willingness and ability to pay for infrastructure services is another important constraint in developing countries. It is often believed that large numbers of people on lower incomes will be unable to afford full cost-recovery tariffs for electricity or water, especially if the tariff level reflects the high costs of building greenfield infrastructure. In addition, many people may be perceived as being unwilling to pay for essential infrastructure services for political or social reasons. There is also the issue of 'willingness to charge', a problem caused, for example, by politicians being unwilling to impose tariffs in order to remain popular with voters.[13] Affordability is a particularly important constraint in developing rural infrastructure, where income levels are typically much lower than in urban areas, and where there are fewer opportunities to share costs with corporate customers.

The inability of users to afford infrastructure services is relevant at two levels: first, in terms of the cost of the infrastructure for the project (for example, the laying of water pipes); and second, in terms of the consumption of the infrastructure service. In a PPP structure, tariffs may need to reflect both capital and operating costs. However, there may be cases where tariffs need to reflect consumption only, such as that of the PPP contract in the Chilean water sector, as there was almost universal coverage.[14]

Where user charges cannot be levied to cover costs, there is a need for subsidies to be employed by the government. Government or donor subsidies can take many forms, such as an outright subsidy included in the financial structure of the project or some form of shadow tolls, revenue guarantees or grants rolled into the project contract. Given that consumers can often afford ongoing costs, and in fact often pay much more for informal provision of services, but lack access to funds to meet up-front capital costs, a strong focus on connection/capital subsidies may be appropriate, although there are also cases where consumption subsidies have been provided. For example, in the Chilean case mentioned above, a consumption subsidy targeted at individual customers was provided, based on the actual amount of water consumed by each beneficiary. The subsidy scheme was funded entirely from the central government's budget, expressed as a percentage of the household's bill. In Guinea, a lease contract for water services in the major towns and cities was structured in 1989, and while the government was committed to recovering the cost of the services, it did not want a major tariff shock at the beginning of the contract. For the first six years of the contract, therefore, an IDA credit was used to subsidise a declining share of the private operator's costs, while the water tariff was raised until it covered costs.[15] Further donor support for subsidy provision is discussed in Section 6.

In some cases, cross-subsidies can be structured into the project, so that affordability constraints are taken into account and the project is still bankable. Water sector PPPs where industrial users pay a higher tariff than domestic users are a useful example. In such a structure, industrial users are essentially subsidising domestic consumption.

Another example is that of private finance initiatives in the UK. These are most commonly used for social infrastructure projects, i.e. projects that provide a public service. Under a PFI, the public sector does not own the asset, for example a hospital or a school, but pays the PFI contractor a stream of committed revenue payments for the use of the facilities over the contract period. Thus the charges for the use of the infrastructure service are paid by the government/taxpayers and not by the direct users. This approach may have limited applicability to developing countries, where governments may not have the resources to commit to the revenue payments.

Some governments have set up dedicated 'viability gap schemes', or initiatives that meet the funding gap required to make an economically essential project commercially viable. For example, in 2006 the Government of India instituted a Viability Gap Fund (VGF) and the Government of Pakistan is currently in the process of establishing a similar initiative. Box 5.4 provides a case study of the Indian VGF.

---

**Box 5.4. Lessons from India's Viability Gap Fund[16]**

The Government of India has set up a Viability Gap Fund, which aims to ensure enhanced access to PPP infrastructure by subsidising the capital cost of access. The VGF's objective is thus to meet the funding gap required to make economically essential projects commercially viable. The VGF has been fully operational since January 2006.

To date, 15 projects have obtained VGF approval and have completed the bidding process. The total support approved amounts to Rs32.29 billion (US$646 million), but only Rs610 million (US$12.2 million) has been disbursed. Thirty-one further projects have obtained 'in principle' approval for VGF support of Rs34.22 billion (US$684 million). The government can commit up to 20 per cent of project capital costs as a capital grant. Sponsoring government authorities may commit a further 20 per cent from their own budgets.

A number of key lessons emerge from the VGF's experience to date:

- Annual outlay has been unexpectedly small. This is due to the long time taken to reach technical and financial close, and the lagged disbursement of support in line with debt disbursements.

- All approved VGF proposals have been in the highway/road sector or urban rapid transit projects. Other infrastructure projects have been unviable, poorly structured or did not involve a concession contract.

- It is critical for projects to be bid out in a competitive and transparent manner, so as to determine the smallest capital subsidy requirement.

- The selected private sector sponsor should first invest their equity, as well as identify the debt financiers/lead financial institution, before they become eligible for VGF support.

- The practice of structuring payments so that they are in proportion to debt disbursements is working well. The VGF benefits from the lead financial institution's due diligence and monitoring.

- Support is provided as a capital grant, as it is thought that any element of repayment would increase the financial bid submitted by the concessionaires.

- Sponsoring authorities are accountable for the progress of projects. They must therefore have sufficient capacity to carry out or supervise feasibility studies and submit documentation.

- Despite the fact that the VGF is housed within the Ministry of Finance, 'political capture' has been avoided by having two levels of institutional approval staffed by senior government officials from across departments.

---

### 5.1.9. Size of the economy or sector

The size of the economy or infrastructure sector is also an important constraining factor limiting the development of PPPs for the delivery of infrastructure services. Small size implies lack of economies of scale in project development, as well as a project size which is below the minimum that is efficient. While size is a constraint for public provision of infrastructure services as well, this is particularly so for PPPs, as a small-scale project may be 'unbankable'.

The public and private sectors can help mitigate this constraint through suitable project design and structuring. Regional initiatives can also help improve economies of scale. Box 5.5 elaborates on this constraint in the context of the experience of small island states, particularly the Commonwealth island countries in the LAC region.

## Box 5.5. Constraints on PPPs faced by small island states

Small island states face a number of additional challenges in developing infrastructure PPPs, given their small size. These include:

- **Lack of economies of scale in infrastructure development and delivery**: The small physical size of the islands, and their concomitantly low population levels, implies that the total level of infrastructure required may be below the minimum efficient size. High fixed costs for infrastructure may mean that investors do not break even (i.e. the project is not bankable), given low consumption levels. For example, Figure 5.1 illustrates the direct relationship between levels of electricity generation and end-user prices across small island states.[17]

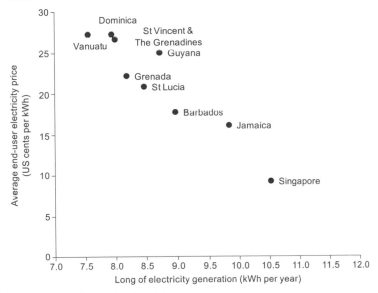

**Figure 5.1** Economies of scale in electricity

The lack of economies of scale is relevant at two levels: (i) in terms of the minimum efficient technical size of the infrastructure asset; and (ii) the high transaction costs of providing the infrastructure service to a limited number of consumers. Difficult island topology and small and sometimes scattered populations further exacerbate this, requiring non-standard solutions that are costlier to develop and maintain than elsewhere. The development of larger regional projects or alternative technologies may provide solutions.

- **Limited number of private sector players:** The greater cost and risk of projects in small islands results in fewer attractive projects for international developers. Consequently, such economies are likely to require greater state support to ensure their success. Solutions that may be considered include offering regional projects to generate greater investor interest among large developers; encouraging the creation of medium-size developers that are appropriate for the scale of the projects; or investigating unconventional technological methods. Other facilitating solutions include defining more relevant procurement criteria; for example, under World Bank procurement guidelines for water and sanitation projects, the private sector bidder needs to have experience of operating local systems for a population of a minimum size that is often larger than the small economy in question. Given the small populations of small island economies, these and other pertinent criteria may be appropriately revised.

- **Difficulty in implementing effective regulation:** The higher cost of infrastructure in small island states makes it especially important to keep price levels competitive. However, conventional regulation is more difficult in small countries for a number of reasons, including: (i) regulatory models cannot be directly copied from elsewhere due to local technical idiosyncrasies; (ii) regulators have high overhead costs that may not be affordable given their small remit; (iii) limited availability of specialist professionals; and (iv) it can be hard to maintain independence in small countries with close links between government and business. However, there are a number of mechanisms that countries can consider in order to make regulators or other infrastructure-related facilities feasible in small island states, including:

  o *Low discretion regulation:* Authorities may create well-defined rules that provide little room for discretion. This is an inexpensive method that requires little skill or independence on the part of the regulator. However, this is likely to be damagingly unresponsive to changes and unanticipated outcomes.

  o *Light regulation:* Operate a small regulator with few staff, supplemented by outside consultants for technical requirements. Multi-sector regulators may also pool fixed costs and are most suitable in countries with constrained technical capacities. For example, Vanuatu has a multi-utility regulator that monitors concession contracts. It employs only four full-time staff, but brings in consultants for quality assurance, training and tariff reviews.

  o *Regional regulatory bodies:* Problems can be tackled at a regional level through:

    - regional forums such as the Organisation of Caribbean Utility Regulators or the East Asia and Pacific Infrastructure Regulatory Forum, that can share common experiences and problems;

    - regional advisory bodies, such as the Eastern Caribbean Telecommunications Regulatory Authority which generate economies of scale by avoiding common tasks, but whose recommendations are non-binding; or

    - binding regional regulators to whom regulation is delegated for the region. It is unlikely, however, that authorities will agree to cede power to this extent.

- **More volatile economies:** Small island economies tend to have per capita GDP and growth rates similar to those of comparable low-income countries. However, their incomes are more volatile than larger ones. They are particularly prone to common shocks through economic diversification and risk of natural disasters. This increases the risk for PPP projects.

However, despite these additional challenges, many Commonwealth small island states have comparatively good infrastructure services, with some examples of PPPs. For example, there are a number of PPPs in island states, including a water concession in Vanuatu, a BOT water project in Barbados and a BOO desalination scheme in Trinidad and Tobago. Private provision of electricity in Caribbean countries has provided higher coverage than in comparable Pacific states.[18]

**Key references**

- Ehrhardt, D and Oliver, C, 'Big Challenges, Small States: Regulatory Options to Overcome Infrastructure Constraints', Gridlines Note No. 24, PPIAF (May 2007). http://www.ppiaf.org/documents/gridlines/24SmIsl.pdf

- Jha, AK (ed.), 'Institutions, Performance, and the Financing of Infrastructure Services in the Caribbean', World Bank Working Paper No. 58 (June 2005). http://www.castalia-advisors.com/files/12383.pdf

### 5.1.10. Summary of key constraints to infrastructure PPPs and mitigation strategies

Figure 5.2 summarises the discussion on the key constraints to infrastructure PPPs and the implications that deter their development.

Table 5.1 summarises relevant mitigation strategies by both the public and private sectors.

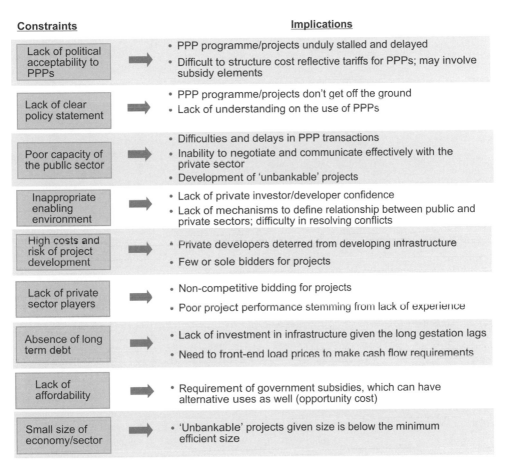

**Figure 5.2.** Constraints to infrastructure PPPs and their implications

**Table 5.1.** Potential public and private sector mitigation strategies for constraints to infrastructure PPPs

| Constraint | Public sector | Private sector |
|---|---|---|
| Lack of political acceptability of PPPs | • Create awareness on the benefits of PPPs<br>• Show commitment to PPPs through supportive policy and enabling framework<br>• Organise stakeholder consultations for consensus building | • Work with the public sector to build consensus and support for the PPP project<br>• Organise stakeholder consultations for consensus building |
| Lack of a clear policy statement | • Develop policy statements and appropriate guidelines | • Business groups to lobby government |
| Weak capacity of the public sector | • Centre of excellence within the public sector in the form of a PPP unit<br>• Staff training<br>• Hiring external advisers<br>• Use of MCAs where appropriate | |
| Inappropriate enabling environment in terms of legal, regulatory and institutional framework | • Develop supportive enabling environment<br>• Regional frameworks<br>• International institutions<br>• Work on relevant supportive legislation, regulation and institutional requirements in contract design and structure | • Work on relevant supportive legislation, regulation and institutional requirements in contract design and structure |
| High costs and risks of project development facing the private sector | • Development of project development vehicles<br>• Encourage local developers<br>• Develop supportive enabling environment to reduce risks | • Access donor-funded project development facilities |
| Lack of private sector players | • Development of bankable projects and effective marketing<br>• Due diligence where there is a limited number of bidders | |
| Absence of long-term debt | • Development of project financing vehicles<br>• Overall macro policies to support capital and credit market development<br>• Sovereign guarantees | • Access credit guarantees/DFI finance |
| Inability of users to afford service fees | • Viability gap funding schemes<br>• Provision of shadow tolls/revenue guarantees<br>• Overall macro policies to support economic growth | • Contract design<br>• Efficient development of infrastructure to minimise costs<br>• Access OBA |
| Size of the economy/ sector | • Suitable project design and structuring<br>• Regional initiatives<br>• Encourage local bidders | • Suitable project design and structuring<br>• Regional initiatives |

## 5.2. PPP units

PPP units are specialist agencies or cells/departments that aim to build government capacity in PPPs. They can perform a range of different functions, providing support across the stages of the project cycle. More recently, beyond this 'classic' approach to a PPP unit, its role has been interpreted more broadly as a means of addressing any number of PPP process support requirements.

Typical priorities for PPP unit support are:

- The development of appropriate PPP policies, their promotion and, sometimes, their enforcement;

- Centralised project development and transaction support – the packaging of opportunities and their marketing; and

- The development of appropriate direct and contingent financial support for projects, including ensuring that government obligations are appropriately accounted for.

Over the past decade, PPP units have become an important part of the infrastructure development agenda in OECD countries. Many governments across the developing world have also introduced units, and several countries, including Kenya and Tanzania, are now in the process of establishing them.

A number of lessons can be drawn from the PPP units that exist. However, their core functions, institutional fit, design and structure are not directly replicable in different countries. PPP units need to be carefully designed to reflect the key constraints and issues for infrastructure PPPs in a particular country. In addition, while they have considerable merits, PPP units should not be viewed as a solution to all the constraints that face infrastructure PPPs. There may be other institutional solutions for particular problems that cannot be covered in this way.

Box 5.6 provides some broad lessons from global experience of PPP units.

**Box 5.6. Lessons learned from global experience of PPP units**

International experience of PPP units in both developed and developing countries shows that they are neither necessary nor sufficient to create successful infrastructure PPPs. However, if they are carefully designed and structured, PPP units can provide considerable support to progress a country's infrastructure PPP plan. The variety of units to date provides useful lessons for the future and highlights fundamental issues that must be considered before a unit is established, as presented below.

**Need for political support**

A high level of political support is crucial to ensure the success of a PPP unit. During its initial design and implementation stages, it is extremely important that the unit has a 'champion' who can promote its establishment within the overall government structure. Once established, the unit needs to have strong political commitment to ensure that it can discharge its roles and responsibilities effectively.

The World Bank and PPIAF (2007) provide an insightful review of eight PPP units; they found that units in the UK, South Africa, Portugal and Victoria, Australia have thrived with strong government support, whereas PPP units in the Philippines, Bangladesh and Jamaica have been much less successful, due to lack of political commitment.

**A functional and institutional structure that takes into account potential conflicts of interest**

PPP units can perform a range of different functions; however, some of their roles involve potential conflicts of interest. For example:

- *Developing policy versus implementation (for instance, through a transaction capability)*: These are typically best kept separate, as the former involves 'setting the stage', while the latter involves a high degree of sponsorship of individual projects.
- *Transacting and then monitoring or ensuring contract compliance* do not go well together, as they can involve the monitoring of own design; and
- *Project design and development versus public funding/financing*: As project development involves promotion by the sponsor of the project, there may be considerable pressure to fund an activity even if it is not bankable.

If conflicts of interest are evident, confidence in the whole PPP approach will be undermined. Thus, if these activities are housed together, they must be appropriately ring-fenced. In more mature PPP regimes with sufficient scale, roles can be separated into different institutions, as they are, for example, in the UK, with functions split between the Treasury Task Force for PPP and Partnerships UK. Any conflicts between the unit and existing line ministries or departments must also be minimised.

**Institutional location of the unit**

The institutional location of the unit has considerable implications for its effectiveness. This not only links up with the conflicts of interest issue highlighted above. On the one hand, it is important that any unit has the right level of sponsorship and on the other hand, it must not become overly politicised or part of an individual's or group's power base. The location of a unit must fit as seamlessly as possible with other institutions. They must avoid replication, conflict or creating another level of red-tape.

As a PPP unit works across infrastructure sectors, it is usually located in a cross-sectoral ministry such as finance or planning. In certain cases, the unit may be well placed as a free-standing institution. However, free-standing units do not benefit from the associated authority and cachet provided by host institutions. In Portugal, Parpública is successful as a separate body, but most of its staff are hired from the Ministry of Finance.

PPP units may be set up at central or state government level, as appropriate. In India, for example, given the relatively large number of PPP transactions, the government has decided to set up PPP cells at both central and state level.

### Development and retention of relevant infrastructure PPP skills

To function effectively, PPP units must be able to assess, structure and review PPP infrastructure projects, and require a clear understanding and experience of issues such as risk allocation and financial structuring.

The skills required for this, and those that are acquired through transaction experience, are highly valued by the private sector, making it difficult to retain them in-house or procure them externally. Where PPP units have been constrained in this manner, they have used a number of creative solutions, including:

- Use of consultants for short-term (South Africa, Bangladesh) or long-term (the Philippines BOT centre, Pakistan) contracts;
- Consultants hired as advisers for specific tasks (Partnerships Victoria, Parpública, Portugal);
- Internal negotiation based upon 'special skills';
- Performance-based contracts or bonuses; and
- Secondments from the private sector (UK Treasury PPP Task Force).

The dangers of relying on learning-as-doing and leakage of internally developed skills mean that there is an emphasis on the use of external skills. For example, the first head of the South African PPP Unit was brought in from the World Bank, and others came on secondment from Partnerships UK. However, these are expensive solutions and incentives must be aligned to motivate staff to take the right risks while still providing good value for money.

## Notes

1. In addition, in some countries public sector officials are wary of PPPs, viewing the involvement of the private sector as a loss of control for themselves.

2. Harris, C, Hodges, C, Schur M and Shukla, P, 'Infrastructure Projects: A Review of Cancelled Projects', Public Policy for the Private Sector, Note No. 252, World Bank (January 2003).

3. This took place in the wider context of political opposition to irrigation reforms and the government's coca eradication policy.

4. Including the India Infrastructure Finance Company Ltd, which provides long-term finance for infrastructure projects, and the Viability Gap Funding Scheme, which supports the financial viability of projects.

5. Government of Pakistan, *Pakistan Policy on Public Private Partnerships: Private Participation in Infrastructure for Better Public Services*, April 2009.

6. http://www.infrastructureaustralia.gov.au/files/National_PPP_Guidelines_Overview_Dec_08.pdf

7. http://app.mof.gov.sg/data/cmsresource/PPP/Public%20Private%20Partnership%20 Handbook%20.pdf

8. In some cases this has been overcome through the use of international bilateral trade agreements.

9. There are a number of other reasons why there may be few or no bidders, such as weak government capacity, lack of affordability and high risk.

10. Section 6 discusses donor facilities for infrastructure finance, including debt financing and guarantee facilities.

11. The trend towards establishing dedicated infrastructure financing facilities is more recent. Governments have, of course, been providing guarantees to improve access to, and reduce the cost of, debt financing. Annex 5 provides examples where sovereign guarantees have enhanced the financing structure of projects. However, these guarantees have implications for government budget management.

12. As of September 2008, 71 projects across all sectors, mostly in road and power, reached financial close. The IIFCL allocated Rs11.8 billion (US$262 million) to these projects, the total cost of which exceeded Rs1,097 billion (US$24 billion). Source: IIFCL Newsletter, October 2008.

13. This can, however, be averted by conducting surveys to establish that the population is willing and able to pay for the infrastructure service.

14. Brook, PJ and Smith, SM (eds), 'Contracting for Public Services – Output-based Aid and its Applications', World Bank and IFC (August 2001).

15. Ibid.

16. For further details of the Government of India VGF, see Indian Department of Economic Affairs, 'Scheme and Guidelines for Financial Support to Public Private Partnerships in Infrastructure' (2008).
http://www.pppinindia.com/pdf/scheme_Guidelines_Financial_Support_PPP_ Infrastructure-english.pdf

17. Ibid.

18. Ehrhardt D and Oliver C (May 2007).

## Key references

### PPP units

World Bank and PPIAF, 'Public–private Partnership Units: Lessons for their Design and Use in Infrastructure', PPIAF and EASSD/World Bank (2007).
http://www.ppiaf.org/documents/other_publications/PPP_units_paper.pdf

Sanghi et al., 'Designing and Using Public–private Partnership Units in Infrastructure: Lessons from Case Studies Around the World', Gridlines Note No. 27, PPIAF (2007).
http://www.ppiaf.org/documents/gridlines/27PPP.pdf

Dutz et al., 'Public–private Partnership Units: What Are They and What Do They Do?', Public Policy for the Private Sector, Note No. 311, The World Bank Group, Financial and Private Sector Development Vice Presidency (2006). http://rru.worldbank.org/documents/ publicpolicyjournal/311Dutz_Harris_Dhingra_Shugart.pdf

## Links to selected Commonwealth PPP units

Partnerships Victoria (Australia): http://www.partnerships.vic.gov.au/

PPP Unit, South Africa: http://www.ppp.gov.za/

Partnerships UK: http://www.partnershipsuk.org.uk/

HM Treasury PPP Policy Team: http://www.hm-treasury.gov.uk/ppp_policy_team.htm

Malta PPP Unit: http://finance.gov.mt/page.aspx?site=MFIN&page=ppp

IIFC (Bangladesh): http://www.iifc.net/

Indian Department of Economic Affairs PPP Cell: http://finmin.nic.in/the_ministry/dept_eco_affairs/ppp/ppp_index.html

Philippines BOT Center: http://www.botcenter.gov.ph/

PPP Initiative, Ministry of Finance, Singapore: http://app.mof.gov.sg/ppp.aspx

Infrastructure Australia: http://www.infrastructureaustralia.gov.au/

Partnerships British Columbia: http://www.partnershipsbc.ca/

UNESCAP and FDI.net maintain more comprehensive directories of PPP units and related organisations: http://www.unescap.org/ttdw/ppp/PPPUnits.html and http://www.fdi.net/spotlight/spotlight_detail.cfm?spid=42&cid=12304

## PPP standardised contracts

Indian Model Concession Agreements: http://infrastructure.gov.in/mca.htm

HM Treasury, UK Standardised PPP Contracts. http://www.hm-treasury.gov.uk/ppp_standardised_contracts.htm

## Financing for infrastructure projects

Klingebiel, D and Ruster, J, 'Why Infrastructure Financing Facilities Often Fall Short of Their Objectives', World Bank Policy Research Working Paper 2358 (2000). http://www-wds.worldbank.org/external/default/WDSContentServer/IW3P/IB/2000/07/07/000094946_00062305373440/Rendered/PDF/multi_page.pdf

## Detailed case studies of infrastructure financing facilities

Alam, M (ed.), *Municipal Infrastructure Financing: Innovative Practices from Developing Countries*, Commonwealth Secretariat (2010). ISBN: 9781849290036 http://publications.thecommonwealth.org/municipal-infrastructure-financing-686-p.aspx

Overview of private sector involvement in the delivery of municipal services, focusing on four case studies from the Commonwealth.

Peterson GE, 'Unlocking Land Values to Finance Urban Infrastructure', Trends and Policy Options No. 7, World Bank/PPIAF. http://www.ppiaf.org/content/view/479/485/

A practical guide that looks at case studies and lessons learned from experience in land-based finance and its role in urban capital budgets.

## Unsolicited proposals

Hodges, J, 'Unsolicited Proposals – Competitive Solutions for Private Infrastructure', Public Policy for the Private Sector, Note No. 258, World Bank (2003). http://rru.worldbank.org/documents/publicpolicyjournal/258Hodge-031103.pdf

Explores methods used by governments to harness unsolicited proposals, while retaining competitive pressures.

Hodges, J and Dellacha, G, 'Unsolicited Infrastructure Proposals: How Some Countries Introduce Competition and Transparency', Gridlines Note No. 19, PPIAF (2007). http://www.ppiaf.org/documents/gridlines/19Unsolisitedproposals.pdf

An updated review of strategies for dealing with unsolicited proposals.

### Affordability/output-based aid

Halpern, J and Mumssen, Y, 'Lessons Learned in Infrastructure Services Provision: Reaching the Poor', GPOBA (2006). http://www.gpoba.org/gpoba/node/126

A discussion of lessons learned in providing infrastructure services for poor households.

Brook, PJ and Smith, SM (eds), *Contracting for Public Services – Output-based Aid and its Applications*, World Bank and IFC (2001). http://rru.worldbank.org/Features/OBABook.aspx

Gerner, F and Sinclair, S, 'Connecting Residential Households to Natural Gas: An Economic and Financial Analysis', GPOBA (2006). http://www.gpoba.org/gpoba/node/127

Analysis of costs and benefits of switching residential households to natural gas and options for increasing domestic connections.

Navarro, M and Tavares, L, 'Output-based Aid in Cambodia: Getting Private Operators and Local Communities to Help Deliver Water to the Poor – The Experience to Date', GPOBA (2008). http://www.gpoba.org/gpoba/node/129

An examination of the output-based aid pilot in small towns in Cambodia, one of the first OBA water supply pilots to be initiated.

# 6

# Donor initiatives to support infrastructure PPPs

## Summarising the section

- A number of donor facilities have been set up to support infrastructure PPPs in developing countries, including for project preparation, financing and funding.

- Project preparation facilities are mainly of three types: (i) facilities that provide advice to the government, such as the PPIAF and DevCo; (ii) facilities that play the role of a principal and take on the risks and costs of early stage project preparation, including InfraCo and InfraVentures; and (iii) facilities that provide funding for the different stages of the project development process, such as the Global Partnership for Output-Based Aid (GPOBA).

- Absence of long-term financing for infrastructure is one of the key constraints in developing countries; in response, donors have set up financing facilities such as the Emerging Africa Infrastructure Fund. Some IFIs also provide loan/debt products for infrastructure. These are usually commercially priced products, offered on a non- or limited-recourse basis.

- The two main types of donor guarantees for infrastructure financing are credit guarantees and political risk guarantees (PRGs).

- Donors also provide assistance for the funding of infrastructure projects. In particular, output-based aid donor programmes provide explicit performance-based capital subsidies to reduce the cost of connecting poorer households to networks.

As discussed in Section 5, developing countries face key constraints that have limited the quantity and quality of infrastructure PPPs. In response to these constraints, donor organisations have set up interventions to promote the successful implementation of PPPs. This section describes some of these, including:

- project preparation facilities;
- infrastructure financing facilities;
- guarantee facilities; and
- infrastructure funding facilities.

These facilities can be accessed by Commonwealth governments to support infrastructure PPPs in their own countries. This section provides a general overview of the type of facilities and nature of support provided and Annex 4 gives a more detailed list of the individual facilities, including their sectoral and geographic focus.

## 6.1. Project preparation facilities

A range of donor facilities provide support across the stages of the project development cycle (see Section 4.2 for the cycle). At the highest level, these can be classified into three types of support:

**Advisory:** As the name suggests, the key role of advisory facilities is to provide advice to governments on project preparation for infrastructure PPPs. Such facilities recognise the constraint imposed by limited government capacity and hence aim to support the government through one or more stages of the project development process.

**Principal:** Unlike advisory support, some donor-funded facilities play the role of a principal, i.e. the facility takes on the risk and associated costs of early stage project development and develops the project for private sector investment. These facilities also help circumvent the problems caused by limited government capacity and relieve the constraint of limited PPP project development.

**Funding for project preparation:** A third type of support provided by some facilities is funding for the different stages of the project development cycle. Funding may be available for the public and/or the private sector.

Each of these types of support is discussed in further detail below. It should also be noted that some facilities provide both advisory and funding support.

### 6.1.1. Advisory role

Advisory project preparation facilities form the largest category of donor-funded project preparation facilities. Examples of these facilities include the following:

- The **Public–private Infrastructure Advisory Facility**[1] focuses on providing advisory support for the development of an enabling environment for infrastructure PPPs (see Box 6.1 for an example of the type of support provided by the PPIAF).

- **DevCo**[2] provides transactions advisory services to the government to support the implementation of a PPP transaction. (DevCo also comprises a non-core window on small-scale infrastructure programmes (SSIPs), which supports technical assistance and advisory services to encourage the development and expansion of small-scale infrastructure providers.)

- The **African Capacity Building Foundation**[3] aims to build capacity in the core public sector through institutional strengthening and human capacity development.

- The **Water and Sanitation Program (WSP)**[4] provides technical assistance support to governments for policy and institutional development in the water and sanitation sectors in sub-Saharan Africa. WSP also provides technical assistance support for investment and pilot approaches in the sector.

Thus, different advisory facilities focus on different stages of the project cycle, with some having a specific geographic or sectoral focus. Further examples are listed in Annex 4.

While some facilities provide *grant-based* support, others require a *cost contribution* (i.e. support is provided on the basis that the facility needs to recover part or all of its costs). In addition, some facilities may provide *linked* support (i.e. support from the facility requires a commitment to receive the facility's own products or services, either now or at a later stage of the project) and others may provide *unlinked support*, i.e. support is provided without the need to commit to any product or service from the facility itself (other than funding, the procurement rules mentioned above and/or ongoing engagement of the facility's task manager).

---

**Box 6.1. PPIAF advisory support for the development of a PPP framework in Malawi**

The Government of Malawi engaged the PPIAF to provide assistance in developing policies, laws and regulations for PPPs. This helped the government to:

1. Develop policies, laws and regulations that define the scope of authority within the various spheres of government to enter into PPP contracts;

2. Design an institutional set up to support and streamline PPP implementation, which will be guided by a set of institutional development principles.

In 2006, the team of consultants conducted extensive field research, interviews and reviews of existing reports in order to formulate a comprehensive government plan for the creation of a PPP policy and legal and institutional frameworks. At the end of this research and analysis period, the team prepared a draft Cabinet paper proposing specific actions that could be undertaken by government in order to establish such PPP frameworks. Following the completion of this assignment, the government plans to prepare detailed operating procedures and guidelines, illustrating the steps to be followed in the implementation of a PPP project, processes for approval and model transaction documents.

*Source:* PPIAF, www.ppiaf.org

---

## 6.1.2. Role of a principal

As mentioned above, there are a number of advisory facilities, each of which has its own core area of focus. However, more recently, the constraint of limited PPP project development, due to its high risks and costs, has been increasingly recognised; in response, donor-funded facilities have been designed to play the role of a principal and develop projects for private sector investment. **InfraCo Africa**[5] and **InfraCo Asia**, funded by PIDG,[6] and **InfraVentures**,[7] supported by the IFC, are important examples. These facilities are essentially structured as project development companies that take on the risks and associated costs of early stage project development, preparing projects for investment by the private sector.

### 6.1.3. Provision of funding support

Some donor-funded facilities provide funding for project preparation to the public and/or private sector. Examples include the ACP-EU Energy Facility,[8] which provides supplementary project preparation funds for energy sector projects and the PIDG Technical Assistance Facility (TAF),[9] which provides funds for PIDG-supported projects. The funding may be grant based or a cost contribution, and may be linked or unlinked, as discussed above.

## 6.2. Infrastructure financing facilities

Lack of long-term finance for infrastructure projects is one of the key constraints faced by developing countries. In response, specialist donor-backed financing funds such as the Emerging Africa Infrastructure Fund (EAIF) have been set up (see Box 6.2).

---

**Box 6.2. Emerging Africa Infrastructure Fund**[10]

www.emergingafricafund.com

The EAIF is a US$498.5 million debt fund established by the PIDG group of donors in 2002 to address the scarcity of long-term debt available to infrastructure projects in sub-Saharan Africa. It provides long-term (up to 15 years) US dollar- or Euro-denominated loans of US$10–36.5 million, suitable for private sector projects, which are not typically available in local credit markets.

The EAIF lends on commercial terms, demonstrating the viability of long-term lending in the region. Despite operating on private sector principles, it attempts to boost its impact by focusing on projects that promote economic growth, poverty reduction and other social goals. Its remit covers support for greenfield projects, refurbishment, upgrade or expansion across telecom, transport, energy and certain other infrastructure sectors.

As at March 2009, the EAIF has provided support of US$443 million to 22 projects, and nearly US$120 million has already been repaid. An example of EAIF projects is the US$35 million 15-year senior loan to the Bugoye Hydro Power Plant in Uganda in 2008. This 13MW project is expected to generate 82GWh each year. Its total costs are projected to be US$56 million, US$16 million of which is covered by grants and sponsor equity. The EAIF provided the loan to Tronder Power Ltd, the Special Purpose Vehicle (SPV) established to develop, construct and operate the project. Its principle investors are TrønderEnergi (a Norwegian hydro power expert) and Norfund (the Norwegian government's development fund). The Norwegian government is financing the 6km 33kV line connecting the plant to the transmission network.

This project will have a region-wide impact through extending access, improving reliability and reducing the need for 'rolling blackouts'. The remote location of the station will also reduce losses from the transmission network. It is cheap and green power will be substitute for polluting and expensive diesel generation, especially as the government has cut subsidies for diesel generation and reduced the unit cost of electricity. The project will also promote skills transfer to local workers and the development of a domestic hydropower sector. Five hundred workers will be employed during the construction phase and ten on a permanent basis.

---

In addition, a number of International Financial Institutions (IFIs) also provide loan/debt products for infrastructure. These are commercially priced products offered by the IFIs to private sector borrowers, with an interest rate, tenor and repayment schedule that reflect the overall risks of the project. IFI loans are typically offered on a non- or limited- recourse basis (i.e. the lender does not have recourse to the project sponsor in the event of default), and require some upfront commitment fees. Most IFI loans are disbursed in foreign currency (US dollars or euros) as against a local currency loan, which is subject to exchange rate risks. Loans can be *senior* or *subordinated* – as the name suggests, senior loans have a higher priority over claims than subordinated debt (and are therefore less risky and bear a lower rate of return). Subordinated debt can be offered by the IFIs as a means of attracting senior debt from the private sector.

The main providers of long-term finance are *Development Finance Institutions (DFIs)*, which are specialist financial institutions established primarily to provide finance to the private sector in developing countries, such as the IFC, the German investment and development company, DEG and the French Development Company, Proparco.[11]

*Bilateral development banks*, such as the Japan Bank for International Cooperation (JBIC) and German Development Bank (KfW), and *multilateral development banks*, such as the World Bank, International Bank for Reconstruction and Development (IBRD), IDA and European Investment Bank (EIB), may also provide financing for infrastructure PPP projects. However, most of their activities are focused on public infrastructure projects. Some multilateral development banks have established special windows for private sector lending.

## 6.3. Guarantee facilities

Closely linked to the above discussion on infrastructure financing facilities are donor facilities that provide guarantees for PPP infrastructure projects – and hence help facilitate both equity financing for the project, as well as debt financing of a suitable price and tenor.[12]

A guarantee facility assumes that banks and other providers of finance are willing to provide longer term finance if the key risks facing the lender or investor can be reduced or mitigated. These facilities provide financial products such as insurance or guarantees which protect lenders and investors in the event of default. This enhances the creditworthiness of the investment and helps to attract greater private sector investment.[13]

In return for providing a guarantee, the facility charges a fee or premium, which reflects the project's risks. Figure 6.1 presents a simple diagrammatic representation of how a guarantee works.

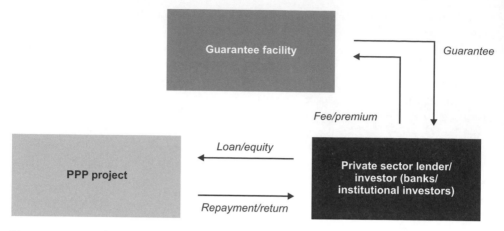

**Figure 6.1.** Typical structure of a guarantee

Donor guarantee facilities provide a range of different types of guarantee based on the type of finance provided, the underlying cause of the risk to be covered and the extent of coverage of potential losses. These are discussed in Table 6.1 below.

**Table 6.1.** Guarantees for infrastructure financing

| Criteria | Type | Description |
|---|---|---|
| Type of finance | Equity financing | Guarantees can be provided for equity or debt providers of finance. |
|  | Debt financing |  |
| Cause of risk | Political risk | Political risks include risks arising from war, civil disturbances, etc. and are usually the responsibility of the government, as well as macroeconomic risks such as exchange rate and interest rate volatility risks. |
|  | Commercial risk | Commercial risks include contract performance risks, most of which are directly under the control of the private sector service provider, as well as construction and market risks, where other factors and influences can have an impact. |
| Extent of coverage | Full | Guarantees can cover part of the total financing or the entire amount. |
|  | Partial |  |

Given the range of guarantees described above, the two main types of guarantees offered by donors' facilities are:

**Credit guarantees:** These cover debt service default, in the case of both political and commercial risks. Thus credit guarantees help improve the borrower's market access and terms of the debt. A number of multilateral development banks such as the

African Development Bank (AfDB) and the Asian Development Bank (ADB) as well as DFIs such as the IFC provide credit guarantees (mostly Partial Credit Guarantees or PCGs).

**Political risk guarantees or political risk insurance (PRI):** These cover losses arising from political risks. PRGs usually cover the full amount of the debt, while PRIs can insure equity investors or lenders. Multilateral development banks such as the World Bank and ADB provide PRGs. There are also specialised agencies for PRI, such as the World Bank Multilateral Investment Guarantee Agency (MIGA).

In addition, export credit guarantees (ECGs) cover losses by exporters or lenders financing projects, tied to the export of goods and services; these may cover aspects of both political and commercial risks. ECGs are normally tied to the nationality of the exporters (and sometimes to that of the project sponsors or lenders), such as those provided by most of the European export credit agencies. However, untied guarantees are also available from a few bilateral agencies, such as the Japan Bank for International Cooperation.

More details on donor guarantee facilities are provided in Annex 4. For an example of a donor-funded guarantee facility support, see Box 6.3. Donor guarantees are often provided in conjunction with guarantees from private sector institutions, and play a 'crowding-in' role, as discussed in Box 6.4.

---

**Box 6.3. GuarantCo support for Indian transport infrastructure finance**

Most road freight in India is carried by small owner-operators. They are often unable to compete with larger operators as they are increasingly constrained by poor access to finance. Their small size makes it difficult to obtain credit from traditional sources, so they may have to resort to informal lenders to compete and meet new environmental regulations. GuarantCo, together with The Netherlands Development Finance Company (FMO), has decided to support specialist truck finance companies, whose existing supply of loans is overwhelmed by demand from drivers. GuarantCo's support comes in the form of a US$18.3 million rupee guarantee for capital market securitisation of these truck loans.

Under the scheme, truck loans from specialist lenders are transferred to a special purpose company, which raises bonds from domestic investors. Adverse selection is minimised by specialist lenders retaining first loss risk defaults on their loans. GuarantCo and FMO provide a cash-backed second loss guarantee on the funds.

Securitising truck loans in this manner should have the effect of lowering the cost of finance for truck operators and extend access from a constrained position. It is estimated that the scheme will allow the extension of loans to an additional 64,000 trucks, all of which will have to meet more demanding environmental standards than the existing fleet.

*Source:* PIDG Annual Report 2008, www.pidg.org

---

Box 6.4. Guarantees provided by private financial entities

In addition to the donor facilities that extend guarantees for infrastructure PPPs, a number of private financial institutions also provide risk-mitigating instruments. One such group of private financial entities are monoline insurers, such as MBIA, AMBAC and FSA. These are highly-rated companies that provide guarantees to structured debt issued by lower-rated sovereigns and corporations in exchange for insurance premiums. Such guarantees allow borrowers to issue higher-rated bonds, and may therefore attract a wider range of investors and result in significantly lower interest costs. A second group of private guarantors are the political risk insurers such as AIG, Chubb and Zurich, which work in a similar way to donors that provide PRIs.

One advantage to employing the services of private insurers is that, unlike many donor facilities, these entities are not limited by the borrower's nationality, which makes their products more accessible. That said, private insurers tend to have more stringent credit limits compared to donors, which may restrict the extent to which they are willing to work with higher-risk issuers.

Given their differences in risk appetite and coverage, the donors and private insurers can be mobilised in a complementary fashion to structure a more financially-attractive deal. One such example is the West African Gas Pipeline Project, which received US$50 million PRG from IDA, US$75 million PRI from MIGA and US$125 million PRI from Steadfast Insurance Company.

Another project which benefited from a complementary approach is the Rutas del Pacifico toll road in Chile. An innovative 'co-guarantee mechanism' was developed for this project, whereby the Inter-American Development Bank (IDB) was the guarantor of record, not only for its account but also for the FSA which acted as the private co-guarantor. The IDB provided US$75 million full-wrap financial guarantee, and the FSA co-guaranteed the remaining amount of about US$200 million and benefited from the IDB's preferred creditor status.

**Key references**

Matsukawa, T and Odo H, *Review of Risk Mitigation Instruments for Infrastructure Financing and Recent Trends and Developments*, World Bank (2007).
http://www.ppiaf.org/documents/trends_and_policy/Riskmitigationinstruments.pdf

## 6.4. Infrastructure funding facilities

As against 'financing' of infrastructure, which refers to debt and equity for the construction and development of the infrastructure, 'funding' of an infrastructure project refers to payments for the use of the infrastructure service. As discussed in Section 5.1, a constraint faced in many developing countries is limited affordability for much-needed infrastructure services, rendering the infrastructure project unsustainable.

Two types of subsidies may be provided:

1. **Capital subsidies,** or subsidies for the funding of the capital costs of the infrastructure. These are typically one-off, or sometimes multiple payment, to buy down the costs of capital provision.

2. **Operating subsidies**, or funding for subsidising the use of the infrastructure services. These are often a series of payments that support operating costs and are used to fund public or merit goods where it is difficult or inappropriate to charge users the full cost of the service provision.

Donor support for infrastructure funding is provided indirectly through budgetary and other support – either grants or concessionary lending – by multilateral development banks, including the World Bank and the ADB.

In addition, other specific donor facilities targeted at infrastructure funding include *output-based aid facilities* such as the Global Partnership for Output-Based Aid[14] and the PIDG TAF OBA window.[15] Output-based aid is a strategy for using explicit performance-based subsidies to support the delivery of basic services where policy concerns justify public funding to complement or replace user fees.[16] Thus, OBA facilities help fund economically desirable but commercially unbankable projects, where the price paid for the infrastructure service does not cover their cost or where risks are too high for the private sector to bear. OBA programmes usually focus on capital subsidies in order to reduce the cost of connecting poorer households to networks.

## Notes

1. http://www.ppiaf.org/
2. http://www.ifc.org/ifcext/psa.nsf/content/Devco
3. http://www.acbf-pact.org/
4. http://www.wsp.org/
5. http://www.infracoafrica.com/
6. http://www.pidg.org/
7. http://www.ifc.org/
8. http://ec.europa.eu/europeaid/where/acp/regional-cooperation/energy/index_en.htm
9. http://www.pidg.org/organisationProfile.asp?NavID=40&step=4&contentID=9
10. PIDG Annual Report 2008, http://www.pidg.org/uploads/public/documents/library/PIDG/PIDG%20Annual%20Reports%20and%20Handbook/PIDG%20Annual%20Report%202008.pdf
11. Over time, the nature of DFIs has changed – mainly from fully publicly owned entities such as IFC to institutions such as FMO (Netherlands Development Finance Company), which is only partially government owned.
12. In the absence of guarantees, project risks can be so high that the commensurate interest rate or dividend would render the project unbankable.
13. Guarantee facilities also encourage local capital market development, as private lenders are encouraged to provide finance.
14. http://www.gpoba.org/
15. While GPOBA can provide funding for all developing countries (IDA or IDA blend countries), the TAF OBA window is restricted to PIDG-supported PPP projects. Both GPOBA and the TAF OBA window provide project preparation support in that they

provide technical assistance for projects that are to be developed using the OBA approach, as well as providing direct funding of the OBA subsidy.

16. Affordability concerns for particular groups of users, positive externalities or the infeasibility of imposing direct user fees represent examples of the types of policy concerns that have motivated governments to use public funds to support the delivery of basic services.

## Key references

PPIAF and ICA, *Infrastructure Project Preparation Facilities: Africa User's Guide* (2006). http://www.ppiaf.org/documents/recent_publications/InfrastructureProjectPreparation FacilitiesUserGuideEnglish.pdf

Provides a description of the infrastructure project development process and the main activities involved, as well as providing details on available donor-funded facilities for project preparation support.

PPIAF and ICA, *Donor Debt and Equity Financing for Infrastructure: User Guide Africa* (2007). http://www.ppiaf.org/documents/other_publications/equityfinancingbookeng.pdf

Describes the main donor instruments and facilities available for financing infrastructure projects.

Matsukawa, T and Odo H, *Review of Risk Mitigation Instruments for Infrastructure Financing and Recent Trends and Developments*, World Bank (2007). http://www.ppiaf.org/documents/trends_and_policy/Riskmitigationinstruments.pdf

Reviews guarantees and insurance, providing a broad overview with further links for practitioners.

# 7

# Recent PPP experience in Commonwealth developing countries

## Summarising the section

- A number of Commonwealth countries suffer from a large infrastructure deficit, with considerable variation between countries.

- Private sector participation in infrastructure in Commonwealth developing countries is becoming increasingly important. 431 projects involving investments of US$109.2 billion reached financial close over the period 2000-2007. Many of these projects were in India and Malaysia, but there have been a growing number of transactions in other Commonwealth countries as well.

- Greenfield projects have dominated in Commonwealth developing countries. In more recent years, however, the number of concession projects in Commonwealth developing countries has risen (and subsequently fallen back again). Divestitures appear to be far less prominent in Commonwealth developing countries compared with developing countries as a whole.

- The energy sector has seen the largest number of transactions in Commonwealth countries over the period 1990-2007.

- The experience of PPP transactions across Commonwealth developing countries, and within sectors in each country, has varied substantially, based on the nature and extent of the constraints to infrastructure PPPs. In addition, different models have been adopted in different country and sector contexts. These are important examples of both good and bad practice, as well as presenting many interesting lessons for the future.

This section discusses recent experience with infrastructure PPPs in Commonwealth developing countries.[1] They include a diverse mix of countries, from large states such as India and Nigeria to small island states such as the Caribbean islands; from fast-growing economies such as those of India, Mozambique and Tanzania to slower growing economies with near zero or negative GDP growth rates in some years such as Lesotho and Guyana. Some of the countries involved, such as India, Malaysia and Nigeria, have considerable experience of infrastructure PPPs; others, like some African states, are only just embarking on their national PPP programmes. The overall PPP experience provides important lessons for Commonwealth countries. This is discussed in Section 8.

This section first outlines the current background to infrastructure PPPs in terms of the infrastructure gap and some measures of the PPP enabling environment, and goes on to describe broad trends and select PPP transaction experience across sectors and in selected Commonwealth countries.

## 7.1. The infrastructure gap

In many low-income Commonwealth countries, as in the rest of the developing world, there is a large infrastructure gap. Existing infrastructure is incapable of meeting the demands of growing populations and is a major constraint to economic and social development. Without significant infrastructure development, this will only get worse as demands for services rise with economic growth and rural-urban migration.

Table 7.1 sets out some measures of the infrastructure gap in selected Commonwealth developing countries. Annex 3 provides a more complete dataset for all 48 Commonwealth developing countries.

**Table 7.1.** The infrastructure gap in selected Commonwealth countries[2]

| Region | Country | Electric power consumption[a] | Paved roads[b] (%) | Improved sanitation facilities, urban[c] (%) | Improved water source[d] (%) |
|--------|---------|------------------|------------|-----------------------|------------------|
| EAP | Brunei Darussalam | 8,173.8 | 77.2 | | 99.0 |
| | Malaysia | 3,387.6 | 79.8 | 95.0 | 99.0 |
| | Papua New Guinea | | 3.5 | 67.0 | 40.0 |
| LAC | Antigua and Barbuda | | 33.0 | 98.0 | |
| | Jamaica | 2,453.2 | 73.3 | 82.0 | 93.0 |
| | Trinidad and Tobago | 5,005.9 | 51.1 | 92.0 | 94.0 |
| SAR | Bangladesh | 146.0 | 10.0 | 48.0 | 80.0 |
| | India | 502.8 | 47.4 | 52.0 | 89.0 |
| | Sri Lanka | 400.1 | 81.0 | 89.0 | 82.0 |
| SSA | Cameroon | 185.6 | 8.4 | 58.0 | 70.0 |
| | Ghana | 303.6 | 14.9 | 15.0 | 80.0 |
| | Kenya | 145.3 | 14.1 | 19.0 | 57.0 |
| | Nigeria | 116.4 | 15.0 | 35.0 | 47.0 |
| | Tanzania | 58.8 | 8.6 | 31.0 | 55.0 |

[a] kWh per capita; [b] Percentage of total roads; [c] Percentage of urban population with access; [d] Percentage of population with access.

Table 7.1 illustrates the infrastructure challenge across Commonwealth countries today. While some infrastructure deficits, such as poor access to water and sanitation, directly impact on development, other deficits, such as limited access to electricity, result in missed economic opportunities and consequently impact on overall development. For example, only around 8 per cent of roads are paved in Tanzania and Cameroon, an infrastructure gap that constrains businesses, as well as access to vital health and education services. Approximately 50 per cent of the population in Kenya, Nigeria and Tanzania have access to an improved water source, with a concomitant impact on disease and hygiene levels, particularly for women and children.

There is also considerable diversity among Commonwealth countries. For example, average electricity consumption for all Commonwealth countries is 1,684.7 kWh per capita: some countries, such as Malaysia, have a much higher consumption, while in others, such as Tanzania, consumption is far lower.

A study by Africa Infrastructure Country Diagnostic (AICD) estimates that if African countries could improve their infrastructure so that it was as good as that of Mauritius, they would benefit from an additional 2.2 per cent per capita GDP growth each year. They would gain an additional 0.4 per cent if their infrastructure was comparable to that of South Korea.[3] Enterprise surveys carried out by the World Bank also present some interesting results: in 2006, Indian firms reported losing 6.62 per cent of sales due to power outages, and in Uganda the loss was even higher at 10 per cent. In Kenya over 30 per cent and in Nigeria over 75 per cent of firms identified transport as a major constraint.[4]

## 7.2. Enabling environment for PPPs

The enabling environment for infrastructure PPPs varies substantially among Commonwealth developing countries. While some countries have more supportive enabling environments, other countries have still to develop a facilitating environment.

As discussed in Section 4.1, the enabling environment comprises a number of different elements, including policy, legal and regulatory frameworks. While an assessment of these frameworks is beyond the scope of this Reference Guide, other overall indicators, such as the IFC's Doing Business Indicators[5] and measures of political risk (Oxford Analytica/Aon),[6] provide a useful reference point. Table 7.2 provides the four highest and lowest ranking countries according to the IFC rankings and their Oxford

Table 7.2. Doing business and political risk indicators in Commonwealth countries[7]

| | Country | Overall ease of doing business ranking (1–181) | Oxford Analytica/Aon Political risk level |
|---|---|---|---|
| Highest ranking Commonwealth countries | Malaysia | 20 | Medium |
| | Mauritius | 24 | Medium-low |
| | South Africa | 32 | Medium |
| | St Lucia | 34 | Medium-low |
| Lower ranking Commonwealth countries | Malawi | 134 | Medium-high |
| | Mozambique | 141 | Medium-high |
| | Sierra Leone | 156 | Medium-high |
| | Cameroon | 164 | Medium |

Analytica/Aon-perceived political risk levels. More details for all Commonwealth developing countries are provided in Annex 3.

A number of African countries received low scores in the overall ranking of 181 countries covered by the IFC Doing Business Indicators. However several, including Senegal, Burkina Faso and Botswana, have improved their rankings over time.

The Oxford Analytica/Aon Political Risk Map reflects an important component of the enabling environment, impacting on private sector investor confidence. The 2009 list designates three Commonwealth countries, Kenya, Nigeria and Pakistan, as high risk.[8] A number of the small island states in the LAC region, for example Trinidad and Tobago, and St Lucia, are accorded a medium-low rank. Further details are provided in Annex 3.

Table 7.2 also demonstrates a correlation between the ease of doing business and the political risk level, with most countries that rank high on the former indicator being ranked medium-low or medium in terms of political risk, and most countries with a low ease of doing business rank being accorded a medium-high level of political risk.

## 7.3. Trends in private sector participation in infrastructure

Private sector participation in infrastructure in Commonwealth developing countries is becoming increasingly important. In the 1990s, a total of 314 projects, with investments valued at US$125.3 billion, reached financial close; 431 projects with investments of US$109.2 billion reached financial close between 2000 and 2007. In particular, from 2005 to 2007, infrastructure projects with private participation in Commonwealth developing countries represented 37.5 per cent of the total number of projects reaching financial close and 34.6 per cent of total investment commitments across all developing countries.

However, this trend is dominated by India and Malaysia, with the former having the largest number of projects over the period 1990–2007 in terms of both number and value (see Figure 7.1).

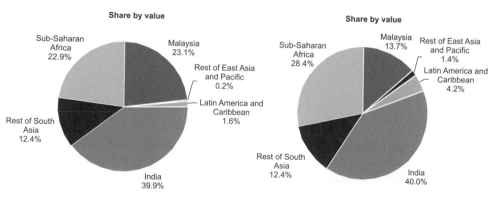

**Figure 7.1.** Global distribution of infrastructure projects with private participation in Commonwealth countries, 1990–2007[9]

Public–Private Partnerships Policy and Practice

However, since 2000 there have also been a number of transactions in other Commonwealth countries. Table 7.3 shows the number of infrastructure projects with private participation that have reached financial close in the years 2000–2008 in Commonwealth developing countries other than India and Malaysia.

**Table 7.3.** Infrastructure projects with private participation that reached financial close in 2000–2008 in Commonwealth developing countries (excluding India and Malaysia) [10]

| Country | Number of projects |
| --- | --- |
| Nigeria | 49 |
| Pakistan | 47 |
| South Africa | 32 |
| Bangladesh | 23 |
| Sri Lanka | 22 |
| Tanzania | 21 |
| Kenya | 16 |
| Ghana | 15 |
| Mozambique | 15 |
| Uganda | 15 |

Figure 7.2 provides a comparison of infrastructure trends by type of contract between the Commonwealth and the rest of the developing world.

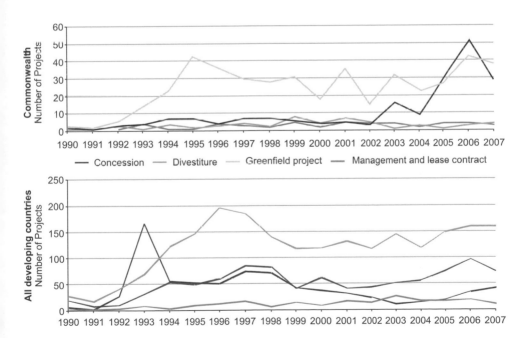

**Figure 7.2.** Number of infrastructure projects by type of private sector participation across Commonwealth countries and all developing countries, 1990–2007 [11]

As Figure 7.2 shows, greenfield projects have dominated. However, in more recent years the number of concession projects in Commonwealth countries increased (and showed a subsequent fall). Divestitures appear to be far less prominent in Commonwealth developing countries compared with developing countries as a whole. As mentioned above, the number of Commonwealth projects is dominated by India and Malaysia; however, the trends by contract excluding these two countries are similar, with greenfield projects being the most frequent type, particularly in the 1990s, and concessions experiencing a sharp peak in 2005.

In terms of sector, transport BOTs and energy IPPs dominated in India. In Malaysia, most projects were in the road and electricity sectors. The energy sector saw the largest number of transactions in all other Commonwealth countries over the period 1990–2007.

## 7.4. PPP transaction experience across core infrastructure sectors

The experience of PPP transactions across Commonwealth developing countries, and within sectors in each country, has varied substantially, based on the nature and extent of the constraints to infrastructure PPPs, as discussed in Section 5.1. In addition, various models have been adopted in different country and sector contexts, presenting important examples of both good and bad practice, as well as many interesting lessons for the future. A detailed examination of the different models employed is beyond the scope of this Guide. However, some specific examples are discussed in this section and examined in more detail in Annex 5.

In the energy sector, independent power projects have dominated infrastructure PPPs in most countries. Box 7.1 provides a discussion of the experience of IPPs in Africa.

**Box 7.1. IPPs in Africa**

IPPs are privately financed greenfield generation projects, typically supported by limited or non-recourse loans and long-term power purchase agreements. They are governed by contract and do not normally require independent regulation.

IPPs emerged as a new model for African power systems in the 1990s, adding capacity to bolster predominantly state-owned energy sectors or set up as part of wholesale energy sector unbundling and reform. They were considered to be a 'quick and relatively easy fix to persistent supply constraints, and could also potentially serve to benchmark state-owned supply and gradually introduce competition'.[12] Over the course of the decade they gained increasing support from international development institutions, receiving preference over state-owned operations. Support for African IPPs peaked in 1997, with US$1.8 billion of IPP investment being committed.[13] Despite their subsequent decline, IPPs remain a viable option in many countries. They contribute over 50 per cent of the electricity generated in Tanzania. Kenya and Nigeria have also been active in pursuing IPPs.

*Examples of Commonwealth IPPs in Africa*

**Kenya**     Westmont (46MW US$35m), Iberafrica (56MW US$35m), OrPower4 (13MW US$54m), Tsavo (75MW US$85m)

**Tanzania**  IPTL (100MW US$120m), Songas (180MW US$316m), Mtwara (12MW US$8.2m)

**Nigeria**   AES Barge (270MW US$240m), Okpai (450MW US$462m)

Forty IPPs had been commissioned in Africa by 2007, with varying degrees of success. Gratwick and Eberhard (2008) found that across these projects certain factors influenced the likelihood of renegotiation or failure. There was an increased likelihood of renegotiation or failure where there was a perceived imbalance between the project sponsor and the host government. On the other hand, projects clearly benefited from favourable enabling environment factors and where more 'development-minded' firms and DFIs were involved.

**Key references**

- Gratwick, KL and Eberhard, A (2008), 'An Analysis of Independent Power Projects in Africa: Understanding Development and Investment Outcomes', *Development Policy Review*, 26 (3): 309–338.
  http://www.gsb.uct.ac.za/files/IPPinAfrica.pdf

The Meghnaghat power project in Bangladesh also presents an interesting example of a successful large-scale IPP awarded through a competitive bidding process and financed both by donor organisations and a government-owned financial institution, IDCOL.[14] A Power Purchase Agreement (PPA) from the Bangladesh Power Development Board (BPDB) to take or pay for all electricity generated up to a plant load factor of 85 per cent made the deal attractive to the private sector. The plant commenced commercial operations in 2002 and has increased power reliability at a reasonable cost.

Energy sector PPPs have also been undertaken in the transmission and distribution sectors. The Tala transmission project in India is the first interstate transmission project undertaken via a PPP and is also the first BOT electricity transmission line outside the LAC region. The project highlights the importance of keeping in mind private sector incentives when structuring a PPP transaction, as the regulators increased the allowable IRR for the private investors. The energy distribution sector has had fewer transactions, although there have recently been several PPPs in India. In addition, in 2005 the Ugandan electricity distribution system was concessioned as a joint venture between CDC and Eskom (the 'Umeme concession'). Experience has been mixed with this contract. There has been some progress in investment and connectivity with the introduction of the PPP; however, system losses have not decreased, tariffs have repeatedly risen and there have been difficulties related to its structure as a joint venture.

In the transport sector, the annuity-based contracts employed in the roads sector in India present an interesting model. Under this model, traffic/demand risk is allocated to the government, which was instrumental in attracting private sector participation in the initial years of PPPs in the sector. Annex 5 provides an example of India's Panagarh-Palsit highway project, awarded on an annuity basis. The scheme forms part of the Golden Quadrilateral Project, India's main highways development, at a total cost of US$69 million. The financing package has a debt-equity ratio of 2:1, a higher than usual ratio compared to typical toll-based projects, as the annuity payments are considered to be a secure and stable source of funding by the financial community. However, the project became operational five months behind schedule, mainly because of difficulties in securing land – an issue that remains an important constraint in PPP projects in India and globally. In recent years, however, with greater development of both the private sector and local credit markets, the Government of India has focused on BOT-based road contracts.

Another interesting example is that of Highway 2000, a two-phase 230km multi-lane toll road project running from Jamaica's capital, Kingston, to Montego Bay, with a spur from Bushy Park to Ocho Rios. It reached financial close in 2002 as a 35-year BOT, to be completed at an estimated total cost of US$850 million. Two regulatory bodies have been established to monitor the concession: the Toll Authority and the Toll Regulator. Although the project as a whole is considered to be a success, the institutions created to monitor the single toll road are considered to be far in excess of requirements.

Airport PPPs have also gained considerable importance, especially since 2000. There have been concession and greenfield airport PPPs in India, Pakistan, Bangladesh, Malaysia, Jamaica, Nigeria and South Africa. The experience of the Nigerian airport BOT is particularly interesting, given the delays in project operations (stemming from both the cancellation of the original contract and its re-awarding to the current operator, as well as the difficulty faced by the current operator in achieving financial close). Currently, all domestic flights continue to operate from the old airport terminal, putting significant pressure on the ability of the private sponsor to recover its investments and thus placing the financial viability of the project at risk (see Annex 5). This illustrates the difficulty of enforcing contractual agreements in some developing countries.

A major transaction in the railways sector is the Kenya-Uganda rail concession, which was awarded to the Rift Valley Railways (RVR) consortium for 25 years in December 2006. The project has run into considerable operational and legal difficulties, which have significantly hampered the likelihood of success. Issues relating to lack of investment and improvements in operational effectiveness have led the governments to consider cancellation of the contract. However, more recently the parties have reached an out-of-court settlement, whereby RVR will continue to be the concessionaire in exchange for the dilution of Sheltam's (the main sponsor) shareholdings from 35 to 10 per cent. This case study highlights the importance of attracting 'competent' private companies for the successful implementation of a contract. In this case, there were concerns that Sheltam lacked the experience of running a complex railway network and therefore was not in a position to enhance cash flows sufficiently to generate the required investment resources. In addition, the different approaches followed by the Kenyan and Ugandan governments point to the political dimension of running a cross-border PPP contract, and the difficulties that may arise in achieving co-operation between governments.

The water and sanitation sectors have seen the smallest number of PPPs among core infrastructure sectors. The main PPP transactions in this sector have been in India, Malaysia and South Africa, where there have been some BOT (and associated variant) contracts for treatment plants, as well as several concessions. (These include four concessions in Malaysia, including the Sybas water distribution concession; the Greater Nelspruit Utility Company in South Africa; and the Latur Water Supply Scheme in India.) Apart from these, there have only been a handful of management and lease contracts in the water and sanitation sector in other Commonwealth countries. Management contracts such as the New Tiruppur project in India are based on charging a higher tariff for industrial users to subsidise domestic consumption. The Dar es Salaam water distribution contract in Tanzania was a lease contract that has now been cancelled. The transaction provides important lessons on the difficulty of structuring, developing and implementing PPPs in the water sector. Considerable care and detail needs to be applied in structuring a PPP transaction, with a thorough feasibility study and appropriate risk mitigation measures, to ensure the financial viability and success of the transaction. The project also highlights the impact of political processes on transactions – an election was scheduled in Tanzania at the time the project was going forward.

Table 7.4 summarises some of the examples discussed above (see also Annex 5).

**Table 7.4.** Lessons learned from a sample of key transactions in Commonwealth countries

| Project Name | Country | Type of PPI | Sector | Total investment (US$ m) | Key lessons |
|---|---|---|---|---|---|
| Dar es Salaam Water Distribution (2003) *Cancelled* | Tanzania | Lease contract | Water and sanitation | 8.5 | The transaction was cancelled because the concessionaire did not perform adequately and there was insufficient support from government bodies. The experience points towards the need for considerable care and detail in structuring a PPP transaction, with a thorough feasibility study and appropriate risk mitigation measures in place, to ensure the financial viability and success of the transaction. |
| Point Lisas Desalination Plant (1999) | Trinidad and Tobago | Greenfield – BOO | Water and sanitation | 120 | There have been disputes between the private operator and the Trinidad Water and Sewerage Authority (WASA) regarding an increase in tariffs; this has placed increasing strain on the financial viability of the project. The experience reflects the difficulty of implementing a water PPP, given that tariffs tend to be a highly politicised issue. There have also been issues regarding the attitude of the public towards the project, reflecting the need to undertake an effective public relations campaign to inform the general public of the benefits of the project. However, overall operational performance has improved, reflecting the greater efficiency brought in by the private sector. |
| Kenya-Uganda Railways (2006) | Kenya and Uganda | Concession | Transport | 404 | The project has run into operational difficulties since its inception. There are concerns that Sheltam, the leader of the winning consortium, lacked experience of running a complex railway network. Sheltam has subsequently seen its shareholding diluted to below 35 per cent (previously 61 per cent). The lesson is that successful implementation of a contract depends very much on attracting competent private companies. Differing approaches undertaken by the Kenyan and Ugandan governments on contract performance also highlight the difficulty of implementing cross-border infrastructure projects. |
| Murtala Muhammed Airport Two (2006) | Nigeria | Greenfield – BOT | Transport | 200 | The initial winning bidder saw its contract revoked within six months, as the government was not happy that no construction had taken place since the signing of the contract. This points to the importance of managing politicians' expectations and setting realistic goals on timelines. The project also demonstrates the difficulty of enforcing contractual agreements, as domestic |

Table 7.4. (continued)

| Project Name | Country | Type of PPI | Sector | Total investment (US$ m) | Key lessons |
|---|---|---|---|---|---|
| | | | | | flights did not move to the new terminal once operational, as was originally envisaged under the contract. This has put the financial viability of the project on high risk. |
| Panagarh-Palsit Highway Project (2001) | India | Greenfield – BOT | Transport | 69 | The annuity method used in this transaction fixes the government's payments to the private sector at the beginning of the contract, and hence allocates revenue risk to the government. This makes the deal more attractive to the private sector, but places an additional burden on the government. |
| Meghnaghat Power Project (2001) | Bangladesh | Greenfield – BOO | Energy | 300 | The project is the first ever competitively-bid power project supported by the private sector in Bangladesh. An agreement with the Power Development Board to take or pay for all electricity generated up to a specified plant load factor enhanced the attractiveness of the project to the private sector. |
| Tala Transmission Project (2004) | India | Greenfield – BOT | Energy | 269 | This is the first BOT electricity transmission line outside the LAC region. There was limited initial interest from the private sector, so the electricity regulator increased the allowable IRR for private investors as a way of attracting more interest, demonstrating that it is important to structure a PPP transaction in such a way that it is attractive to the private sector. In addition, to make up for state electricity boards' poor payment records, it was necessary for the Power Grid Corp of India to assure 100 per cent payment to the private sponsor for transmitting power to the state boards. This shows that having risk mitigation measures in the PPP structure may be important to secure private sector interest. |
| National Referral Hospital (2008) | Lesotho | Greenfield – BOT | Health | 100 | The project received strong support from the government at the highest level. This positive signalling effect allowed the government to secure the services of a consortium led by an international healthcare provider with hospital PPP experience. The operating costs of the new facility will be similar to those at the existing hospital and therefore patients will not need to pay extra to use the new hospital. This shows that it is possible to structure a financially attractive deal for the private sector without having to increase end user charges. |

## 7.5. Case studies of PPP experience in selected Commonwealth countries

This final section discusses the experience of three Commonwealth countries in implementing their PPP programmes. The case studies cover:

- The state of Victoria, Australia, where PPPs have been successfully facilitated by the well-known PPP unit Partnerships Victoria;

- South Africa, an example of a developing Commonwealth country that has achieved considerable success in implementing its PPP agenda; and

- Bangladesh, a country which has had some success in PPPs in the energy sector thus far and is now looking towards further developing its PPP agenda.

### 7.5.1. Victoria, Australia

Australia's federal structure means that most PPP activity is run by the individual states. As of December 2008, Victoria was the most active Australian state in terms of the number of PPP projects contracted (18), just ahead of neighbouring New South Wales (17).[15]

The composition of the Victorian PPP portfolio is heavily based on social PFI projects, although it has pursued a small number of core infrastructure projects in the transport, and water and sanitation sectors. This focus on core infrastructure PPP projects has been even more pronounced in the other Australian states, where there have been a higher proportion of road and water projects.

Maguire and Malinovitch (2005)[16] divide the evolution of PPP policy in Victoria into three stages:

- **Late 1980s–1992: Off balance sheet financing.** The motivation for PPPs was to gain off balance sheet financing for projects outside the limits set by the Australian loan council. The PPPs in this period had little impact on service delivery arrangements. Private finance was utilised, but was backed by government indemnities and guarantees, which limited risk transfer. Consequently, projects were brought forward, but were often structured in an inefficient manner that was later costly to unwind. Examples of projects from this period are the St Vincent's Hospital redevelopment (1991) and the Melbourne Magistrates Court Complex.

- **1993–1999: Belief in competition and efficiency of the private sector.** An infrastructure investment policy for Victoria was introduced in 1994. This shifted the motivation for PPP to the pursuit of private sector efficiency and risk transfer. Projects involved high levels of risk transfer and were no longer supported by significant guarantees from the government. This produced some large, unsustainable projects, created in a system of weak evaluation and assessment. Projects from this period include the Melbourne CityLink road project (1996) and Port Philip Prison (1996).

- **2000 to present: Value for money in the public interest and optimal risk transfer.**
  The Victoria Department of Treasury and Finance set up Partnerships Victoria[17] in 2000. Their first project was the Victoria County Court in 2002, typical of the social PFI-style projects they have pursued since then, with a strong emphasis on value for money and optimal risk transfer through whole-of-life-costing. Projects were implemented under Partnerships Victoria policy and guidance material, including the use of public sector comparator analysis and standardised contract documentation. Other examples from this period include the Eastlink, Mitcham-Frankston Freeway (2004) and Echua/Rochester Wastewater Treatment Plant (2004).

Victoria, together with the other states, has entered a further stage since 2008 – the process of integration and creation of a national market for PPPs. The National PPP Forum[18] was established in 2004 to pool knowledge and resources, and to share lessons learned in each state. The biggest step towards integration was the introduction of national PPP policy and guidelines in December 2008.[19] PPPs in Victoria since January 2009 must now comply with these national policies, supplemented by Partnerships Victoria policy in areas where the guidelines allow state-level flexibility.[20] One of the requirements of the new national guidelines is that PPP must be considered as a procurement option for any project involving capital expenditure of over A$50 million. One of the first projects to be completed under the guidelines is a A$3.5 billion desalination plant at Wonthaggi, expected to reach financial close in September 2009.

### 7.5.2. South Africa

The South African experience with PPPs has been noted worldwide, especially since the establishment of its PPP Unit in 2001. Compared to other developing Commonwealth countries, South Africa was a relatively early mover, borrowing significantly from the Partnerships UK approach. Between 1980 and 2006, 24 projects involving private sector participation reached financial close in the core infrastructure sectors of energy, transport, and water and sanitation.[21] Of these, 16 projects were initiated before 2001 (i.e. before the establishment of the PPP Unit). The South Africa PPP Unit reported a further 16 PPP projects in the health, education, tourism and other sectors as at January 2009 and 45 projects in the pipeline at both national and municipal levels.[22] Apart from one cancelled project in the water and sanitation sector in 1995, there have been no cancellations or outright project failures.

The beginnings of an integrated national PPP strategy came in 1997 with the establishment of an interdepartmental task team to develop policy and reforms to facilitate PPPs. This was supported by the setting up of the Municipal Infrastructure Investment Unit in 1998 to provide municipalities with technical and grant assistance. Before the full PPP framework was operational, several pilot PPP schemes were undertaken by government departments and municipalities.[23] An important PPP concession project during this period was the N4 toll road (a US$426 million investment reaching financial close in 1997)[24] linking South Africa and Mozambique. This road is an example of a difficult cross-border project that has performed well. Another project from this period was the Bloemfontein prison, one of two prisons reaching financial close in

2000. Plans for 11 PPP prisons were made, but higher costs than expected resulted in only two projects being taken forward.

The Cabinet endorsed a strategic framework for PPPs in 1999 and Treasury regulations for PPPs were issued in 2000. The culmination of this process was the creation of a PPP Unit in the Treasury in 2000 with international support from USAID, the UK Department for International Development (DFID) and the German Agency for Technical Cooperation (GTZ).[25] The Treasury Regulation 16 on PPPs, issued in terms of the Public Finance Management Act (PFMA) in 2004 is the key legislation for PPPs, outlining the procedure, approvals and management of PPPs.[26] The various modules of the PPP Manual and Standardised PPP Provisions are issued as Treasury *PPP Practice Notes* in terms of the PFMA.[27]

The PPP Unit has acted as a focal point for PPPs in the country. It has facilitated the completion of 18 projects, with no failures to date (although the Chapman's Peak Drive toll road has been closed for an extended period following rock slides in June 2008). While it has engaged in some core infrastructure projects (for example transport), the unit's projects have leaned to the social end of PPPs including health, tourism, IT and government accommodation. Typical of this is the first PPP unit-supported project, the R4.5 billion Inkosi Albert Luthuli Hospital, a state-of-the-art, but underutilised hospital near Durban. In contrast to this is the controversial R23.09 billion Gautrain (high-speed train) linking Johannesburg and Pretoria, which reached financial close in 2006. This project has been criticised for its substantially large investment costs as compared to other public transport projects in the country, and as a project that will primarily benefit the well-off.[28]

The South African experience highlights the important role of a well-functioning PPP unit in facilitating PPPs. The unit has received considerable political support, as well as being staffed with highly qualified advisers – both factors contributing favourably to its performance. The country's relatively more sophisticated financial and investment sector and overall enabling environment have also been important supporting factors. However, despite this, the rate of project closure in the country has been slow (about two projects a year), highlighting the inherent complexities in developing PPPs.

### 7.5.3. Bangladesh

Bangladesh's PPP programme commenced in the mid-1990s, when the government adopted a policy of promoting private sector participation in the power sector. Subsequently, and up to 2007, seven IPP projects have achieved financial close and are currently operational, providing approximately one-quarter of the country's generation capacity.[29] However, their success has been mixed – the large Haripur and Meghnaghat IPPs[30] reaching financial close in 2001 have been regarded as reasonably successful, but questions have been raised about the quality of the projects implemented since then.[31] In addition, over this period, Bangladesh has also undertaken five significant BOO fixed access telecom PPPs and three transport management contracts (a bridge, seaport terminal and airport).[32]

Bangladesh's PPP experience is built on the 2004 Bangladesh Private Sector Infrastructure Guidelines (PSIG).[33] These introduced the Private Infrastructure Committee (PICOM), designed to advance and monitor projects, while also providing a co-ordinating role between departments. PICOM is under the Prime Minister's Office, however, it has been contended that it has not received the political support required thus far. Beyond PICOM there are three main agencies supporting PPP in Bangladesh:

- **Infrastructure Development Company Ltd (IDCOL)**,[34] a government-sponsored company established in 1997 to promote private sector investment in infrastructure. IDCOL provides project finance and financial intermediation services and as of June 2009 had financed 22 (Tk13 billion) infrastructure projects, of which seven were BOO and two were BOT (see Section 5, Box 5.2).

- **Investment Promotion and Financing Facility (IPFF)**,[35] established in 2007 as a five-year investment promotion and financing facility, providing long-term finance for government-endorsed infrastructure. Its focus has been in the energy sector, bringing three BOO power projects to commercial operation and with two further projects nearing completion.

- **Infrastructure Investment Facilitation Centre (IIFC)**,[36] a government-sponsored company established in 1999 to assist government bodies formulate project proposals, screening and technical assistance. It became a fully commercial operation in 2007, when it began operating without any government or donor support. Sanghi et al. (2007)[37] criticises the design of the facility as leading to its limited role, and argues that it has done little to address investor perceptions of risk.

The infrastructure sectors are also supported by independent regulators for the energy and telecoms sectors.

The government recognises that although these initiatives have been useful in supporting PPP infrastructure project development in the country, they are not sufficient to cater to the needs and potential for the country. More recently, it is expected that Bangladesh's PPP programme will gain a renewed focus, with the new government claiming considerable support for the PPP approach. The Minister of Finance, Abul Maal Abdul Muhith, has expressed the government's commitment to support the PPP initiative with five key actions being planned by the end of 2009[38]:

1. reform of guidelines and institutional framework in the 2004 PSIG;

2. establishment of a PPP unit for budget formulation and implementation;

3. creation of a significant budgetary allocation for PPP (proposals for FY2009-10 include Tk21bn for project financing, Tk3bn for Viability Gap Funding and Tk1bn for technical assistance grants;

4. introduction of tax incentives for PPP investors; and

5. increased publicity for the new PPP initiative.

# Notes

1. Of the 54 Commonwealth countries, the four developed countries of the UK, Canada, New Zealand and Australia are not discussed here. Fiji Islands is also not included, as it was suspended from the Commonwealth in 2009. Rwanda is also not included as it joined the Commonwealth after this report was written.

2. Table 7.1 includes the latest available information as of 2008. World Development Indicators database. http://ddp-ext.worldbank.org/ext/DDPQQ/member.do?method=getMembers& userid=1&queryId=135

3. http://siteresources.worldbank.org/INTAFRICA/Resources/AICD_exec_summ_9-30-08a.pdf

4. http://www.enterprisesurveys.org/

5. IFC, *Doing Business 2009*, http://www.doingbusiness.org/

6. Oxford Analytica/Aon Political Risk Map 2009, http://www.aon.com/risk-services/political-risk-map/index.html

7. IFC, op. cit. and Oxford Analytica/Aon, op. cit.

8. The risk ratings are: high, medium-high, medium, medium-low and low.

9. http://ppi.worldbank.org/

10. http://ppi.worldbank.org/

11. http://ppi.worldbank.org/

12. Gratwick and Eberhard (2008).

13. Ibid.

14. IDCOL provided a loan of US$80 million, the largest loan ever made by a Bangladeshi financial institution. In addition, the ADB made available its PRG scheme for the first time for a US$70 million loan from a syndicate of commercial banks.

15. http://www.pppforum.gov.au/national_pipeline/projects_contracted.aspx

16. Maguire, G and Malinovitch, A, 'Development of PPPs in Victoria', *Australian Accounting Review*, Vol. 14, No. 2. (2004). http://www.partnerships.vic.gov.au/CA25708500035EB6/WebObj/DevelopmentofPPPsinVictoria/$File/Development%20of%20PPPs%20in%20Victoria.pdf

17. http://www.partnerships.vic.gov.au/

18. http://www.pppforum.gov.au/

19. http://www.infrastructureaustralia.gov.au/public_private_partnership_policy_guidelines.aspx

20. http://www.partnerships.vic.gov.au/CA25708500035EB6/WebObj/PartnershipsVictoriaStatement-February2009/$File/Partnerships%20Victoria%20Statement%20-%20February%202009.pdf

21. World Bank and PPIAF database.

22. http://www.ppp.gov.za/Documents/QuarterlyPubs/Feb_2009.pdf

23. Toll roads by the SA National Roads Agency, prisons by the Department of Public Works and Correctional Services, two municipalities (for water projects) and South African National Parks.

24. World Bank and PPIAF database.

25. The PPP unit was originally staffed by five professional staff, but its staffing complement has now grown to approximately 15.

26. http://www.ppp.gov.za/Documents/ppp_legis/Reg16_January2004.pdf

27. http://www.ppp.gov.za/PPPLegislation.html

28. Yescombe, ER, 'Public Private Partnerships: Principles of Policy and Finance', Butterworth-Heinemann (2007), pp. 47–48.

29. World Bank and PPIAF database.

30. See Annex 5 for a detailed case study of the Meghnaghat IPP.

31. Sanghi et al., 'Designing and Using Public–private Partnership Units in Infrastructure: Lessons from Case Studies Around the World', Gridlines Note No. 27, PPIAF (2007). http://www.ppiaf.org/documents/gridlines/27PPP.pdf

32. World Bank and PPIAF database.

33. http://www.bangladeshgateway.org/egovernment/Guideline-BOi.pdf

34. http://www.idcol.org/

35. http://www.bangladesh-bank.org/

36. http://www.iifc.net/

37. Sanghi et al. (2007), op. cit.

38. http://mof.gov.bd/en/budget/09_10/ppp/ppp_09_10_en.pdf

## Key references

### Project case studies and best practices

Gratwick, KL and Eberhard, A, 'An Analysis of Independent Power Projects in Africa: Understanding Development and Investment Outcomes', Development Policy Review, 26 (3): 309–338 (2008). http://www.gsb.uct.ac.za/files/IPPinAfrica.pdf

Analyses 40 IPPs across eight African countries, uncovering factors behind their success or failure.

Ministry of Urban Development (India) and Confederation of Indian Industry, Compendium on Public Private Partnership in Urban Infrastructure – Case Studies (2008). http://www.indiaurbanportal.in/bestpractice/books/PPP_Urban_Infra_moudcii.pdf

Twenty-six case studies of urban infrastructure PPPs in India, with varying levels of detail.

3-i Infrastructure Network, India Infrastructure Report 2001–08. http://3inetwork.org/reports/reports1.shtml

Substantive annual reports on infrastructure development in India, covering rural and urban infrastructure sectors and drawing on detailed case studies.

European Commission, Guidelines for Successful PPPs (2003) and Resource Book on PPP Case Studies (2004). http://ec.europa.eu/regional_policy/sources/docgener/guides/ppp_en.pdf http://ec.europa.eu/regional_policy/sources/docgener/guides/pppresourcebook.pdf

Guidelines for Successful PPPs highlights some of the most important issues to be considered when implementing PPPs. The guidelines are supplemented by 23 European case studies across the water and transport sectors that demonstrate several of the issues discussed in the earlier Guide.

ADB, *Developing Best Practices for Promoting Private Sector Investment in Infrastructure – Airports and Air Traffic Control/Ports/Power/Roads/Water Supply* (2000).
http://www.adb.org/Documents/Books/Developing_Best_Practices/Airports/default.asp
http://www.adb.org/Documents/Books/Developing_Best_Practices/Ports/default.asp
http://www.adb.org/Documents/Books/Developing_Best_Practices/Power/default.asp
http://www.adb.org/Documents/Books/Developing_Best_Practices/Roads/default.asp
http://www.adb.org/Documents/Books/Developing_Best_Practices/Water_Supply/default.asp

Five reports commissioned by the ADB on best practices to encourage private sector participation across five areas. Each report covers detailed sector characteristics and lessons to be learned.

Harris, C, 'Infrastructure Projects: A Review of Cancelled Private Projects', Public Policy for the Private Sector, Note No. 252, World Bank (2003).
http://rru.worldbank.org/Documents/PublicPolicyJournal/252Harris-010303.pdf

A note on failures examining the trends behind the data.

## Experience of small island states

World Bank, 'Institutions, Performance, and the Financing of Infrastructure Services in the Caribbean', World Bank Working Paper No. 58 (2005).
http://www.castalia-advisors.com/files/12383.pdf

A review of infrastructure sectors in 15 Caribbean counties, using performance benchmarks to draw out policy lessons and recommendations.

Ehrhardt, D and Oliver, C, 'Big Challenges, Small States: Regulatory Options to Overcome Infrastructure Constraints', Gridlines Note No. 24, PPIAF (2007).
http://www.ppiaf.org/documents/gridlines/24SmIsl.pdf

A Gridlines report synthesising lessons from experience in the Asia-Pacific region.

World Bank, *Doing Business in Small Island Developing States* (2009).
http://www.doingbusiness.org/documents/subnational/DB2009_Small_Island_developing_states.pdf

The second report focusing on the business environment of 33 small island states, drawing on the Doing Business Indicators database and focusing on best practice.

# 8

# Key lessons learned and emerging best practices on PPPs

The experience of PPPs in Commonwealth countries shows that successful projects can deliver significant benefits in terms of increased quantity and quality of infrastructure services. Moreover this can be achieved at lower overall cost for customers and taxpayers if suitable incentives are in place for the private partner to deliver efficiency improvements. On the other hand, when PPPs fail, the costs can be high, resulting in protracted and expensive legal disputes and the loss of political support for private sector involvement in infrastructure. Failures can also imply loss of government funding and consequently a decline in spending on other much-needed infrastructure services. In the worst cases, customers may suffer through service disruptions or unaffordable increases in tariffs.

Listing the factors attributable to successful PPPs is relatively straightforward (see Box 8.1). But these are not sufficient conditions. Every project will raise a different set of issues that must be dealt with by capable and experienced individuals from both the public and private sectors. Challenges are likely to arise throughout the project life cycle, from the project development phase through construction and operation (i.e. well beyond contract signing). Many of the key lessons on PPPs are therefore related to the need to take a long-term view when designing and implementing a PPP programme.

---

**Box 8.1. Success factors for PPPs**

- Strong political will
- Underlying economics of the project are attractive
- The project is well-designed and structured
- Capable private sector sponsor
- Access to suitable sources of finance/guarantees
- Robust legal and institutional framework for PPPs
- Strong public sector capacity

---

The experience of PPPs in developing countries (for example in the specific case studies presented in Annex 5) raises three main sets of lessons, discussed below.

**Lesson 1: *PPPs should be designed with long-term sustainability and value for money considerations in mind.***

It is widely recognised that many countries, including OECD markets, are attracted to PPP solutions because they offer access to private capital. Raising funds on capital markets can help governments avoid short-term budgetary constraints by spreading the up-front costs of infrastructure investment over the lifetime of the project. In emerging markets, where fiscal capacity is often seriously limited, PPPs can help governments tackle the infrastructure gap and provide services to those not previously reached by the public sector.

But it would be a mistake to view PPPs as only, or mainly, about raising capital. The success of a PPP programme should be assessed against the quantity, quality and cost of infrastructure services provided to the public over the long term. There is a danger that an approach to PPPs focused on the raising of capital will fail to properly assess or allocate the underlying risks in a project, with the result that the government may not end up getting value for money. In the worst cases, this may lead to the failure of the project, causing service disruptions and potentially high costs for government.

Key to ensuring long-run sustainability and value for money of PPPs are the following:

- Robust feasibility analysis;
- Proper due diligence in selecting a strong private sector sponsor;
- Good project and contract design.

### Robust feasibility analysis is essential

In the early years of modern PPP programmes in Europe and North America, a common mistake was for government and project sponsors to overestimate future revenues on PPP contracts. This was especially the case for toll road concessions, where traffic forecasts were over-optimistic – for example, more than half the Mexican toll roads reached less than 50 per cent of the forecasted volumes and the M1/M15 toll road in Hungary achieved less than 60 per cent of projected traffic flows in its initial years of operation.[1] Many contracts ran into difficulties, with the sponsor being unable to fund maintenance programmes because of lower than expected traffic volumes.

Nowadays there is more awareness of the importance of robust feasibility analysis which incorporates various scenarios about key revenue and cost drivers. But there are still examples of projects that fail because bidders were over-optimistic about future performance (for example the East Coast rail concession in the UK in 2009 – see Box 3.3).

In emerging markets there is often the additional challenge of a lack of data to inform a feasibility analysis. For example, reliable information on the number of potential customers for a service and the level of tariffs they are willing and able to pay is typically unavailable. This implies there will often be a need to spend relatively more time and effort at the feasibility stage in emerging markets to ensure that a proper case can be made for structuring a project as a PPP.

*Proper due diligence is required when selecting a private sector sponsor*

A common mistake when selecting a private partner is to focus on a limited number of variables (e.g. lowest cost tariff) without making a wider assessment of the capability of the sponsor to deal with unexpected events as they arise and implement the PPP contract successfully over the long term. This was arguably one of the main failings of the Kenya-Uganda rail concession and even of the Tanzania City Water transaction.

Of course, attracting the right sponsor and getting the best deal for the public sector is linked to the fundamental attractiveness of the project and how effectively it is marketed. In some situations it may not be possible to attract more than one competent bidder, in which case the government should undertake careful due diligence to determine whether or not the contract will deliver value for money. South Africa is an example where VfM considerations are built into the PPP legislative framework (see Box 8.2).

---

**Box 8.2. South Africa Treasury Regulation 16 – Public–private Partnerships, issued in terms of the Public Finance Management Act, 1999**

(Gazette No. 25915, 16 January 2004)

**Contracting PPP agreements – Treasury Approval: III**

After the procurement procedure has been concluded but before the accounting officer or accounting authority of an institution concludes a PPP agreement, that accounting officer or accounting authority must obtain approval from the relevant treasury –

(a) that the PPP agreement meets the requirements of affordability, value for money and substantial technical, operational and financial risk transfer as approved in terms of regulation 16.4.2 or as revised in terms of regulation 16.4.4;

(b) for a management plan that explains the capacity of the institution, and its proposed mechanisms and procedures, to effectively implement, manage, enforce, monitor and report on the PPP; and

(c) that a satisfactory due diligence including a legal due diligence has been completed in respect of the accounting officer's or accounting authority and the proposed private party in relation to matters of their respective competence and capacity to enter into the PPP agreement.

*Source:* http://www.ppp.gov.za/Documents/ppp_legis/Reg16_January2004.pdf

---

*A PPP approach may not be the optimal solution if sustainability and value for money cannot be assured*

Risk allocation, incentives and affordability are the three key aspects for the 'bankability' of a project; their consideration in the project structure will distinguish a 'good' from a 'bad' project. Projects need to be 'bankable' to attract private sector interest. Related to good project design is that it is interpreted clearly in the contract. Good contract design warrants that: (i) the processes and procedures for the PPP are clearly spelt out; and (ii) the measures for evaluating the performance of the PPP are clearly laid out.

Given the above, it is important to recognise that at times the PPP approach may not be the best one to follow. There will some projects where a PPP approach is not considered suitable, even though a private sponsor may want to invest, because long-term sustainability or value for money cannot be assured with sufficient certainty. The City Water project (Tanzania) is an example where the underlying economics of the project were unproven from the start (weak feasibility analysis based on poor data) and the private sponsor allegedly lacked suitable experience in operating this type of concession (poor due diligence on sponsor). With hindsight it might have been preferable for the government to have delayed awarding a contract to the private sector until more data had been gathered about the willingness of customers to pay user fees for improved services. This would also have allowed more time for the development of a PPP legal and regulatory framework, which could have encouraged additional bidders for the concession.

### Lesson 2: PPPs should be viewed as long-term commercial relationships between the public and private sectors, and not one-off procurement exercises or sales transactions.

A related lesson is that the role of government in a PPP remains important over the full life cycle of the project. This is a major difference to traditional outsourcing arrangements where the public sector typically runs a one-off procurement exercise and then steps back to allow the private contractor to implement the contract. It also distinguishes true PPPs (see Section 3) from privatisations or divestitures, where, again, the public sector's role is limited to a regulatory role after the introduction of the private sector.

The long-term nature of PPPs has implications for the PPP framework, ongoing management of the contract and the skills and experience needed in the public sector.

### Establish a flexible PPP framework

Although the lack of a PPP framework does not prevent PPPs from going ahead, it does reduce their chances of long-term success. The main reason is that without a suitable framework the PPP contract for a specific project must attempt to capture all eventualities that may arise over the lifetime of the project. Since PPPs typically have a life cycle of at least 15 years beyond financial close, this is almost impossible to achieve. Under a strict contractual approach there is a risk of a rapid descent into arbitration if events occur which materially impact on the performance of the contract. This issue has been discussed at length in Section 4.1, as well as highlighted as an important constraint to infrastructure PPPs in Section 5.1.

The best way of avoiding this situation is to have a PPP framework that establishes broad principles for ongoing dialogue and co-operation between the public and private sectors beyond contract signature. The framework should include a process for renegotiation where unexpected events occur which are beyond the control of either party – for example, as highlighted by the EBRD in the core principles for a modern concession law in Box 4.2 above. In situations where the PPP framework is absent or underdeveloped, flexibility should be designed into the contract itself.

### Ensure effective ongoing management of the PPP contract

As mentioned above, the role of the government in a PPP is important over the full life of the project. Post-financial close, efficient contract management and monitoring are key to the success of the project. The government needs to manage the PPP contract in such a way that it delivers the desired outcomes for the public sector and value for money. Central to this is the monitoring of the performance of the PPP (one of the key risks usually transferred to the private sector in a PPP). A good monitoring system (also built into the contract) is important to keep track of deviations, if any, and consequently forms the base for public action, as may be required.

The suitable institutional framework for monitoring of PPP contracts depends upon the complexity and number of transactions. As highlighted in Box 4.9 above, there can be a number of different options, but the key lesson is that the institutional framework should be 'fit for purpose'.

### The public sector needs staff with appropriate business skills and experience

'People matter' – evidence from the World Bank shows that a successful partnership between the public and private sectors depends to a large extent on the people involved in the project.[2] Naturally it is important that both parties have the right skills and experience to execute the PPP project development process successfully. In particular, public sector employees involved in negotiating and managing PPPs benefit from having commercial, i.e. business, experience or training. (There is, of course, still a need for specialist legal, technical and financial skills which can be accessed through long-term secondments of external experts and through contracting professional advisers for specific projects.) Where there is weak public sector capacity, the potential for a suitably designed PPP unit can offer much advantage.

It also matters that there is regular and effective communication between the public and private sectors: this will be easier if both parties share a commercial approach to the partnership rather than a legalistic one.

### Lesson 3: PPPs are inherently complex, costly and time-consuming to develop properly. A rushed project often becomes a failed project.

A third set of lessons arises from the fact that PPPs are almost always complex transactions. As set out in Section 4.2, the project development phase alone typically lasts three years (often longer for greenfield projects) before finance is secured and groundbreaking can commence. This timetable sits uncomfortably with short-term political horizons. There can be a temptation for governments to short circuit the project development process in order to deliver on public expectations of improved services from a PPP programme. A high level of political support, as well as suitable management of political and public expectations on PPPs, is crucial to their success. In addition, given the complexity of PPPs, expert advice is very important.

### High-level political support is essential

This is essential for the success of a PPP, especially during the project development stage when there is potential for significant delays if there is not a champion within the government who can drive through required legislation, and licence and land allocation agreements. A strong PPP unit can play an important role in pushing PPP projects up the political agenda, but there may still be occasions when high-level political support (say from ministers) may be necessary. Strong government commitment to PPPs is essential to secure private sector confidence.

### It is important to manage political expectations about the time it takes to design and execute a PPP project properly

In particular, it is important to avoid 'over-selling' PPP projects early in the project life cycle because of the risk of creating unrealistic expectations of what can be delivered and by when. Ministers will need to be persuaded to support greenfield projects, despite the fact that operations are unlikely to commence within one or two electoral cycles.

One way of building public support for a PPP programme is to focus on a small number of 'easy wins' for the initial round of projects (e.g. in the power or transport sectors rather than in water and sanitation). This is also likely to have benefits in terms of building capacity and experience within the public sector about how to develop PPPs. As experience in India has shown, the demonstration effect of successful PPPs can be very powerful in encouraging government and the private sector to support other transactions.

### Expert advice is expensive but necessary

Legal, technical and financial advisers for PPP projects can be expensive, reflecting the fact that professionals with international experience of working on PPPs are in scarce supply. Advisory fees will typically account for between 5 and 10 per cent of the total project cost. However, assuming professional services are competitively procured, this investment is essential to ensure the project is properly designed and structured. It is especially important that the public sector has access to high-quality advisers to make sure there is an equitable sharing of costs and risks with the private sector.

Box 8.3 presents India's approach to the empanelment of transactions advisers for PPP projects. In addition, Section 6 and Annex 4 describe some of the international facilities that are available to governments to pay for technical assistance.

Box 8.3. Empanelment of transaction advisers for PPPs in India[3]

The Government of India has adopted a policy to facilitate private investment in infrastructure and recognises the importance of appropriate advisory support for the implementation of PPP transactions. Accordingly, the government has finalised a panel of pre-qualified transaction advisers to assist public sector agencies in PPP transactions.

The purpose of the panel is to:

- Streamline the tendering process for the engagement of transaction advisers for PPPs;
- Enable fast access to firms that have pre-qualified against relevant criteria; and
- Ensure transparency and accountability through clear definition of the processes and the role and responsibilities of the agencies and the private sector.

The evaluation for empanelment of transaction advisers has been undertaken on the basis of two-stage evaluation criteria, which requires each agency to satisfy minimum threshold requirements of annual turnover and human resource capability. Applicants who have satisfied the threshold requirement have been evaluated for their capability and experience in discharging a lead role in transactions and providing commercial, financial and legislative advice.

The panel is available to all sponsoring authorities, including central, state and municipal governments and their agencies in India who are undertaking PPP transactions.

## Notes

1. Harris (2003), op. cit.
2. World Bank, *Does Private Sector Participation Improve Performance in Electricity and Water Distribution?* (2009).
3. http://www.pppinindia.com/pdf/User_Guide_for_Tr_Ads_final_approved.pdf

# ANNEX 1

# Frequently Asked Questions on PPPs

1. What is a PPP? How is it different from public procurement or privatisation?

2. What are the key benefits of PPPs?

3. How can PPPs be structured to achieve public policy goals? Do PPPs always lead to an increase in user charges?

4. When is PPP an appropriate approach for delivery of infrastructure services?

5. What are the differing objectives and risks facing governments and investors in a PPP?

6. What type of risks can be allocated to the private sector? How much risk is the private sector willing to take in lower-income countries?

7. What are the different payment mechanisms for PPPs?

8. How can competitive pressure be ensured throughout the bidding process? What should be done if there is only one bidder?

9. How much time and cost is involved in developing PPP projects?

10. Why have there been so few successful PPPs in the lower-income countries of the Commonwealth?

11. How is the global financial crisis affecting PPP projects in emerging markets?

12. What are the most common mistakes to avoid when considering and developing PPP transactions?

13. What are the main reasons for the failure of PPP contracts?

## 1. What is a PPP? How is it different from public procurement or privatisation?

It is easy to become confused by the ever-increasing number of definitions and synonyms for PPPs. The working definition used in this Reference Guide (Section 3.1) captures the key defining feature of a PPP: 'A PPP is a long-term contractual arrangement for the delivery of public services where there is a **significant degree of risk sharing between the public and private sectors**'. Thus, a contract wherein both the public and private sectors have a significant stake, and consequently share the risks in delivering the infrastructure services, is a PPP.

This definition of a PPP also alludes to its other characterisations, namely:

- It is a **long-term** contract, typically for a period of 10 to 20 years (although there are some PPPs that may be of a shorter duration of, say, three to five years);

- It is a **partnership** agreement between the public and private sectors, in that both parties have a mutual interest and a unified commitment.

These three characteristics define a PPP and distinguish it from others forms of private participation in infrastructure. Variations of these characteristics in terms of the degree of risk sharing or the number of years of the contract, define the different types of PPP models, such as concessions, BOTs and DBFOs.

Unhelpfully, the term PPP has come to refer to anything between pure private provision and pure government provision. However, there are key differences between PPPs and these two methods of infrastructure service delivery. Pure private provision, or privatisation, involves the transfer of responsibility for asset construction and ownership, service delivery and revenue collection to the private sector. Thus the private sector bears 100 per cent of the risks of infrastructure service delivery. The role of government is restricted to regulation. On the other hand, pure public provision (also often referred to as 'traditional public procurement') refers to the contracting out of infrastructure services by the government to private sector contractors, with the public sector retaining almost 100 per cent of the risk. Under these contracts, there are few efficiency incentives, unlike in a PPP wherein payments are linked to specific performance criteria. For example, under a PPP contract for a road, payments may be made on the basis of a certain specific quality of the road surface, whereas in the case of traditional procurement, the payments may be linked to the number of kilometres of road area.

## 2. What are the key benefits of PPPs?

Governments around the word have embraced PPPs because they offer three main types of benefits:

- The ability to **develop new infrastructure services** despite short-term fiscal constraints;

- **Value for money** through efficiencies in procurement, construction and operation; and

- Improved **service quality and innovation** through use of private sector expertise and performance incentives.

However, these benefits will only be achieved if the project is properly designed and structured from the outset.

## 3. How can PPPs be structured to achieve public policy goals? Do PPPs always lead to an increase in user charges?

By allocating different risks to the entity best able to manage them, PPPs can be structured to achieve a range of public policy goals, including the acceleration of new infrastructure investment, improved efficiency in operations and management leading to lower cost service provision, access to advanced technologies and know-how not available to the public sector, and contractually enforced social and environmental standards. Where these goals are not achieved ex post it will typically be the result of poor contractual design or project structure.

Involving the private sector in infrastructure generally entails a shift towards full cost-recovery, which can mean higher tariffs in situations where state-owned enterprises were previously subsidised by the taxpayer. However, tariff increases are by no means inevitable, for four key reasons:

- If the PPP is well-structured, involving the private sector achieves efficiencies which drive down long-term costs – this is at the core of the benefits of a PPP, in which private sector innovation and greater efficiency will potentially lower the costs of infrastructure service delivery;

- The government may continue to pay for services through annual payments to the private service provider (i.e. services for the consumer remain free at the point of delivery) – this can be structured as a PFI type contract, or in the form of shadow tolls, revenue guarantees, etc. by the government to the private operator;

- The service provider may cross-subsidise by charging lower fees to those less able to pay and increasing charges for corporate customers – as has often been the case for energy and water sector PPPs, wherein a higher tariff is charged for industrial/ urban users to subsidise use by domestic/rural consumers;

- The government may decide to channel explicit subsidies to the poorest user groups in order to facilitate affordability of the infrastructure service.

Overall, it is unlikely that a PPP will lead to higher costs for services, but payment for the service from direct users and indirect contributors, such as taxpayers, may change.

## 4. When is PPP an appropriate approach for delivery of infrastructure services?

It is important to recognise that a PPP is one of many options available to the government for the delivery of an infrastructure service (the others include direct public sector provision, contracting of the private sector and other forms of private participation, such as service contracts and privatisations). When deciding whether a PPP is the appropriate approach, it is important to assess whether these other options offer greater benefits to taxpayers and customers.

The key criteria for assessing whether a PPP is an appropriate approach include the following:

- **Does the project offer value for money to the public sector?** It is important to compare the costs of alternative methods of provision of the infrastructure service to ensure that the PPP offers value for money for the public sector. There may be cases where public sector provision (or any other model) may be the preferred approach. For example, the UK Treasury notes that in certain instances the PFI procurement structure is unlikely to deliver value for money, such as when equity and accountability in public service delivery cannot be met or where authorities require a significant degree of short-term flexibility due to fast-changing service requirements (for example, in information technology projects). This is also the case when the investment is small and the benefits of PFI do not justify the significant costs incurred during the PFI procurement process (for projects of less than £20 million capital value).

- **Do the project economics add up and is the project 'bankable'?** In assessing the appropriateness of a PPP approach, it is important to structure the project in such a way that it is bankable. For example, where affordability of the infrastructure service is a key constraint, a PPP approach may not be the most appropriate option unless the government can guarantee the payments for the infrastructure service (whether directly through fixed payments or through some guarantee for a minimum level of revenue). Or the project may be so risky that the cost of the investment may be far too high in relation to the expected return from the project.

- **Is a supportive enabling environment in place to facilitate the PPP?** If a supportive legal and regulatory framework for PPPs is not in place, following the PPP approach needs to be carefully considered, as it may lead to inefficient project development and operation. While some PPPs have gone ahead without the support of an enabling framework, it is questionable whether this was the most appropriate and efficient solution. Closely related to this is the level of capacity in the country (both in the public and private sectors). There needs to be capacity within government to develop, procure and manage the PPP contract, as well as good quality sponsors who are able to deliver the project outcomes efficiently.

- **Is the country infrastructure sector suitable for PPPs?** Some infrastructure sectors may be more suitable than others for the PPP approach in general and specific types of PPP in particular. It has usually been the case that private participation in a country is first introduced in the telecoms sector and only slowly introduced into the water sector, given the political sensitivities around charging for water services.

- **Is the infrastructure sector/asset of strategic importance to the country?** There may be certain infrastructure sectors/assets that are of strategic importance to the security of a country. In these cases, the PPP route may not be the most appropriate. For example, roads near territorial boundaries where there is an ongoing dispute may not be appropriate for PPPs – not least because the risks for private sector investors would be too high.

## 5. What are the differing objectives and risks facing governments and investors in a PPP?

The government, sponsors and investors all have different objectives and consequently face different risks under a PPP arrangement:

- The key concerns for the **government** are whether the service is delivered and the PPP offers value for money. A related concern is contingent liabilities, both during project development up to financial close and during the construction and operational phases of the project (note that even where the government does not provide an explicit guarantee for a PPP project it will typically be expected to step in and pick up the cost in cases where projects fail).

- **Investors and lenders** are most interested in ensuring that their capital gets repaid over the lifetime of the project with a suitable return. Hence, the key risks from the perspective of the investors are unexpected reductions in the project revenues, increases in costs and consequent delays or default on loan repayments or dividends. These risks can be managed through robust feasibility analysis, the introduction of competent management and the use of various guarantee mechanisms (e.g. to hedge interest rate or currency risk). Investors will also seek insurance against expropriation and other political risks over which they have no direct control.

## 6. What type of risks can be allocated to the private sector? How much risk is the private sector willing to take in lower-income countries?

The private sector is typically willing to accept construction and operating risks, over which it can exercise a reasonable degree of control. The level of demand risk the private sector is willing to bear depends critically on the quality of data underpinning market studies. Typically, investors will require some form of minimum revenue guarantee from governments or international agencies; these can take the form of ridership guarantees for transport projects or off-take agreements backed by a creditworthy entity for utility services. The private sector will not typically accept political or *force majeure* risk.

In developing countries, investors are likely to demand a higher financial return for accepting construction and operating risks. They are also unlikely to accept significant demand risk because of low quality data on demand volumes and willingness to pay. The higher cost of PPP projects and the greater degree of risk that needs to be held by the public sector (or international agencies) should be weighed against the benefits of delivering much-needed infrastructure services in situations where the alternative is often no service provision.

## 7. What are the different payment mechanisms for PPPs?

Payment mechanisms refer to the modalities for payment for the infrastructure services, i.e. the mechanisms through which private operators earn their revenues. They are instrumental in delivering effective risk transfer and provide a means to re-align private profit motives and achieve efficient public service provision.

Most payment mechanisms can be split into two broad categories: direct user charges and availability/performance-based payments.

### User charges

This payment mechanism places a strong emphasis on the transfer of demand risk to the private sector. The private operator sells services directly to consumers (usually the general public or businesses) and charges a fee or toll for these services. Common examples include toll roads and water utilities.

### Availability performance-based payments

These mechanisms have a much lower degree of demand risk transfer and place greater emphasis on the transfer of construction and performance risk. Optional payment mechanisms include:

- **Availability-based payments:** Payments are based upon the availability of a facility when required. This mechanism is common for PFI-based projects in the UK such as hospitals or schools. Penalties may be incurred if the facility is unavailable. However, the definition of what constitutes availability must incorporate its varying degrees and the varying impacts that it may have (e.g. closing a bridge in the rush hour compared with in the middle of the night).

- **Performance-based payments:** Governments may provide financial support to PPP projects in the form of shadow tolls or guarantees for a minimum level of revenue. These are usually linked to the performance of the project, but may also be provided for directly in the PPP contract.

### Other mechanisms

The above mechanisms are broad types, and it is likely that a project may be a hybrid of both approaches. For example, the mechanisms for the UK PFI project to set up the Liverpool Women's Hospital information support system are 70 per cent availability, 20 per cent performance and 10 per cent usage. Toll roads may often have an availability element supporting their user charges.

In addition, output-based aid (usually provided by donor agencies) provides an important source of funding for PPP infrastructure projects.

### 8. How can competitive pressure be ensured throughout the bidding process? What should be done if there is only one bidder?

Competition in the bidding process is key to achieving value for money for the government, as the private sector will find innovative ways of delivering the infrastructure service at the lowest possible cost. However, a competitive environment needs to be carefully structured in order to ensure appropriate incentives; for example, if renegotiations are the norm in the country, the private sector bidders may be incentivised to provide an over-aggressive bid, in the belief that the contract may be renegotiated for more realistic terms at a later date.

There are a number of ways through which the government can ensure greater competitive pressure in the bidding stage:

- **First**, the project should be marketed well, so that the private sector is made aware of the project and thus its potential to submit a bid. Different media/options may be followed, such as roadshows or advertisements in the print media;

- **Second**, the procurement process and all relevant project information should be clearly provided to the private sector so as to reduce the costs of bidding and consequently encourage its participation;

- **Third**, the duration of the procurement process should be reasonable. In some countries, procurement of the private sector sponsor has taken a few years, which can drive away the private sector because of the additional costs incurred, as well as changes in circumstances which may impact on the terms of their bid.

However, there may be cases where a project has a sole bidder. In such cases, the following measures may be considered:

- **Repackaging the project:** Limited private sector interest may be due to the underlying project economics not adding up. There may then be advantages in the government repackaging the project to make it more attractive to the private sector, thereby soliciting a greater number of competitive bids.

- **Detailed due diligence of the sole bidder:** If a single bid has been received for the project, the government should carry out a detailed due diligence on the bid/sponsor to ensure that it is getting a good deal. Although this may not be the lowest priced bid, given the absence of competitive pressure, there are other aspects to be considered, such as the cost of running an additional procurement exercise and whether or not the private sector in the country is developed enough to result in a number of bidders for one project. Thus in certain circumstances, it may make sense to explore the sole bid further through a detailed assessment of the capabilities, creditworthiness and experience of the sponsor. This is key to ensuring the success of the project.

## 9. How much time and cost is involved in developing PPP projects?

PPP projects are inherently complex and resource intensive. There are few short cuts to designing and structuring PPPs properly because of the need to identify and allocate risks that will generally be specific to the project, the sector and the country. The minimum cost of developing a PPP is likely to be US$3–5 million; for this reason pursuing small projects (e.g. projects less than US$20 million in total value) makes limited sense from a value for money perspective. The timeframe from concept to financial close is typically between three and five years and can be longer for especially complex or risky transactions.

For larger projects, the amount spent on advisory fees should be considered an investment that will be returned over the lifetime of the project through cost and efficiency savings brought about by private sector participation. Of course, if the contract is poorly designed these savings might not be achieved, or they might accrue entirely to the private investor. That is why it is important that governments have access to high quality advisers to ensure they can negotiate a fair deal with private sponsors.

Although the time and cost of developing a PPP project may appear high, this should be weighed against the fact that governments, especially in lower-income developing countries, have often failed to deliver essential infrastructure services to the majority of the population over a period of many decades, and that where infrastructure services have been provided, they have often been of low quality and relied on heavy public subsidies.

## 10. Why have there been so few successful PPPs in the lower-income countries of the Commonwealth?

There are two main reasons. First, the costs and risks of developing PPPs in poorer countries are typically much higher than elsewhere. As a result, sponsors are reluctant to invest significant time and resources in developing projects which may not deliver an acceptable financial rate of return. Second, projects in poorer countries tend to be smaller in size (often less than US$100 million), which means the absolute financial returns available are insufficiently attractive to large infrastructure investors.

Solutions to these problems include establishing (publicly-backed) project development facilities to help design and structure bankable projects; using international facilities to access long-term finance and help mitigate project risks; and tapping domestic capital markets for investment, supported by credit guarantees.

## 11. How is the global financial crisis affecting PPP projects in emerging markets?

The global economic and financial crisis is having a major adverse impact on private sector infrastructure investment in low-income developing countries. First, there has been a general reduction in risk appetite for infrastructure assets in developing countries, especially in relation to greenfield projects. Second, there has been a reduction in the availability and a sharp increase in the real cost of debt, especially longer-term debt. Third, there has been a related reduction in the availability of equity for greenfield investments arising from a refocusing by public and private equity investors on recapitalising existing businesses rather than investing in new ones.

Consequently, it has become significantly more difficult for project sponsors to raise the financing required to get PPPs to financial close. This is especially the case for projects in smaller economies and those without a track record of successfully completed transactions. Until long-term liquidity returns to the markets, we are likely to see a sharp decline in the number of infrastructure PPPs in developing countries. Those transactions that do proceed are likely to have to rely heavily on the development finance institutions as anchor investors. Where commercial debt is available, it will generally require the support of credit guarantees (e.g. from GuarantCo) to persuade lenders to reduce the cost of funds and extend tenors beyond three or four years.

At the time of writing, major uncertainties remain as to how long it will take for liquidity to return to the markets, and as to the extent to which, during the interim, the DFIs will be willing and able to step in to help fill the financing gap. The good news is that collectively the DFIs have strong balance sheets, having accumulated large reserves during the boom years of the last decade. There have also been announcements of major new initiatives to support infrastructure investments in developing countries (e.g. the IFC's Infrastructure Crisis Facility). Now is the time for the DFIs to play the counter-cyclical role for which they were designed.

## 12. What are the most common mistakes to avoid when considering and developing PPP transactions?

PPP project development is a complex, expensive and time-consuming process. Every effort must be made to make the process as efficient as possible. Some common mistakes to avoid when developing a PPP are:

- Lack of a project champion within the public sector;
- Lack of ownership and leadership of the project among the project developers (public or private sector);
- Lack of detailed feasibility studies (to be carried out by relevant experts);
- Overly ambitious project development timeframe;
- Selecting advisers on the basis of cost only, without a detailed consideration of their quality and experience;
- Lack of effective engagement with relevant stakeholders.

## 13. What are the main reasons for the failure of PPP contracts?

PPP contracts can fail for a number of reasons. Some of the most common reasons for their failure are:

- Poor feasibility analysis, particularly in terms of forecasting demand for the infrastructure service. A number of PPP contracts have failed because revenues have fallen well short of projections. In some cases this is the result of inadequate feasibility analysis or aggressive bidding.
- Weak private sector sponsor in terms of lack of skills and experience to deliver the infrastructure services.

- An inappropriate enabling environment in terms of a poor legal and regulatory framework, as well as weak enforcement capacity.

- Lack of a proper contract management and monitoring framework by the public sector, from the initial project development and procurement stages through to post-financial close phases of construction and operation.

- Political issues related to the application or increase of tariffs for the use of the infrastructure service. This has particularly been the case for water sector projects in developing countries.

Macroeconomic shocks, such as a financial crisis or foreign exchange fluctuations, may reduce the profitability of the project and lead to its ultimate failure.

# ANNEX 2

# Trends in private participation in infrastructure in low and middle income countries, 1990–2007[1]

## Summary of key trends

- Private participation in infrastructure in low- and middle-income countries has increased considerably since 1990.

- EAP and LAC project numbers decreased following the late-1990s economic crises.

- Median project size decreased in the early 2000s, recovering to around US$100 million in 2007.

- Concessions and management contracts grew steadily since 1990, but remain a minority.

- The number and value of projects in sub-Saharan Africa lag behind most other regions.

- Commonwealth projects are dominated by India and Malaysia, leading to low levels of divestitures and increases in concessions since 2002 within the group.

- Around 5 per cent of all projects reaching financial closure between 1990 and 2007 have been cancelled, at an average of 6.9 years after financial close.

## Overview

Private participation in infrastructure has become increasingly important in low- and middle-income countries since 1990.[2] Progress is highlighted by 58 projects reaching financial close in only eight countries in 1990, compared to 288 projects across 64 countries in 2007.[3]

However, while the growth of private participation in infrastructure has been remarkable, the trend from 1990 has not been uniform. Figure A2.1 reveals the large fluctuations that have occurred in the value of new private sector investment commitments since 1990.[4]

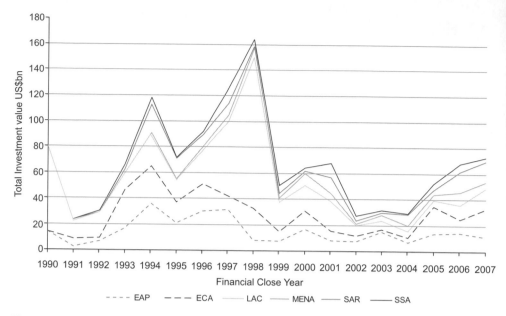

**Figure A2.1.** Investment commitments in low- and middle-income countries, 1990–2007

As Figure A2.1 shows, there was a near sixfold increase in investment commitments, from US$23.7 billion in 1991 to a peak of US$164.8 billion in 1998. Rapid growth in LAC projects fuelled this boom. The decline that followed was strongly influenced by currency and debt crises in the EAP and LAC regions.[5] Investment commitments temporarily stabilised at this level before halving again during the recession of the early 2000s. Private sector investments have increased since 2002 to reach US$73 billion of new committed investments in 2007.

The trend in the value of investment commitments depends on both the number of projects reaching financial closure and their size. Figure A2.2 shows the former, tracking the number of projects that reached financial close in each year from 1990 to 2007.

Public–Private Partnerships Policy and Practice

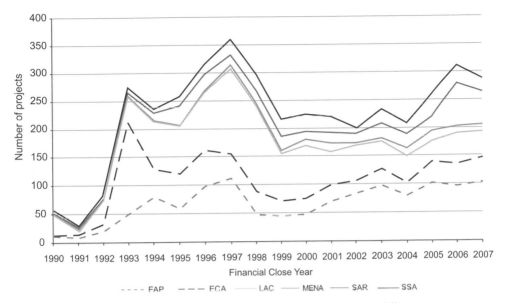

**Figure A2.2.** Number of projects reaching financial close in low- and middle-income countries, 1990–2007

Figure A2.2 shows that despite the 1998 peak in total value of investment commitments, the number of projects rapidly decreased, particularly in the EAP region. While there was a boom and bust in project numbers in the 1990s, there has been a greater degree of stability in the number of projects since 2000, and an increase since 2004.

Figure A2.3 shows the changing median project size over the period.[6]

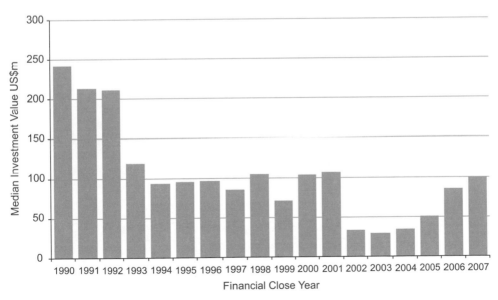

**Figure A2.3.** Median and investment value in infrastructure projects involving private sector participation, 1990–2007

Median project commitments were high in the early 1990s compared to the 2000s, with some large divestitures driving the higher project value (for example, the US$33.1 billion Telefonos de Mexico divestiture in 1990). However since 1993 the median project value has held steady around US$100 million, with a further fall in 2002. This latter downward adjustment was caused by several factors, including:

- local economic crises and turbulence;

- the bursting of the dot com bubble;

- the decline of some large investors (including Enron); and

- a shift towards a larger number of management and lease contracts.

The figures above also show differences in the nature of the declines in investment commitments following the late 1990s and early 2000s recessions. The decrease in total investment commitments in the late 1990s was the result of reductions in both the number of projects and their size. On the other hand, the reduction following 2001 appears to have been predominantly caused by a reduction in project size, with little change in project numbers. The cutback in size also persisted longer than in the late 1990s only returning to the US$100 million mark in 2007.

Finally, Figure A2.4 shows the number of projects by type of private sector participation over the period 1990 to 2007.

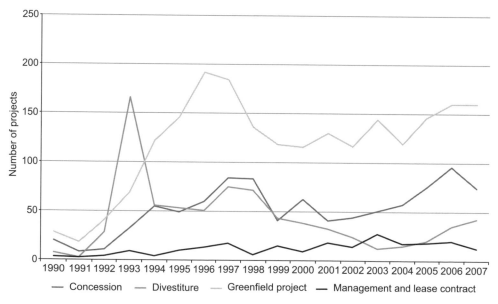

**Figure A2.4.** Number of projects reaching financial close by type of private sector participation, 1990–2007

Figure A2.4 shows relatively steady growth in concessions, and management and lease contracts since 1990. The number of divestitures and greenfield projects grew rapidly in the first half of the 1990s, but then declined to lower levels soon after reaching their peaks. Greenfield projects have been the most frequent type of private sector participation since the late 1990s.

## Trends by region

The overall picture painted above reflects both the growing awareness and application of private sector participation in infrastructure projects globally, but also its sensitivity to macroeconomic shocks. Further details can be explored when regions are examined individually.

Historically, the LAC and EAP regions have led in the use of private sector participation. They accounted for approximately 60 per cent of both projects and investment commitments between 1990 and 2007. However, their shares have dipped since 2004, with transactions being spread more evenly across regions. LAC reached its private sector investment peak in 1998, only to fall and settle at 13 per cent of this value in 2007. The mid-1990s boom was largely based on Brazilian telecom and energy divestitures. The emphasis has now shifted to transport concessions and greenfield energy projects. Although the absolute number of these types of projects was higher in earlier years, they now represent a greater proportion of the total projects, given the lower number of divestitures. The EAP region had the largest number of projects involving private sector participation in 2007, but at only the fourth highest value. China dominates this region, with 63.1 per cent of all projects from 1990 to 2007. However, in terms of value, Malaysia, the Philippines, Indonesia and Thailand are also major players.

Projects in South Asia region (SAR) countries generated US$16.0 billion of commitments in 2007, the third largest value by region. This represents a rapid growth from only US$1.7 billion in 2003, and was propelled by increased private participation in both the energy and transport sectors. The development of transport projects involving private sector participation has made a large impact in SAR. The sector comprised less than 6 per cent of regional private sector commitments from 1990 to 2004, but contributed 43 per cent from 2005 to 2007.

Sub-Saharan Africa has traditionally lagged behind most other regions, both in terms of the number and value of projects implemented. This trend has not changed. Private sector participation in infrastructure projects across the region expanded rapidly through the 1990s, only to realise a sharp fall in 2002. It recovered to its peak level in 2005, from which it slightly receded as the number of transport projects decreased. However, growth in the region has been steadier than in other regions. This can be partly attributed to the high proportion of low-income countries, as these have been more robust to shocks (see Figure A2.5). Private sector participation in infrastructure has also been relatively low in the Middle East and North Africa (MENA) region.

Europe and Central Asian (ECA) countries generated the highest value of infrastructure projects involving private sector participation in 2007 for only the third time since 1990. Russian energy divestitures boosted figures in a region where investment commitments have been particularly volatile. The number of projects has gradually risen over time to 43, but is overshadowed by the 1993 peak of 162.[7]

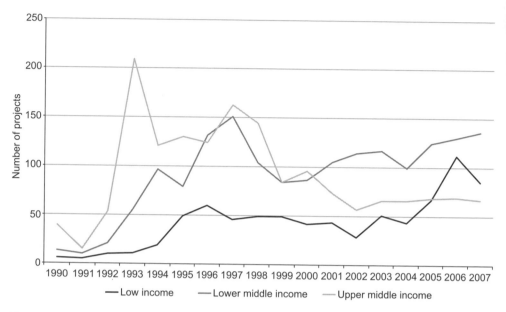

**Figure A2.5.** Number of projects involving private sector participation reaching financial close by income group, 1990–2007

The portfolio of private sector participation in infrastructure projects across Commonwealth countries covers a wide range of projects and locations. However, it is dominated by Malaysia and India, who together accounted for 63 per cent of total Commonwealth country investment commitments in the period 1990–2007 by value, as shown in Figure A2.6. In part because of efforts in these countries, Commonwealth countries represent a significant proportion of all these transactions in recent years. From 2005 to 2007, Commonwealth countries generated 37.5 per cent of projects reaching financial close and 34.6 per cent of total investment commitments. The recent increase in Commonwealth concession projects and the comparatively low level of divestitures in the group (Figure A2.7) is also largely influenced by activities in these two countries.

Public–Private Partnerships Policy and Practice

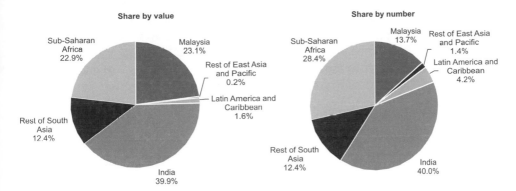

**Figure A2.6.** Global distribution of Commonwealth infrastructure projects involving private sector participation, 1990–2007

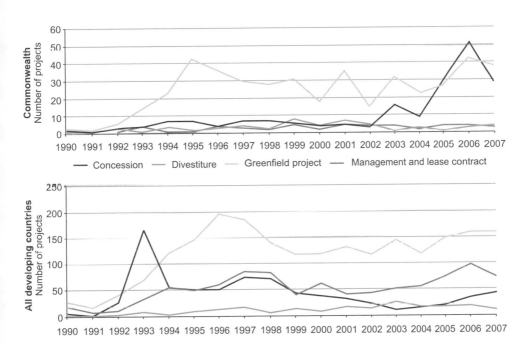

**Figure A2.7.** Type of private sector participation across Commonwealth countries and all developing countries, 1990–2007

## Distribution by country

A closer examination of the regional data reveals that the spread of private sector participation is not evenly distributed among countries within regions. These differences are illustrated in Table A2.1.

Private sector involvement has been concentrated in a small number of countries, but with a long tail of countries with fewer projects. This, however, does not mean that smaller countries have not been active relative to their size. Chile, Argentina and Malaysia are the top three countries in terms of number of projects per capita.[8] Dominica has the highest number of projects per capita, with three for its population of just over 73,000 (the equivalent of over 41 projects per million people).

**Table A2.1.** Top ten countries by project commitments, project number and projects per head, 1990–2007

| Country | Value US$ billion | Share (%) | Country | No. of projects | Share (%) | Country | Projects per million people[9] |
|---|---|---|---|---|---|---|---|
| Brazil | 67.2 | 18.1 | China | 337 | 20.9 | Chile | 7.80 |
| China | 35.6 | 9.6 | Brazil | 143 | 8.9 | Argentina | 4.64 |
| India | 33.9 | 9.1 | India | 98 | 6.1 | Malaysia | 4.23 |
| Argentina | 25.9 | 7.0 | Argentina | 91 | 5.6 | Colombia | 2.97 |
| Philippines | 18.3 | 4.9 | Russia | 88 | 5.5 | Russia | 2.19 |
| Russia | 17.4 | 4.7 | Philippines | 62 | 3.8 | Kazakhstan | 2.16 |
| Malaysia | 14.3 | 3.9 | Thailand | 51 | 3.2 | Ecuador | 2.04 |
| Indonesia | 13.6 | 3.6 | Mexico | 48 | 3.0 | Guatemala | 1.96 |
| Thailand | 11.0 | 3.0 | Chile | 43 | 2.7 | Peru | 1.95 |
| Mexico | 10.0 | 2.7 | Colombia | 34 | 2.1 | Brazil | 1.72 |
| **Total top ten** | **247.1** | **66.5** | **Total top ten** | **995** | **61.6** | | |
| Grand total | 371.5 | | Grand total | 1,614 | | | |

## Trends by sector

Both trends and type vary considerably between sectors. Figure A2.8 presents the overall trends by sector and Figure A2.9 provides details on the type of private sector participation by sector.

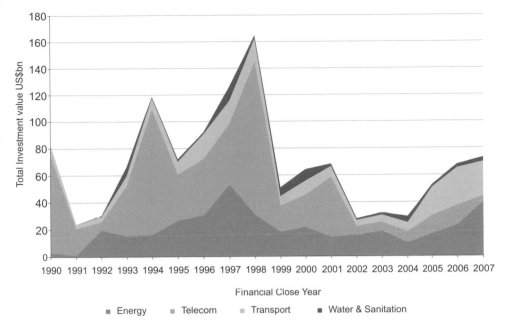

**Figure A2.8.** Value of investment commitments by sector, 1990–2007

As can be seen in Figure A2.8, telecoms have dominated the value of investment commitments in infrastructure projects with private sector participation since 1990, with water and sanitation projects attracting the lowest investment commitments.

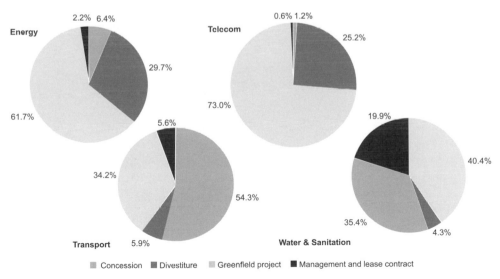

**Figure A2.9.** Share of number of project types by sector, 1990–2007

Figure A2.9 shows that the majority of energy projects have been in the form of greenfield projects, nearly 75 per cent of which were in electricity generation. Most of the remainder are divestitures, 40 per cent of which are also in generation, a further reflection of the high number of generation projects in energy as a whole (58%). The pattern is similar in the telecom sector, but with mobile access projects dominating. Divestitures were much less popular in the 2000s than at the mid-1990s peak of energy and telecom privatisation throughout upper-middle income countries.

A high proportion of greenfield projects have been in the transport, and water and sanitation sectors. However, concessions dominate in these two sectors. Additionally, a significant proportion of water and sanitation projects have been management or lease contracts.

## Trends in failed projects

Out of the sample of 4,078 private infrastructure deals reaching financial close between 1990 and 2007, 194 were cancelled. These represented 4.76 per cent of all deals. The cancellation rate in Commonwealth countries in the sample was lower at 4.16 per cent. Cancelled projects had investment commitments of US$63.4 billion, 5.10 per cent of the total value committed. Projects were cancelled on average 6.9 years after financial close (see Figure A2.10).

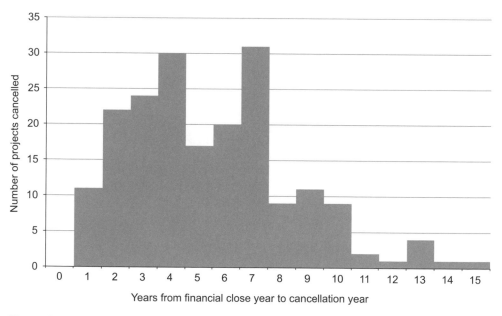

**Figure A2.10.** Frequency of years from financial closure until cancellation

Figure A2.10 shows that no projects were cancelled in the year in which they were negotiated. The majority of cancelled projects are terminated between two and seven years after financial close.

Figure A2.11 shows differences in project status across sector and region.

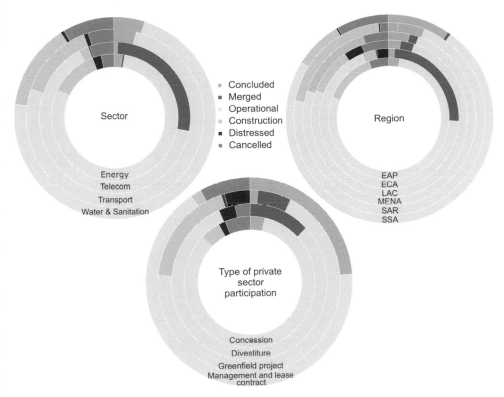

Figure A2.11. Project status by sector, region and type as at end of 2007

It is not surprising that failure rates vary along lines of sector, region and type, as shown in Figure A2.11. The highest rates of cancellation occurred in the water and sanitation sector, the sub-Saharan region and in management and lease contracts. Eight per cent of projects in each of these categories reaching financial close in the period 1990–2007 had been cancelled by the end of 2007. Cancellation, however, is only one kind of failure and the data do not capture the number of projects that have been renegotiated or the varying degrees of distress.

## Notes

1. The data in this annex has been sourced from the World Bank/PPIAF Private Participation in Infrastructure database available at http://ppi.worldbank.org/ and covers energy, telecom, transport, and water and sanitation projects in low- and middle-income countries (i.e. those with Gross National Income (GNI) per capita of less than US$11,455 in 2007, as defined by the World Bank).

2. While there was some activity prior to 1990, levels were comparatively low.

3. This reflects the number of new projects, not the number active at the time.

4. The graph depicts investment commitments as against investment payments per year.

5. Total investment commitments declined by nearly US$114 billion in 1998 as crises emerged in LAC.

6. The average size of projects per year is sensitive to a small number of very large projects in a number of years. The skewed nature of the distribution of values can be seen in the difference in 1998 between the mean value of US$590.6 million, compared to the median of US$105 million. Since 2000, the distribution has narrowed but is still skewed, with the mean being around US$140 million above the median.

7. Russian telecom or energy divestitures accounted for 151 of these. If Russian transactions are omitted, the number of transactions in the ECA region follows the global trend more closely.

8. Restricted to countries with populations of over 10 million people to counter anomalous values from small island states.

9. For countries with populations of over 10 million people.

# ANNEX 3

# Some useful indicators for Commonwealth developing countries

## Infrastructure gap

**Table A3.1.** The infrastructure gap in Commonwealth countries[1, 2]

| Region | Country | Electric power consumption (kWh per capita) | Improved sanitation facilities (% of urban population with access) | Improved water source (% of population with access) | Paved roads (% of total roads) |
|---|---|---|---|---|---|
| EAP | Brunei Darussalam | 8,173.8 | | 99.0 | 77.2 |
| | Kiribati | | 46.0 | 65.0 | |
| | Malaysia | 3,387.6 | 95.0 | 99.0 | 79.8 |
| | Papua New Guinea | | 67.0 | 40.0 | 3.5 |
| | Samoa | | 100.0 | 88.0 | 14.2 |
| | Solomon Islands | | 98.0 | 70.0 | 2.4 |
| | Tonga | | 98.0 | 100.0 | 27.0 |
| | Vanuatu | | | | 23.9 |
| | *EAP region* | *1,668.9* | *75.1* | *87.4* | *34.3* |
| LAC | Antigua and Barbuda | | 98.0 | | 33.0 |
| | Bahamas, The | | 100.0 | | 57.4 |
| | Belize | | | | 17.0 |
| | Dominica | | | | 50.4 |
| | Grenada | | 96.0 | | 61.0 |
| | Guyana | | 85.0 | 93.0 | 7.4 |
| | Jamaica | 2,453.2 | 82.0 | 93.0 | 73.3 |
| | St Kitts and Nevis | | 96.0 | 99.0 | |
| | St Lucia | | | 98.0 | |
| | St Vincent and the Grenadines | | | | 70.0 |
| | Trinidad and Tobago | 5,005.9 | 92.0 | 94.0 | 51.1 |
| | *LAC region* | *1,808.2* | *86.2* | *91.4* | *42.3* |

| Region | Country | Electric power consumption (kWh per capita) | Improved sanitation facilities (% of urban population with access) | Improved water source (% of population with access) | Paved roads (% of total roads) |
|---|---|---|---|---|---|
| SAR | Bangladesh | 146.0 | 48.0 | 80.0 | 10.0 |
| | India | 502.8 | 52.0 | 89.0 | 47.4 |
| | Maldives | | 100.0 | 83.0 | |
| | Pakistan | 480.1 | 90.0 | 90.0 | 65.4 |
| | Sri Lanka | 400.1 | 89.0 | 82.0 | 81.0 |
| | *Whole SAR region* | *453.2* | *56.7* | *86.9* | *56.9* |
| SSA | Botswana | 1,419.1 | 60.0 | 96.0 | 32.6 |
| | Cameroon | 185.6 | 58.0 | 70.0 | 8.4 |
| | Gambia, The | | 50.0 | 86.0 | 19.3 |
| | Ghana | 303.6 | 15.0 | 80.0 | 14.9 |
| | Kenya | 145.3 | 19.0 | 57.0 | 14.1 |
| | Lesotho | | 43.0 | 78.0 | 18.3 |
| | Malawi | | 51.0 | 76.0 | 45.0 |
| | Mauritius | | 95.0 | 100.0 | 100.0 |
| | Mozambique | 461.4 | 53.0 | 42.0 | 18.7 |
| | Namibia | 1,545.5 | 66.0 | 93.0 | 12.8 |
| | Nigeria | 116.4 | 35.0 | 47.0 | 15.0 |
| | Seychelles | | | | 96.0 |
| | Sierra Leone | | 20.0 | 53.0 | 8.0 |
| | South Africa | 4,809.9 | 66.0 | 93.0 | 17.3 |
| | Swaziland | | 64.0 | 60.0 | 30.0 |
| | Tanzania | 58.8 | 31.0 | 55.0 | 8.6 |
| | Uganda | | 29.0 | 64.0 | 23.0 |
| | Zambia | 729.6 | 55.0 | 58.0 | 22.0 |
| | *Whole SSA region* | *530.9* | *42.3* | *58.4* | *11.9* |
| | **Average for Commonwealth countries** | **1,684.7** | **66.9** | **78.5** | **35.7** |

# Doing business indicators

**Table A3.2.** Doing Business Indicators in Commonwealth countries[3]

| Region | Country | Overall ease of doing business ranking (1–181) | Ranking within sample (1–42) | Protecting investors ranking (1–181) | Enforcing contracts ranking (1–181) | Getting credit ranking (1–181) |
|---|---|---|---|---|---|---|
| EAP | Brunei Darussalam | 88 | 24 | 113 | 157 | 109 |
| | Kiribati | 79 | 19 | 38 | 75 | 131 |
| | Malaysia | 20 | 1 | 4 | 59 | 1 |
| | Papua New Guinea | 95 | 26 | 38 | 162 | 131 |
| | Samoa | 64 | 12 | 24 | 79 | 123 |
| | Solomon Islands | 89 | 25 | 53 | 108 | 145 |
| | Tonga | 43 | 7 | 104 | 57 | 109 |
| | Vanuatu | 60 | 10 | 70 | 67 | 84 |
| LAC | Antigua and Barbuda | 42 | 6 | 24 | 73 | 109 |
| | Bahamas, The | 55 | 9 | 104 | 120 | 68 |
| | Belize | 78 | 18 | 113 | 168 | 84 |
| | Dominica | 74 | 16 | 24 | 164 | 68 |
| | Grenada | 84 | 22 | 24 | 163 | 68 |
| | Guyana | 105 | 30 | 70 | 73 | 145 |
| | Jamaica | 63 | 11 | 70 | 127 | 84 |
| | St Kitts and Nevis | 67 | 14 | 24 | 114 | 84 |
| | St Lucia | 34 | 4 | 24 | 161 | 84 |
| | St Vincent and the Grenadines | 66 | 13 | 24 | 109 | 84 |
| | Trinidad and Tobago | 80 | 20 | 18 | 167 | 28 |
| SAR | Bangladesh | 110 | 32 | 18 | 178 | 59 |
| | India | 122 | 35 | 38 | 180 | 28 |
| | Maldives | 69 | 15 | 70 | 90 | 145 |
| | Pakistan | 77 | 17 | 24 | 154 | 59 |
| | Sri Lanka | 102 | 28 | 70 | 135 | 68 |
| SSA | Botswana | 38 | 5 | 38 | 92 | 43 |
| | Cameroon | 164 | 42 | 113 | 172 | 131 |
| | Gambia, The | 130 | 38 | 170 | 63 | 131 |
| | Ghana | 87 | 23 | 38 | 50 | 109 |
| | Kenya | 82 | 21 | 88 | 107 | 5 |
| | Lesotho | 123 | 36 | 142 | 104 | 84 |
| | Malawi | 134 | 39 | 70 | 138 | 84 |

| Region | Country | Overall ease of doing business ranking (1–181) | Ranking within sample (1–42) | Protecting investors ranking (1–181) | Enforcing contracts ranking (1–181) | Getting credit ranking (1–181) |
|---|---|---|---|---|---|---|
| | Mauritius | 24 | 2 | 11 | 76 | 84 |
| | Mozambique | 141 | 40 | 38 | 124 | 123 |
| | Namibia | 51 | 8 | 70 | 36 | 12 |
| | Nigeria | 118 | 34 | 53 | 90 | 84 |
| | Seychelles | 104 | 29 | 53 | 62 | 163 |
| | Sierra Leone | 156 | 41 | 53 | 141 | 145 |
| | South Africa | 32 | 3 | 9 | 82 | 2 |
| | Swaziland | 108 | 31 | 178 | 129 | 43 |
| | Tanzania | 127 | 37 | 88 | 33 | 84 |
| | Uganda | 111 | 33 | 126 | 117 | 109 |
| | Zambia | 100 | 27 | 70 | 87 | 68 |

# Economic and political risk indicators

Table A3.3 shows the political risk level of Commonwealth countries, as assessed by Oxford Analytica/Aon. Its judgements are based on a range of factors, including risk of currency inconvertibility and transfer, strikes, riots and civil commotion, war, terrorism, sovereign non-payment, political interference, supply chain interruption, and legal and regulatory risk.[4]

**Table A3.3.** Perceived political risk levels in Commonwealth countries[5]

| Region | Country | Political risk level |
|---|---|---|
| EAP | Brunei Darussalam | Medium-low |
| | Kiribati | Medium-low |
| | Malaysia | Medium |
| | Nauru | Medium-low |
| | Papua New Guinea | Medium-high |
| | Samoa | Medium-low |
| | Solomon Islands | Medium-high |
| | Tonga | Medium-low |
| | Tuvalu | Medium-low |
| | Vanuatu | Medium |
| LAC | Antigua and Barbuda | Medium-low |
| | Bahamas, The | Low |
| | Belize | Medium-high |
| | Dominica | Medium-low |
| | Grenada | Medium-low |
| | Guyana | Medium-high |
| | Jamaica | Medium-high |
| | St Kitts and Nevis | Medium-low |
| | St Lucia | Medium-low |
| | St Vincent and the Grenadines | Medium-low |
| | Trinidad and Tobago | Medium-low |
| SAR | Bangladesh | Medium-high |
| | India | Medium |
| | Maldives | Medium |
| | Pakistan | High |
| | Sri Lanka | Medium-high |
| SSA | Botswana | Medium-low |
| | Cameroon | Medium |
| | Gambia, The | Medium-high |

| Region | Country | Political risk level |
|--------|---------|---------------------|
| | Ghana | Medium |
| | Kenya | High |
| | Lesotho | Medium |
| | Malawi | Medium-high |
| | Mauritius | Medium-low |
| | Mozambique | Medium-high |
| | Namibia | Medium-low |
| | Nigeria | High |
| | Seychelles | Medium-low |
| | Sierra Leone | Medium-high |
| | South Africa | Medium |
| | Swaziland | Medium-high |
| | Tanzania | Medium-high |
| | Uganda | Medium-high |
| | Zambia | Medium-high |

## Notes

1. Table A3.1 includes the latest available information as of 2008. Fields are omitted in cases where no information has been published since 2000.
2. World Development Indicators database
3. *Doing Business 2009.* http://www.doingbusiness.org/
4. http://www.aon.com/
5. Oxford Analytica/Aon Political Risk Map 2009. http://www.aon.com/risk-services/political-risk-map/index.html

# ANNEX 4

# Donor-backed PPP facilities

## Project preparation facilities

Table A4.1 provides a summary of a selection of the key donor PPP project preparation facilities. The table focuses on facilities that support projects in the four main infrastructure sectors.

## Key

Focus areas: 1. Enabling environment; 2. Project definition; 3. Project feasibility; 4. Project structuring; 5. Transaction support; 6. Post-implementation report.

Table A4.1. Project preparation facilities

| Facility name | Description | Focus area | | | | | | Hosted by | Product | Size | Sector | Geography |
|---|---|---|---|---|---|---|---|---|---|---|---|---|
| | | 1 | 2 | 3 | 4 | 5 | 6 | | | | | |
| African Capacity Building Foundation http://www.acbf-pact.org/ | Supports and develops implementation of policies encouraging efficient management of infrastructure | x | x | x | | | x | African Capacity Building Foundation | Grant | US$1.5m–US$4.0m | All sectors | SSA |
| African Catalytic Growth Fund http://www.worldbank.org/afr/ce/acgf/ | Supports programmes in strong performing countries, those committed to reform and regional integration initiatives | x | x | x | x | x | x | World Bank | Grant | US$15m–US$50m | All sectors | SSA |
| African Water Facility http://www.afdb.org/awf/en/ | Initiative to mobilise resources to finance water resources development activities | x | x | x | | | x | African Development Bank and African Ministers' Council on Water | Cost contribution | €50K–€5m | Water and sanitation | Africa only |
| Asian Development Bank http://www.adb.org/ | Provides project/programme preparatory technical assistance (PPTA) grants to help governments identify and prepare feasible projects | x | x | x | x | x | x | Asian Development Bank | Grant | Not available | All sectors | ADB member countries |
| City Development Initiative Asia http://cdia.asia/ | Assists Asian cities to bridge the gap between city development plans and turning those plans into viable investments | x | x | x | x | x | | ADB | Grants and Contributions | Not specified | All Sectors | Asia and the Pacific (based on ADB members) |

| Facility name | Description | Focus area | | | | | | Hosted by | Product | Size | Sector | Geography |
|---|---|---|---|---|---|---|---|---|---|---|---|---|
| | | 1 | 2 | 3 | 4 | 5 | 6 | | | | | |
| DEVCO http://www.ifc.org/ifcext/psa.nsf/content/Devco | Supports transactions in the poorest nations to increase private sector involvement in infrastructure services | x | x | x | x | | | IFC | Grant | Approx US$1m per project | All sectors | Poorest nations by DAC classification |
| Development Bank of South Africa Development Fund http://www.dbsa.org/development%20fund/pages/default.aspx | Aims to address human, institutional and financial capacity constraints to rural and urban development | x | x | x | | | | Development Bank of South Africa | Grant | Not available | Transport, and water and sanitation | South Africa |
| FEMIP Support Fund http://www.eib.org/projects/regions/med/instruments/technical-assistance/support-fund/index.htm | Supports EIB investment activities in the southern Mediterranean countries, assisting promoters during different stages of the project cycle, including feasibility or pre-feasibility studies, project management units and site assessments | x | x | x | x | x | x | European Investment Bank | Grant | US$5K–US$5m | All sectors | FEMIP Mediterranean partner countries |
| FEMIP Trust Fund http://www.eib.org/projects/regions/med/instruments/trust-fund/index.htm | Supports activities upstream of projects such as policy, legal, regulatory and institutional reform, sector development | x | x | | | | | European Investment Bank | Grant | Not specified | All sectors | FEMIP Mediterranean partner countries |

**Table A4.1** (continued)

| Facility name | Description | Focus area | | | | | | Hosted by | Product | Size | Sector | Geography |
|---|---|---|---|---|---|---|---|---|---|---|---|---|
| | | 1 | 2 | 3 | 4 | 5 | 6 | | | | | |
| | strategies, capacity-building and training | | | | | | | | | | | |
| Fund for African Private Sector Assistance http://www.afdb.org/en/topics-sectors/initiatives-partnerships/enhancing-private-sector-assistance-for-africa-epsa-initiative/ | Grants funding for technical assistance and capacity building for public and private the sector | x | x | x | x | | | African Investment Bank | Grant | Not usually expected to exceed US$1m | All sectors | SSA and MENA |
| Global Environment Facility http://www.gefweb.org/ | Supports environmentally friendly projects through its trust fund, the Least Developed Countries Fund and the Special Climate Change Fund | x | x | x | | | x | United Nations Environment Programme | Grant | Wide-ranging from thousands of US$ to over US$100m | All sectors | Global |
| Global Partnership for Output-Based Aid http://www.gpoba.org/ | Increases access to basic infrastructure and services through output-based aid | x | x | x | x | x | | World Bank | Grant | US$25K–US$0.5m | All sectors | Global |
| IDB Project Preparation Facilities http://www.iadb.org/aboutus/ii/op_projectfacility.cfm?lang=en | Several facilities supporting project preparation, including the Project Preparation Facility and the Project Preparation and Execution Facility (PROPEF) | x | x | x | x | x | x | Inter-American Development Bank | Loan | Up to US$5m per project | All sectors | LAC |

**Table A4.1** (continued)

| Facility name | Description | Focus area 1 | 2 | 3 | 4 | 5 | 6 | Hosted by | Product | Size | Sector | Geography |
|---|---|---|---|---|---|---|---|---|---|---|---|---|
| IFC Advisory Services http://www.ifc.org/advisory | Assistance to national and municipal governments for structuring and implementing sustainable private sector participation in infrastructure and social infrastructure | x | x | x | x | x | | IFC | Cost contribution | Not applicable | All sectors | Global |
| IFC Municipal Fund http://www.ifc.org/municipalfund | Technical assistance to enhance capacity and creditworthiness for subnational public sector entities and project implementation assistance | x | x | x | x | x | x | IFC | Cost contribution | No set policy | All sectors | Global |
| InfraCo http://www.infraco.com/ | Privately managed infrastructure development company providing risk capital | x | x | x | x | | | PIDG | Infrastructure company | | All sectors | Africa and Asia |
| InfraVentures http://www.ifc.org/ | Provides risk capital to fund the early stages of development of infrastructure projects to bring projects to the financing stage | x | x | x | x | x | | IFC | Project development fund | | All sectors | IDA countries |

**Table A4.1** (continued)

| Facility name | Description | Focus area 1 | 2 | 3 | 4 | 5 | 6 | Hosted by | Product | Size | Sector | Geography |
|---|---|---|---|---|---|---|---|---|---|---|---|---|
| Islamic Development Bank Technical Assistance Facility http://www.isdb.org/ | Assists preparation and implementation of projects and policies for development of institutions or human resources | x | x | x | x | x | x | Islamic Development Bank | Cost contribution | Public sector up to ID300K, private sector up to ID100K | All sectors | IDB countries |
| NEPAD IPPF http://www.nepad.org/ | Assist preparation of high quality, viable regional infrastructure projects | | x | x | x | | | African Development Bank | Cost contribution | US$5K–US$0.5m | All sectors | Africa |
| NEPAD PPFS http://www.dbsa.org/ | Finance studies and project preparation activities in support of NEPAD projects | x | x | x | x | x | | Development Bank of South Africa | Cost contribution | US$5K–US$0.3m | All sectors | Africa |
| Nigerian Technical Cooperation Fund http://ww.dtca-ng.org/ | Grants to assist development projects and programmes that benefit regional members of the African Development Bank | x | x | x | x | x | x | African Development Bank | Cost contribution | Annual limit of US$2.5m | All sectors | AfDB member countries |
| PHRD Technical Assistance Grant Program http://www.worldbank.org/rmc/phrd/phrdbr2.htm | Technical assistance and grant activities for World Bank supported projects and programmes | x | x | x | x | x | | World Bank | Grant | Not normally above US$1m | All sectors | Global |
| PIDG Technical Assistance Fund http://www.pidg.org/ | Builds local capacities and the ability of public and private sector clients | x | x | x | x | x | x | PIDG | Grant | US$3m–US$5m annual | All sectors | Global |

**Table A4.1** (continued)

| Facility name | Description | Focus area | | | | | | Hosted by | Product | Size | Sector | Geography |
|---|---|---|---|---|---|---|---|---|---|---|---|---|
| | | 1 | 2 | 3 | 4 | 5 | 6 | | | | | |
| | to attract private capital to infrastructure financing | | | | | | | | | budget – likely to increase | | |
| Public–private Infrastructure Advisory Facility (PPIAF) http://www.ppiaf.org/ | Provides technical assistance to governments on strategies and measures to tap potential of private involvement in infrastructure, and identifies and disseminates best practices | x | x | | | | | World Bank | Grant | Up to US$1m, but below US$75K is encouraged | All sectors | DAC aid recipient countries |
| Slum Upgrading Facility http://www.unhabitat.org/content.asp?typeid=19&catid=293&cid=3130 | Assistance and implementation of local housing and related projects to attract domestic commercial capital | | | | x | x | x | UN-HABITAT | Grant | US$2m–US$3m per country | Transport, and water and sanitation | ACP countries |
| Sustainable Energy Finance Initiative (SEFI) Transaction Support Facility http://www.sefi.unep.org/ | Advisory support for investment in sustainable energy projects | | | | x | x | x | United Nations Environment Programme and Basle Agency for Sustainable Energy | Grant | US$50K per financial institution for 5–10 project evaluations | Energy | North Africa |
| The Water and Sanitation Program http://www.wsp.org/ | Gives impartial advice to governments on improving access to water and sanitation facilities | x | x | x | x | x | | World Bank | Grant | Typically US$5K–US$0.35m but no limits | Water and sanitation | All except ECA |

# Infrastructure financing institutions and facilities

Table A4.2 provides brief profiles of infrastructure financing facilities provided by institutions such as multilateral and bilateral development banks and development finance institutions.

Table A4.2. Financing facilities

| Institution name | Product type | Geography | Sector | Investment size | Other details |
|---|---|---|---|---|---|
| Actis www.act.is | Equity | Africa, China, Latin America, south and south-east Asia | All sectors (less preferred: ICT internet and water) | Minimum: US$20m Maximum: US$75–100m | Expected equity return of more than 14 per cent; Minimum 50 per cent shareholding required; Voting rights, board representation and protection against change of control in ownership required |
| Deutsche Investitions und Entwicklungsgesellschaft (DEG) www.deginvest.de | Equity | Developing countries | All sectors except oil and gas | Minimum: €5m Maximum: €20m | Minimum 5 per cent and maximum 49 per cent shareholding preferred; Minority shareholding required; Prefers not to be the largest shareholder; Voting rights, board representation and protection against change of control in ownership preferred |
|  | Debt | Developing countries | All sectors except oil and gas | Minimum: €10m Maximum: €25m | Maximum 30 per cent of total project; €denominated only, at market interest rates; Untied; Tenor: 4–15 years |
| The Netherlands Development Finance Company (FMO) www.fmo.nl | Equity | All World Bank members except high-income countries and EU states | All sectors | Maximum: €7.75m | Minority shareholding required |
|  | Debt | All World Bank members except | All sectors | Minimum: €1-2m Maximum: €15–20m | Preferably in foreign currency, but local currency is permitted at market interest rates |

**Table A4.2** (continued)

| Institution name | Product type | Geography | Sector | Investment size | Other details |
|---|---|---|---|---|---|
| | | high-income countries and EU states | | | Untied<br>Preferred tenor: 3–15 years<br>Security in form of sovereign guarantee, recourse to sponsor, etc. is preferred |
| Globeleq<br>www.globeleq.com | Equity | Africa, the Americas, Asia | Electricity (generation, transmission and distribution) | Minimum: US$20m<br>Maximum: US$100m | Expected equity return: 15–20 per cent<br>Minimum 51 per cent and maximum 100 per cent shareholding preferred<br>Voting rights, board representation and protection against change of control in ownership required |
| International Finance Corporation (IFC)<br>www.ifc.org | Equity | Developing countries that are IFC members | All sectors | Minimum: US$1m (preferred) | Maximum 50 per cent of project (25 per cent if investing in company)<br>Maximum 20 per cent shareholding preferred<br>Minority shareholding required<br>Prefers not to be the largest shareholder |
| | Debt | Developing countries that are IFC members | All sectors | Not applicable | Preferably in foreign currency but local currency is permitted, at market interest rates<br>Tied<br>Preferred tenor: 7–12 years<br>Security in form of recourse to sponsor and other guarantees is preferred |
| Promotion et Participation pour la Coopération économique (PROPARCO)<br>www.proparco.fr | Equity | All ODA recipient countries on the OECD's DAC list | All sectors (oil and gas not preferred)[1] | Required minimum and maximum: €0.5m and €10m<br>Preferred minimum and maximum: €3m and €6m | Expected equity return: 10–20 per cent<br>Minimum 5 per cent and maximum 20 per cent shareholding preferred<br>Minority shareholding required<br>Cannot be the largest shareholder<br>Voting rights and protection against change of control in ownership required |

**Table A4.2** (continued)

| Institution name | Product type | Geography | Sector | Investment size | Other details |
|---|---|---|---|---|---|
| | Debt | All ODA recipient countries on the OECD's DAC list | All sectors | Required minimum and maximum: €7m and €50m<br><br>Preferred minimum and maximum: €10m and €20m | Preferably in € but other foreign currencies are permitted. Local currency is permitted if convertible/swap<br>Interest rate: Libor/Euribor + (1–5%)<br>Untied<br>Preferred tenor: 5–15 years<br>Security in form of guarantees is required |
| East African Development Bank (EADB) www.eadb.org | Equity | Burundi, Kenya, Rwanda, Tanzania and Uganda | All sectors | Not applicable | Maximum 25 per cent shareholding preferred<br>Minority shareholding required |
| | Debt | Burundi, Kenya, Rwanda, Tanzania and Uganda | All sectors | Not applicable | Maximum 50 per cent of total project<br>Foreign and local currency permitted, at market interest rates<br>Untied<br>Tenor: 5–12 years<br>Security in form of guarantees is required |
| Emerging Africa Infrastructure Fund (EAIF) www.emergingafricafund.com | Debt | Sub-Saharan Africa | All sectors except oil and gas upstream (ICT (mobile) preferred) | Minimum: US$10m<br>Maximum: US$30m | Foreign currency denominated<br>Variable interest rates: Libor/Euribor + (3–6%)<br>Untied<br>Preferred tenor: 10–15 years<br>Guarantees required (preferably sovereign guarantee or recourse to sponsor)<br>Financial covenants: Maximum gearing of 2.3 |
| Agence Française de Développement (AFD) www.afd.fr | Debt | Africa (excluding Libya), Middle East (excluding | All sectors | Not applicable | Preferably in foreign currency but local currency is permitted<br>Untied |

**Table A4.2** (continued)

| Institution name | Product type | Geography | Sector | Investment size | Other details |
|---|---|---|---|---|---|
| | | Saudi Arabia, Oman, UAE), the Caribbean, Belize. Suriname, Guyana, French Guiana, Brazil, Pacific and Indian Ocean countries, Afghanistan. Pakistan, India, China, Thailand, Cambodia, Lao PDR, Vietnam, Indonesia, Papua New Guinea | | | Maximum tenor: 20–30 years Security in the form of sovereign guarantee or other guarantees is preferred |
| African Development Bank www.afdb.org | Equity | Africa | All sectors | Minimum: US$3m | Maximum 25 per cent of total project Maximum 25 per cent shareholding Voting rights and board representation permitted |
| | Debt | Africa | All sectors | Not applicable | Maximum 33 per cent of total project US$, €, £, JPY or ZAR-denominated, at market rates Tenor: 5–15 years Security in form of recourse to sponsor permitted, other guarantee preferred |
| Cotonou Investment Facility www.eib.org | Equity | Africa, Caribbean and Pacific | All sectors | Minimum: €5m (preferred) Maximum: €20m (preferred) | Required rate of return: 15 per cent (flexible, depending on industry and investment stage) Maximum 50 per cent of total project for direct investment, 25 per cent for fund investment |

Table A4.2 (continued)

| Institution name | Product type | Geography | Sector | Investment size | Other details |
|---|---|---|---|---|---|
| | | | | | Minimum 10 per cent and maximum 49 per cent shareholding preferred<br>Minority shareholding required<br>Voting rights and protection against change of control in ownership required |
| | Debt | Africa, Caribbean and Pacific | All sectors | Minimum: €5m (preferred) | Maximum 50 per cent of total project required<br>Foreign and local currency permitted<br>Interest rate: Libor/Euribor + (1–5%)<br>Untied<br>Preferred tenor: 5–25 years<br>Security in form of sovereign guarantee preferred |
| European Investment Bank (EIB) www.eib.org | Equity | Asia, Latin America, Africa, Pacific, Caribbean, Mediterranean, Russia and eastern neighbourhood | All sectors | Minimum: €5m (preferred)<br>Maximum: €20m (preferred) | Required rate of return: 15 per cent (flexible, depending on industry and investment stage)<br>Maximum 50 per cent of total project for direct investment, 25 per cent for fund investment<br>Minimum 10 per cent and maximum 49 per cent shareholding preferred<br>Minority shareholding required<br>Voting rights and protection against change of control in ownership required |
| | Debt | Asia, Latin America, Africa, Pacific, Caribbean, Mediterranean, Russia and eastern neighbourhood | All sectors | Minimum: €5m (preferred) | Maximum 50 per cent of total project required<br>Foreign currency permitted<br>Interest rate: Libor/Euribor + (1%–5%)<br>Untied<br>Preferred tenor: 5–25 years<br>Security in form of sovereign guarantee required |

**Table A4.2** (continued)

| Institution name | Product type | Geography | Sector | Investment size | Other details |
|---|---|---|---|---|---|
| Japan Bank for International Cooperation (JBIC) www.jbic.go.jp | Equity | Developing countries | All sectors | n/a | Maximum 25 per cent of total investment Cannot be the single largest Japanese shareholder |
| | Debt | Developing countries | All sectors (preferred: electricity and transport) | Preferential terms are applied for each income category | JPY denominated, at interest rate of 0.01–2.3 per cent Can be tied or untied Preferred tenor: 15–40 years Sovereign guarantee required |
| Asian Development Bank www.adb.org | Equity | Developing ADB member countries | All sectors (those supplying basic needs and services to wide segment of population are prioritised) | Maximum: US$75m | Maximum 25 per cent of the total share capital Does not seek a controlling stake Voting rights required, reserves right for board representation |
| | Debt | Developing ADB member countries | All sectors (those supplying basic needs and services to wide segment of population are prioritised) | Maximum: US$250m (US$400m if guaranteed by an entity with credit rating of A- or better) | Maximum 25 per cent of total costs or assets (if costs/assets are more than US$50m) Maximum 50 per cent of total costs or assets (if costs/assets are less than US$50m) Maximum 70 per cent of costs or assets (if guaranteed by an entity with credit rating of A- or better) Foreign currency denominated only[2], at market rates Tenor: Up to 15 years |

**Table A4.2** (continued)

| Institution name | Product type | Geography | Sector | Investment size | Other details |
|---|---|---|---|---|---|
| Inter-American Development Bank www.iadb.org | Debt | Borrowing member countries of IDB[3] | All sectors | Maximum: US$200m | US$ or local currency denominated, at market rates<br>Tenor: 5–15 years (may be extended to 30 years) |
| Overseas Private Investment Corporation (OPIC) www.opic.gov | Debt | Worldwide | All sectors | Minimum: US$100,000 Maximum: US$250m | Maximum 75 per cent of total investment<br>Interest rate: Risk-free rate + (2–6%)<br>Direct loans available only for projects sponsored by US small and medium enterprises<br>Preferred debt-to-equity ratio in the range of 60:40<br>US company must have ownership interest of at least 25 per cent in the overseas investment<br>Preferably more than 50 per cent of voting rights to be held by private sector<br>Tenor: 3–15 years<br>Security in form of guarantees is required |

*Key sources:* Infrastructure Consortium for Africa and PPIAF, *Donor Debt and Equity Financing for Infrastructure: User Guide Africa* (2007); various institution websites.

Public–Private Partnerships Policy and Practice

## Guarantee facilities

Table A4.3 provides brief profiles of multilateral and bilateral guarantee facilities that are available for infrastructure financing.

Table A4.3. Multilateral and bilateral guarantee facilities

| Institution name | Instrument name | Instrument type | Eligible borrowers and projects | Eligible beneficiaries | Eligible forms of investment |
|---|---|---|---|---|---|
| World Bank, International Bank for Reconstruction and Development (IBRD) and International Development Association (IDA) www.worldbank.org | IBRD Partial Risk Guarantee (PRG) IDA PRG IBRD Enclave PRG IBRD Partial Credit Guarantee (PCG) IBRD Policy-Based Guarantee (PBG) | Debt guarantee | New investments in a developing member country;[4] IBRD Enclave PRG: Foreign currency-earning projects in IDA-only countries PBG: sovereign for fiscal support PCG: sovereign/public borrowers for new investments[6] | Private lenders[5] | Debt (loans, bonds or other financial instruments with characteristics of commercial debt, including local currency debt) |
| International Finance Corporation (IFC) www.ifc.org | Partial Credit Guarantee (PCG) | Debt guarantee | Private sector projects in developing member countries;[7] new investments or a pool of new assets in developing member countries;[8] meet development objectives of the host country, technically, environmentally and socially sound | Private lenders | Debt (loans, bonds or other financial instruments with characteristics of commercial debt, including local currency debt) |
| Multilateral Investment Guarantee Agency (MIGA) www.miga.org | Investment Guarantee | Political risk insurance | New cross-border investments (originating in a MIGA member country, destined for any developing member country); meet development objectives | Entities operating on a commercial basis | Equity, shareholder loans, non-shareholder loans,[9] loan guarantees by shareholders, other instruments such as performance bonds, |

Table A4.3 (continued)

| Institution name | Instrument name | Instrument type | Eligible borrowers and projects | Eligible beneficiaries | Eligible forms of investment |
|---|---|---|---|---|---|
| | | | of the host country; technically, economically and financially viable, environmentally viable and socially sound | | leases, franchising and licensing agreements. All investments must have a minimum tenor of three years |
| African Development Bank (AfDB) www.afdb.org | Partial Risk Guarantee (PRG) Partial Credit Guarantee (PCG) Policy-Based Guarantee (PBG) | Debt guarantee | Any public or private sector project eligible for AfDB financing; PBG eligibility is same as for policy-based loans; must meet AfDB environmental requirements | Private lenders | Debt (loans, bonds, other financial instruments such as commercial paper, local currency debt included) |
| Asian Development Bank (ADB) www.adb.org | Political Risk Guarantee (PRG) Partial Credit Guarantee (PCG) | Debt guarantee | Greenfield and expansion projects that can be public or private sector operations (includes state-owned enterprises) | Lenders operating on a commercial basis (includes public and private insurers and re-insurers) | Loans, including commercial bank loans, loans by shareholders, loans guaranteed by shareholders, bond holders and other traded debt instruments |
| European Bank for Reconstruction and Development (EBRD) www.ebrd.com | Political Risk Guarantee (PRG)  Trade Finance Facilitation Program (TFP) SME Guarantee Facility  Municipal Finance Facility (MFF) | Debt guarantee | Financial sector strengthening, local capital market development, power, transport, waste water  TFP: Trade finance transactions (state-owned entities precluded) SME: Loans and loan portfolios of local banks and leasing companies MFF: Municipal projects | Sub-sovereigns, approved financial institutions, private sector | Short- and medium-term loans, local and foreign currency bonds, letters of credit, local currency loans |

**Table A4.3** (continued)

| Institution name | Instrument name | Instrument type | Eligible borrowers and projects | Eligible beneficiaries | Eligible forms of investment |
|---|---|---|---|---|---|
| Inter-American Development Bank (IDB) www.iadb.org | Political Risk Guarantee (PRG) | Debt guarantee | Non-sovereign guaranteed entities in borrowing member countries (transactions include greenfield and expansion projects); loans and re-financings for corporate borrowers and sub-sovereigns; capital markets | Private lenders | Loans, bonds (local and foreign currency, project and corporate bonds) |
| | Partial Credit Guarantee (PCG) | | Those eligible for PRG. In addition, sovereign and public borrowing | | Loans, bonds (local and foreign currency, project and corporate bonds, asset backed securities, future flow or loan securitisations) |
| | Trade Finance Facilitation Program (TFFP) | | TFFP: International trade activities | | TFFP: Letters of credit, promissory notes, etc. |
| European Investment Bank (EIB)[10] www.eib.org | Political risk carve-out on guarantees for EIB loans Comprehensive risk coverage instruments for ACP states and in the Mediterranean region | Political risk carve-out on guarantees to EIB (in ALA and ACP countries); credit enhancement guarantees by EIB; portfolio credit risk sharing with local banks | Borrowers in ACP states, certain countries in ALA, the Mediterranean countries | Private companies and institutions, or commercially run public institutions | Long- and medium-term debt (in foreign currency and in selected countries also in local currency), equity and guarantee instruments available in ACP and Mediterranean countries |
| GuarantCo www.guarantco.com | Variety of contingent products, including partial risk | Guarantee | Eligible countries: Low-income and lower-middle-income countries in Africa, Asia, Latin | Bearers or holders of the guaranteed debt instruments | Senior and subordinated or mezzanine debt, in local currency only |

Table A4.3 (continued)

| Institution name | Instrument name | Instrument type | Eligible borrowers and projects | Eligible beneficiaries | Eligible forms of investment |
|---|---|---|---|---|---|
| | and partial credit guarantees, first loss guarantees, tenor extension or liquidity guarantees | | and Central America, and the Caribbean[11] Eligible borrowers: Private, municipal and parastatal infrastructure companies Eligible sectors: Energy supply, water and sanitation, transport, telecoms, urban infrastructure, mining Eligible projects: Construction of new facilities or expansion/refurbishment of existing ones. Must adhere to environmental, social and health standards | (including trustees, financial institutions, insurers, commercial banks, mortgage lenders/insurers, micro-finance institutions (MIs)) | |
| Agence Française de Développement (AFD) www.afd.fr | Political risk coverage | Guarantee | Infrastructure, urban and rural development, rural environment, health, education, local financial market development, in AFD-qualified countries | Lenders, private sector companies | Debt, equity, bond issues |
| | Comprehensive risk coverage | | Private companies and micro-finance institutions in AFD-qualified countries; medium- and long-term loans to private companies and MIs; credit lines for MIs; private housing, small retail businesses, weapons, gambling, tobacco and alcohol activities excluded | | Debt (not working capital) |

**Table A4.3** (continued)

| Institution name | Instrument name | Instrument type | Eligible borrowers and projects | Eligible beneficiaries | Eligible forms of investment |
|---|---|---|---|---|---|
| Deutsche Investitions und Entwicklungsgesellschaft (DEG) www.deginvest.de | Partial and full credit guarantees | Guarantee | Agribusiness, financial sector, infrastructure, manufacturing; eligible borrowers are private sector financial institutions and private sector companies | Private financial institutions | Debt |
| Promotion et Participation pour la Coopération économique (PROPARCO) www.proparco.fr | Guarantees | Bond, loan and liquidity guarantees | Private sector borrowers | Lenders | Bonds, loans (foreign currency and local currency denominated), mutual funds, investment funds, local savings mobilisation funds |
| Japan Bank for International Cooperation (JBIC) www.jbic.go.jp | Political Risk Guarantee (PRG) | Debt guarantee | Private entities; projects supporting economic activities of Japanese companies; projects with JBIC loan participation under co-financing and projects without JBIC loan participation | Private financial institutions (nationals of Japan or Japanese branches of foreign financial institutions); sovereign, public, and private entities (for bond guarantees) | Loans and bonds |
|  | Comprehensive Guarantee (CG) |  | Same as PRG; in addition, sovereign and public entities |  | Loans and bonds (includes local currency bond) |
| The Netherlands Development Finance Company (FMO) www.fmo.nl | Credit Guarantees Partial Credit Guarantees | Guarantee | Commercial businesses in developing countries operating in agriculture, fisheries, mining, agribusiness, manufacturing, | Private sector companies and financial institutions in developing | Trade facilities and letters of credit, commercial paper, capital market transactions (bonds, securitisations). In |

Table A4.3 (continued)

| Institution name | Instrument name | Instrument type | Eligible borrowers and projects | Eligible beneficiaries | Eligible forms of investment |
|---|---|---|---|---|---|
| | | | service sector (including utilities), and banking and insurance | countries | addition to US$ and €, local currency transactions can be guaranteed under special conditions |
| United States Agency for International Development's (USAID's) Development Credit Authority (DCA) www.usaid.gov | Partial credit guarantees | Debt guarantee | Private sector enterprises, sub-sovereign entities; projects must meet local USAID development goals and must not be tied to US export transactions or to US companies; support guaranteed for projects in SME, democracy and governance, natural resource management, agriculture, infrastructure, energy, education and health | Non-sovereign financial institutions (foreign or local), local capital market participants and investors | Debt, loans, leases, bonds, letters of credit or other debt instruments issued by local financial institutions and private sector lenders (denominated in US$ or local currency) |
| Overseas Private Investment Corporation (OPIC) www.opic.gov | Political Risk Insurance (PRI) | Insurance | New investments, privatisations, expansion and modernisation of existing plants | US corporations that are more than 50 per cent owned by US citizens; foreign corporations that are more than 95 per cent owned by eligible investors; other foreign entities that are 100 per cent US owned | Debt, equity, capital and operating leases, contractors and exporter exposures |

**Table A4.3** (continued)

| Institution name | Instrument name | Instrument type | Eligible borrowers and projects | Eligible beneficiaries | Eligible forms of investment |
|---|---|---|---|---|---|
| | Loan guarantees | Loan guarantee | Commercially and financially sound projects in which management has a significant financial risk | Same as above. OPIC expects US investors to own at least 25 per cent of the equity of the project | Loans, guarantees (parent company and third-party loans) |

*Key sources:* Matsukawa, Tomoko and Odo Habeck, *Review of Risk Mitigation Instruments for Infrastructure Financing and Recent Trends and Developments*, World Bank (2007); various institution websites

# Notes

1. Applies to Africa, the Caribbean, Pacific and Indian Ocean islands, Mediterranean countries, Afghanistan, Bangladesh, Cambodia, China, India, Indonesia, Jordan, Lao PDR, Mongolia, Nepal, Pakistan, the Philippines, Sri Lanka, Thailand, Vietnam and Yemen. In other ODA recipient countries, activity is restricted to combating climate change, agro-industry and food security, social sectors (health, education), micro-finance and activities to support French interests.

2. Local currency financing may be available for selected developing member countries.

3. Argentina, The Bahamas, Barbados, Belize, Bolivia, Brazil, Chile, Colombia, Costa Rica, Dominican Republic, Ecuador, El Salvador, Guatemala, Guyana, Haiti, Honduras, Jamaica, Mexico, Nicaragua, Panama, Paraguay, Peru, Suriname, Trinidad and Tobago, Uruguay and Venezuela.

4. Investments must be in compliance with the World Bank's country assistance strategy for each country; technically, economically and financially viable; and environmentally and socially sound.

5. This includes publicly-owned autonomous financial institutions that are established and operate under commercial law for the purpose of pursuing profit.

6. Private entities could be considered.

7. Except at World Bank/IFC Municipal Fund, which assists subnational public sector entities

8. Existing assets may be eligible for risk-sharing facilities or securitisation support.

9. Provided that an equity or quasi-equity investment in the same project is or has been insured by MIGA.

10. Only covers the instruments that are available to non-EU countries, i.e. to ACP, ALA and Mediterranean region countries.

11. As listed in columns I (least developed countries), II (other low-income countries) and III (lower-middle-income countries and territories) of the OECD's *DAC List of ODA Recipients*.

# ANNEX 5

# Case studies on selected infrastructure PPP transactions

........................................................................................................

This annex provides the following selection of case studies on infrastructure PPP transactions with the aim of highlighting key lessons about what makes a specific project succeed or fail.

**Water and sanitation**

Maynilad Water Services, Philippines

Dar es Salaam Water Distribution, Tanzania

Omdurman Water Treatment Plant, Sudan

Point Lisas Desalination Plant, Trinidad and Tobago

**Transport**

Kenya-Uganda Railways, Kenya and Uganda

Murtala Muhammed Airport Two, Nigeria

Panagarh-Palsit Highway Project, India

Cross-Harbour Tunnel, Hong Kong

**Energy**

Meghnaghat Power Project, Bangladesh

Tala Transmission Project, India

**Other**

National Referral Hospital, Lesotho

# Maynilad Water Services, Philippines

**Sector**

| | | |
|---|---|---|
| Transport | | Energy |
| Water and sanitation | X | Other |
| Sub-sector: Utility | | |

**Type of PPP**

| | | |
|---|---|---|
| Concession | X | BOO |
| BOT | | Lease contract |
| Management contract | | |

**Status**

| | | | |
|---|---|---|---|
| Financial close | | Construction | |
| Operations | | Cancelled | X |
| Distressed | | Other | |

| | |
|---|---|
| **Project concept** | The project involved the concession of Metro Manila's Metropolitan Waterworks and Sewerage System (MWSS). For the purposes of the project, the city was divided into two service areas: West Zone and East Zone, with populations of 6.3 million and 4.5 million respectively at the time of the bidding. While the East Zone concession has been a highly publicised success story, the failed West Zone concession, which is the focus of this case study, has received far less attention. The private company was responsible for the management, operation and maintenance of, and investment into, MWSS's West Zone service area. |
| **Procurement details** | The bidding procedure was structured in such a way that the interested consortia had to bid for both the East and West Zone concessions, but could only win one. In addition, each bidding consortium was required to cap foreign shareholding at 40 per cent. The bid criterion was the lowest tariff. Four pre-qualified bidders submitted proposals for both zones. While the consortium led by Ayala offered the lowest bid for both the East and West zones, it was granted the East Zone concession only. The West Zone concession was awarded to a consortium led by Benpres. |
| | The concession was granted for 25 years and the concessionaires took over in August 1997. However, the West Zone concession was terminated in 2005. The Philippine contracting entity was the Philippine Government. |

| Details of sponsor/ company | Maynilad Water Services, the private consortium that won the initial West Zone concession, was a partnership between the Philippine company Benpres (60%) and the French company Lyonnaise des Eaux, fully owned by Suez (40%). |
|---|---|
| Financing and funding structure for the project | The project was expected to cost US$4.5 billion (payments to the government accounted for US$846 million and the balance comprised investment commitments in physical assets).<br><br>The contract also contained a price adjustment mechanism that shared the exchange rate risk between the operators and customers. The operators were required to bear the costs of exchange rate fluctuations upfront, but could recover them from customers over the course of the concession. After the onset of the Asian financial crisis, the operators renegotiated the agreement and established a new mechanism called the Foreign Currency Differential Adjustment, which allowed full and immediate recovery of exchange rate losses from customers. |
| Other stakeholders | The project received multilateral support from the EIB and ADB. The EIB provided a loan of US$55 million and the ADB's total contribution was US$171 million. In addition, the IFC advised and assisted MWSS and the government on bidding procedures. |
| Review of the outcome of the project/VfM assessment | The concession was cancelled in 2005 after a long struggle by Maynilad with serious financial difficulties which arose due to the following factors: |

- Maynilad took over the West Zone services in August 2007, a month after the onset of the Asian financial crisis. As the concessions were structured in such a way that the West Zone concessionaire would assume most of the foreign currency debt of the former public utility, the severe depreciation of the Philippine peso (PHP) greatly increased Maynilad's debt burden.

- In the first two years of the concession, the revenues generated were not enough to cover the concession fee payments. By end-2000, the company managed to increase revenues sufficiently to cover the fee payments, but still did not have enough left over to cover the operational and capital expenditures.

- In the first year of operations, the El Niño phenomenon led to a 35 per cent reduction in water supply.

In terms of operational performance, the Maynilad consortium yielded mixed results:

- Access to piped water increased from 67 to 86 per cent in the West Zone, whereas the national urban average for water coverage grew only modestly. However, the coverage improvements in the East Zone were even more notable, jumping from 49 to 94 per cent.

- Sewerage coverage actually declined from 14 to 10 per cent in the West Zone, compared with a marginal increase from 7 to 10 per cent in the East Zone.

- By the end of 2005, the regulator had allowed tariff adjustments which meant that tariffs in both zones were pushed above pre-PPP levels. However, the tariff was 250 per cent of pre-PPP levels in the West Zone, much higher than the 23 per cent increase in the East Zone.

**Key lessons learned**

- The Maynilad case highlights the value of the competitive tendering process to the community. The eight tariff bids received by the government ranged from 26 to 70 per cent of the prevailing MWSS tariffs, and the winning bids were substantially below the rates charged by the public entity.

- It may be relevant to consider factors other than tariffs when setting the appropriate bidding criteria. While lower tariffs benefit consumers, they may have a detrimental effect on the environment. There is some justification for the notion that in a city like Manila, where there is much wastage of water, it might have been preferable to have a higher tariff structure. It might have been possible to achieve this if the companies had bid on the concession fees and accepted a predetermined tariff structure.

- The case study also highlights the extent to which the operational success of a project depends on the financial position of the consortium. Most of the coverage improvements in the West Zone came early on; progress stagnated after 2001 as Maynilad's financial situation deteriorated.

- The case study points to the fact that despite the presence of capable advisers, unintended consequences can arise from structuring the bidding process in a particular way. In this case, the structure mandated that there must be a separate concessionaire for each zone. Since the Ayala consortium provided the lowest bid for both zones, but could only be awarded the East Zone concession, customers in the West Zone ended up having to pay tariffs that were twice those in the East Zone. (Maynilad's winning bid was PHP4.97 compared with Ayala's winning bid of PHP2.32.) This difference in tariffs for customers in different parts of the city was a politically contentious issue. In addition, had Ayala's bid for the West Zone been accepted, the customers would have ended up facing a tariff of PHP2.51, almost half the tariff that resulted from Maynilad's winning bid.

- An independent regulatory body is essential for the appropriate monitoring and enforcement of PPP agreements. In the Manila case, it was decided that since no national water regulator existed, a regulatory office would be established within MWSS through the concession agreement. The office was to be managed by five members, including a chief regulator, all of whom were to report to the MWSS Board. This set-up not only raised questions about the independence of the regulatory office, but also prevented the agency from building on the skills of other regulatory undertakings of the Philippine Government.

**Key references**
- Asian Development Bank, 'Developing Best Practices for Promoting Private Sector Investment in Infrastructure – Water Supply' (2000).

- Chiplunkar, Anand, Ma. Christina Duenas and Mai Flor, 'Maynilad on the Mend: Rebidding Process Infuses New Life to a Struggling Concessionaire', Asian Development Bank (June 2008).

- Marin, P et al., *Public–private Partnerships for Urban Water Utilities: A Review of Experiences in Developing Countries*, World Bank (December 2008).

- World Bank, *Approaches to Private Participation in Water Services: A Toolkit* (2006).

# Dar es Salaam Water Distribution, Tanzania

**Sector**

| | | |
|---|---|---|
| Transport | | Energy |
| Water and sanitation | X | Other |
| Sub-sector: Water utility with sewerage | | |

**Type of PPP**

| | | | |
|---|---|---|---|
| Concession | | BOO | |
| BOT | | Lease contract | X |
| Management contract | | | |

**Status**

| | | | |
|---|---|---|---|
| Financial close | | Construction | |
| Operations | | Cancelled | X |
| Distressed | | Other | |

| | |
|---|---|
| **Project concept** | The project involved the leasing of Dar es Salaam's Water and Sewerage Authority's (DAWASA) infrastructure for water distribution to a private consortium for operation. The private company was responsible for billing, collecting revenues for the customers, making new connections and performing routine maintenance. Ownership of the infrastructure remained with DAWASA. |
| | Alongside the lease contract, there were two ancillary contracts to install or refurbish pumps at treatment plants, repair transmission mains, supply customer meters and manage 'delegated capital works'. |
| **Procurement details** | Initially, there were three bidders for the project – two French companies and the winning bidder, City Water. The bid criterion was that the contract would go to the company that would charge the lowest tariffs. The two French companies did not submit their final tender and therefore City Water was awarded the contract. |
| | The contract was awarded for a period of ten years, commencing 1 August 2003. However, it was terminated within two years of the start of operations. The Tanzanian contracting entity was the United Republic of Tanzania, represented by DAWASA. |
| | In addition to the main lease contract, ancillary contracts for priority works were also awarded to City Water; the works included refurbishment of pumps at treatment plants and repairs of transmission mains. |
| **Details of sponsor/ company** | The private consortium was led by Biwater, a UK-based water company with 26 a per cent share, together with the Tanzanian local company Super Doll Trailer Manufacturer Company (SDT) with 49 per cent and the German company H.P. Gauff Ingenieure GmbH Co. with 26 per cent. |

| | |
|---|---|
| **Financing and funding structure for the project** | US$8.5 million of investments was to be made in physical assets and payments to the government under the lease contract. Significant further investment was to be undertaken under the ancillary contracts. |
| **Other stakeholders** | The project received multilateral support from the World Bank, AfDB and EIB (total loan amount of US$140 million). DFID also provided support in the form of funding for a consultancy contract to publicise the project. |
| **Review of the outcome of the project/VfM assessment** | The contract was cancelled after two years, followed by complex arbitrations between the Government of Tanzania and City Water under the lease contract, and between the Government of Tanzania and Biwater Gauff (Tanzania) under international law. The lease contract arbitration was awarded in favour of the Government of Tanzania; Biwater's claims for damages under the UK-Tanzania Bilateral Investment Treaty were dismissed. |

City Water did not perform adequately. Project outcomes included:

- Revenue collection targets were not met, with City Water collecting less in revenues than its state-run predecessor. At the same time water bills rose.

- Improvements to the water distribution system (e.g. introduction of a new billing system) were not introduced.

- City Water stopped paying its monthly fee for leasing DAWASA's piping and other infrastructure in July 2004, less than a year into the contract.

- There were also internal management problems, with SDT refusing to put in more equity unless it was given a greater share in the management.

- City Water had a social obligation to contribute to a fund for first-time connections that was never created.

| | |
|---|---|
| **Key lessons learned** | - The City Water example highlights the difficulty of structuring, developing and implementing PPPs in developing countries, particularly in the water sector, where increasing water tariffs to improve the financial viability of projects can be very difficult, as this is a big political issue.[1] |

- One of City Water's primary contentions was that it was provided with flawed assumptions from DAWASA in structuring its financial model, which led to the drop in revenue collections. However, the Tanzanian Government claims that City Water submitted a poorly structured bid and had not anticipated the difficulties involved in the contract. The overall lesson is that given a difficult operating environment, considerable care and attention to detail needs to be applied in structuring a PPP transaction, with appropriate risk mitigation measures in place, to ensure financial viability and the success of the transaction.

- DAWASA's monitoring capacity was very poor – this was not underwritten by the donors that supported DAWASA in the project. The importance of a good monitoring capability so that preventive action can be taken in good time cannot be overemphasised.

- This case study also highlights the disadvantages of non-competitive bidding. With only City Water submitting a proposal at the final tender stage, there was no comparator to evaluate bids on a least-cost basis.

- Another emerging lesson is the problems associated with donor organisations providing support that is conditional on privatisation or higher levels of private sector participation.

- Related to the above two points is that the reality of the contract needs to be viewed in the light of available private expertise to successfully implement the contract. In the case of this contract, there were assessments that Biwater did not have previous experience of running a huge management operation and that the project team was inexperienced.

- Faced with upcoming elections in Tanzania, the government was also under pressure to 'resolve' this contract appropriately. Thus broader political issues can have a significant impact on the outcomes of a transaction.

**Key references**
- International Centre for Settlement of Investment Disputes (ICSID), Case No. Arb/05/22, Biwater Gauff (Tanzania) Ltd. (Claimant) versus United Republic of Tanzania (Respondent), Award document, Rendered by an Arbitral Tribunal Composed of Gary Born, Arbitrator Toby Landau Qc, Arbitrator, Bernard Hanotiau, President, Date of Dispatch to the Parties: 24 July 2008.

- http://www.guardian.co.uk/business/2007/aug/16/imf.internationalaidanddevelopment

- http://www.guardian.co.uk/politics/2005/may/25/uk.world

- http://www.guardian.co.uk/business/2008/jan/11/worldbank.tanzania

- http://www.guardian.co.uk/business/2008/jul/28/utilities.tanzania

- http://allafrica.com/stories/200902021411.html

# Omdurman Water Treatment Plant, Sudan

**Sector**

| | | | |
|---|---|---|---|
| Transport | | Energy | |
| Water and Sanitation | X | Other | |
| Sub-sector: Treatment plant | | | |

**Type of PPP**

| | | | |
|---|---|---|---|
| Concession | | BOO | |
| BOT | X | Lease contract | |
| Management contract | | | |

**Status**

| | | | |
|---|---|---|---|
| Financial close | | Construction | X |
| Operations | | Cancelled | |
| Distressed | | Other | |

| | |
|---|---|
| **Project concept** | The project involved the turnkey construction of the Omdurman water treatment plant and the optimisation of the works in Khartoum, Sudan. The private company was responsible for the construction of the plant, transmission mains, booster pump station, storage reservoirs and the implementation of an integrated network management system. |
| **Procurement details** | Instead of using a competitive and open bidding procedure, the government decided to award the contract through direct negotiation. As a result of this procedure, Biwater secured the contract.<br><br>The contract was awarded for a period of 13 years, commencing in March 2007. The Sudanese contracting entity was the Federal Government. |
| **Details of sponsor/ company** | Biwater is a UK-based water company that has designed and constructed water treatment plants, provided consultancy services and run water systems in over 90 countries. |
| **Financing and funding structure for the project** | US$120.7 million of investments in physical assets. The financing incorporates a significant grant component.<br>The project was supported by Dutch, Malaysian and South African lenders. |
| **Review of the outcome of the project/VfM assessment** | • The delivery of the project is still at an early stage. The treatment plant is currently under construction and is expected to be completed in 2010.<br>• The water treatment plant is projected to supply clean water to 1.5 million people and will be an important step towards the achievement of the Millennium Development Goals in Sudan. |

- The project was one of the four candidates shortlisted for the 'Sustainable Water Award' as a part of the 2009 Global Water Awards.

**Key lessons learned**

- For BOT contracts, it is particularly important to make sure that the public sector is equipped with the skills needed to maintain the project once the contract comes to an end. In the Omdurman case, incorporating an asset management program into the project is likely to improve the long-term sustainability of the project.

- The lack of transparency in the bidding process is a serious impediment to evaluating whether or not the process was a fair one. In a PPP scheme, such lack of transparency may also frustrate the owners of the losing contracts and make them reluctant to take part in any future bidding.

- Water projects generally require substantial support from international agencies, including credit enhancement and grants.

**Key references**

- Biwater, 'Case Study Details and Description'. http://www.biwater.com/casestudies/detail.aspx?id=61

- Global Water Awards, 'Omdurman Water Supply Optimisation Scheme, Sudan'. http://www.globalwaterawards.com/2009/sudan.html

- Water Technology, 'Omdurman Water Supply and Optimisation Scheme, Sudan'. http://www.water-technology.net/contractors/construction/biwater/press11.html

- World Bank, 'Private Participation in Infrastructure (PPI) Project Database', http://ppi.worldbank.org/

# Point Lisas Desalination Plant, Trinidad and Tobago

| Sector | | |
|---|---|---|
| Transport | | Energy |
| Water and sanitation | X | Other |
| Sub-sector: Utility | | |

| Type of PPP | | |
|---|---|---|
| Concession | | BOO X |
| BOT | | Lease contract |
| Management contract | | |

| Status | | |
|---|---|---|
| Financial close | | Construction |
| Operations | X | Cancelled |
| Distressed | | Other |

| | |
|---|---|
| **Project concept** | The project involves the financing, construction and operation of an 110,000 m³/day capacity desalination plant to service the industrial park at Point Lisas on the west coast of Trinidad. Trinidad's Water and Sewerage Authority (WASA) is the sole purchaser of the treated water. WASA on-sells most of the water to industries located in Point Lisas and pumps the excess into the potable supply. |
| **Procurement details** | In 1999, a selection committee acting on behalf of the government awarded the contract for the plant to a joint venture, the Desalination Company of Trinidad and Tobago (Desalcott). |
| | The contract was awarded for a period of 20 years. |
| **Details of sponsor/ company** | Desalcott is a joint venture between the local company Hafeez Karamath Engineering Services Ltd. (60%) and Ionics Inc. (40%), a US-based company specialising in desalination, water re-use and recycling, and industrial ultrapure water services. Ionics was bought by General Electric (GE) in 2004. |
| **Financing and funding structure for the project** | The estimated cost of the project is US$120 million. |
| **Other stakeholders** | Initially, Desalcott attempted to raise financing for the project through the Overseas Private Investment Corporation (OPIC), a US government agency that helps US businesses invest overseas. Eventually, OPIC dropped out of the project as a result of the difficulties securing government guarantees for the project. |

Review of the
outcome of the
project/VfM
assessment

- The plant became fully operational in 2002 and was subsequently expanded in 2004.

- Water from the plant accounts for more than 10 per cent of the total water production in the country.

- It is the largest seawater reverse osmosis system in the western hemisphere.

- The plant was originally designed for 50 per cent overall recovery, but by 2006 it was already operating at around 62 per cent recovery, with significantly lower than expected chemical consumption. The plant operates extremely reliably with an availability of over 95 per cent.

- Despite the positive operational performance, public opinion on the desalination plant has been mixed. The water supply system in Trinidad is quite unreliable and even though the plant has made significant improvements in the supply of water to the industrial area, there is a widespread conviction that WASA is giving foreign-owned companies preferential treatment at the expense of the general public.

- Desalcott's financial situation throughout the first five years of the project was also in contrast to the operational performance of the plant. After winning the contract, it faced significant challenges raising financing and had to start construction without a long-term financing agreement in place. Long-term finance was finally secured in 2003, but this required keeping a significant sum in a reserve account, which left little free cashflow to service Desalcott's obligations to Ionics.

- The project has also been subject to allegations of corruption. The probe began in 2002 after the new government promised an investigation into the contract entered into by the previous administration. It is claimed that the bid process was rigged and that payments to certain Trinidadian officials were made to ensure that Desalcott would win the contract. In 2006, Desalcott's executive chairman Hafeez Karamath was arrested on fraud charges and released on bail.

- There has also been at least one dispute between WASA and the plant owners regarding a proposed escalation in the wholesale price of the water produced. The underlying cause of the disagreement in 2006 was the government's refusal to allow an increase in tariffs according to the formula in its agreement with WASA.

**Key lessons learned**

- This case shows that operational success does not necessarily guarantee public support, and that it may be beneficial to undertake an effective public relations campaign to inform the general public of the benefits of the project. In the Point Lisas case, corruption allegations reinforced public perception that the project was undertaken to benefit foreign companies, as opposed to benefiting the general public.

- As the dispute between WASA and Desalcott shows, implementing PPPs in water sectors in developing countries may be particularly difficult, as increasing water tariffs is a highly political issue. The inability to increase tariffs may put a serious strain on the financial viability of the project.

- The government's reluctance to grant the tariff increase in its agreement with WASA also highlights the difficulty of enforcing the rule of law in some developing countries. The political risk of such violations is likely to deter international companies from taking part in further PPP projects.

- During the tender process, significant attention should be paid to the ability of the private sector to raise financing for the project. While Desalcott did manage to obtain a bridge loan from a local bank after winning the tender, its inability to lock in long-term financing put significant strain on its finances and threatened the viability of the project in its early stages.

**Key references**

- Brand, M, 'Reducing the Dependence of Water Supply Systems on Reliable Rainfall Patterns', Churchill Fellowship Report (January 2007).

- Chase, V, 'Report of the Caribbean Sub-Region', Water Forum of the Americas (September 2008).

- Global Water Intelligence, 'Making the most of a bad deal' (July 2004).

- Global Water Intelligence, 'Sitting on Your Hands' (July 2006).

- Papa, F and Wood, P, 'Investing in Water Infrastructure Projects', Boswell Capital (December 2008).

- *The Trinidad Guardian*, 'GE buys Ionics for US$1.1b', 2 December 2004. http://legacy.guardian.co.tt/archives/2004-12-04/bussguardian5.html

- *The Trinidad Guardian*, 'Karamath on $1m bail', 3 June 2006. http://legacy.guardian.co.tt/archives/2006-06-03/news1.html

- *The Trinidad Guardian*, 'Israeli escapes extradition to T&T', 18 April 2008. http://legacy.guardian.co.tt/archives/2008-04-18/news13.html

- The Water Resources Agency, 'National Report on Integrating the Management of Watersheds and Coastal Areas in Trinidad and Tobago', Ministry of the Environment (March 2001).

# Kenya-Uganda Railways, Kenya and Uganda

| Sector | | |
|---|---|---|
| Transport | X | Energy |
| Water and Sanitation | | Other |
| Sub-sector: Railways | | |

| Type of PPP | | |
|---|---|---|
| Concession | X | BOO |
| BOT | | Lease contract |
| Management contract | | |

| Status | | |
|---|---|---|
| Financial close | | Construction |
| Operations | $X^2$ | Cancelled |
| Distressed | | Other |

| | |
|---|---|
| **Project concept** | The project involves the concession of the railway networks in Kenya and Uganda in order to improve management, operation and financial performance. The concessionaire is responsible for the rehabilitation, operation and maintenance of the railways, which were previously run by the government (Kenya Railways Corporation and Uganda Railways Corporation), as well as providing freight services in both countries for the duration of the contract. The private company is also obliged to run passenger services in Kenya for at least five years. |
| **Procurement details** | While the two concessions for the Kenyan and Ugandan parts of the rail network are legally separate, the tendering process was undertaken jointly by the two governments and the contracts are substantially identical. The concession was awarded as a result of an international, competitive bidding process and the bid criterion was the highest price paid to the government. Two groups bid for the project and the Rift Valley Railways (RVR) Consortium was awarded the concession. The concession was granted for 25 years and the concessionaires took over in December 2006. The Kenyan and Ugandan contracting entities were the countries' two governments. |
| **Details of sponsor/ company** | When RVR was first awarded the concession, it was led by South Africa's Sheltam Rail Company (61%), with the remaining participants being Prime Fuels (Kenya, 15%), Comazar (South Africa, 10%), Mirambo Holding (Tanzania, 10%) and CDIO Institute for African Development Trust (South Africa, 4%). |

In order to overcome the substantial operational and legal difficulties the project has encountered since 2007, the private consortium has been restructured so that Sheltam owns 35 per cent of RVR, while TransCentury of Kenya has a share of 20 per cent and Centum Investment and Babcok and Brown Investment each control 10 per cent. In March 2009, ongoing difficulties forced the parties into a further restructuring of the consortium, whereby Sheltam's share will be diluted from 35 to 10 per cent, and the balance will be taken up by TransCentury and its partners.

<table>
<tr><td>Financing and funding structure for the project</td><td>The project was expected to cost US$404 million, of which US$4 million was made up of payments to the governments and the rest was for investment commitments in physical assets.<br><br>Of the US$404 million, US$111 million was estimated to be the cost for the first five years of the project, of which US$47 million was to be contributed by the consortium in the form of direct equity and internal cash generation. The balance was to be funded by loans from international organisations.<br><br>Overall, the debt-to-equity ratio of the project was envisaged to be about 70:30.</td></tr>
<tr><td>Other stakeholders</td><td>The original deal envisaged IFC and KfW providing loans worth US$32 million each.[3] IFC/DevCo and Canarail acted as advisors to the governments of Kenya and Uganda, respectively. PwC provided assistance to the concession operators. PIDG provided support to DevCo, and additional grants were also obtained through the Technical Assistance Facility. (These funds had not yet been disbursed when this report was written.) In addition, the World Bank provided PRGs of US$45 million for Kenya and US$10 million for Uganda.[4] An IDA credit for US$44 million was made to fund labour retrenchment in Kenya.</td></tr>
<tr><td>Review of the outcome of the project/VfM assessment</td><td>The Kenya-Uganda railway concession is a flagship transport sector PPP in East Africa and won Euromoney's Project Finance Africa Transport Deal of the Year award in 2006. Since then, the project has run into considerable operational and legal difficulties, which have seriously hampered its likelihood of success. Below is a brief list of the issues encountered so far:</td></tr>
</table>

- Contrary to the conditions governing the concession, the consortium has not undertaken any significant investment in structures or rolling stock. As a result, the US$64 million in loans from the IFC and KfW have not been released in full.

- The overall operational effectiveness of the project has also been debatable. For example in Uganda the percentage of freight from Mombasa has not increased as was envisaged. In Kenya, the freight traffic increases stipulated in the concession agreement were not met in the first 12 months of the concession; instead of increasing from 1.5 billion to 1.88 billion net tonne kilometres, freight traffic fell to 1.4 billion kilometres.

- There have also been allegations that the operator failed to make quarterly fee payments to the governments.

- Substantial funds need to be spent on labour retrenchment in both countries. While Kenya received donor funding in order to finance the retrenchment of 6,200 employees, the cost of retrenching 1,000 workers in Uganda was borne directly by the government.

- The Kenyan Government required the consortium to pay US$40 million as proof of investment capability and threatened the cancellation of the contract should the payment not be received on time. In January 2009, RVR won a court order blocking the termination of its contract, which was overturned by the High Court of Kenya. However, the parties seem to have reached an out of court settlement whereby RVR will continue to be the concessionaire in exchange for the dilution of Sheltam's shareholdings from 35 to 10 per cent.

**Key lessons learned**

- This case study highlights the importance of attracting competent private companies to ensure the successful implementation of the contract. In this case, there were concerns that Sheltam lacked the experience of running a complex railway network and therefore was not in a position to enhance cash flows sufficiently to generate the required investment resources. Indeed, the position of Sheltam as the lead investor became a serious impediment to the consortium's ability to raise further funds. In order to dilute Sheltam's share, an agreement was reached in March 2009 to change the terms of the contract and scrap the requirement that the consortium have a lead investor with a minimum shareholding of 35 per cent. While this may make it easier to raise funds, it is also bound to make it more difficult for the Kenyan and Ugandan governments to designate which member of the consortium should assume responsibility for performance.

- While the concessions for the Kenyan and Ugandan parts of the rail network were legally separate, in practice they were dependent on each other for operational and logistical reasons. The efficient implementation of the contract demanded that the two governments take similar positions on issues. As problems arose, the Ugandan Government took a more lenient approach, while the Kenyan Government was more eager to terminate the contract. This experience points to the political dimension of running a cross-border PPP contract and the difficulties that may arise in achieving co-operation between the governments involved.

- In addition, the governments faced increasing political pressure to build a new gauge railway from Mombasa to Uganda, which may have made them more eager to terminate the current concession contract rather than see it succeed. The lesson that can be learned from this is that larger political issues may influence the priorities of the parties involved and negatively impact on the outcome of a transaction.

**Key references**

- Babbar, Suman, 'Partial Risk Guarantees for Kenya-Uganda Joint Railway Concession', World Bank Transport Forum (March 2006).

- *Business Daily Africa*, 'Centum confident of RVR turn-around', 30 June 2008. http://www.bdafrica.com/index.php?Itemid=5812&id=8474&option=com_content&task=view

- *Business Daily Africa*, 'Parties seek to settle rail contract row', 3 April 2009. http://www.bdafrica.com/index.php?option=com_content&task=view&id=13839&Itemid=5838

- International Finance Corporation, 'Kenya Uganda Rail: Summary of Proposed Investment'. http://www.ifc.org/ifcext/spiwebsite1.nsf/DocsByUNIDForPrint/25625BF5269CEC80852571A900749445?opendocument

- Matsukawa, Tomoko and Odo Habeck, 'Review of Risk Mitigation Instruments for Infrastructure Financing and Recent Trends and Developments', World Bank (2007).

- *Railways Africa*, 'Rift Valley Concession', 13 February 2009. http://www.railwaysafrica.com/2009/02/rift-valley-concession/

- *The East African*, 'Railway investors told to cough up $50m as deal gets back on track', 14 November 2008. http://www.theeastafrican.co.ke/news/-/2558/491242/-/s0p0i1z/-/index.html

- *The East African*, 'RVR survives, but Sheltam loses lead investor role', 28 March 2009. http://www.theeastafrican.co.ke/news/-/2558/553914/-/rj1valz/-/index.html

- *The Independent*, 'RVR rail failure threatens main export route', 28 January 2009. http://www.independent.co.ug/index.php/business/business-news/54-business-news/535-rvr-rail-failure-threatens-main-export-route

- World Bank, 'Private Participation in Infrastructure Project Database'. http://ppi.worldbank.org/

# Murtala Muhammed Airport Two, Nigeria[5]

| Sector | | |
|---|---|---|
| Transport | X | Energy |
| Water and Sanitation | | Other |
| Sub-sector: Airports | | |

| Type of PPP | | |
|---|---|---|
| Concession | | BOO |
| BOT | X | Lease contract |
| Management contract | | |

| Status | | |
|---|---|---|
| Financial close | | Construction |
| Operations | X | Cancelled |
| Distressed | | Other |

| | |
|---|---|
| **Project concept** | The project involves the design, construction and operation of a new domestic terminal and ancillary facilities at the Murtala Muhammed Airport in Lagos, following the destruction of the old domestic terminal in a devastating fire in 2000. The new terminal, Murtala Muhammed Airport Two (MMA2), has a land area of 20,000m². The project comprises an airport terminal building, a multi-storey car park and an apron. |
| **Procurement details** | In 2003, the Ministry of Aviation advertised for bids for the project. Among the bidders were Royal Sanderton Ventures Limited and Bi-Courtney Limited. Initially, Sanderton was awarded the contract. However, after no significant construction had started six months after the signing of the contract, the government decided to revoke Sanderton's mandate and award the contract to Bi-Courtney after direct negotiations with the company.<br><br>The contract was awarded for a period of 35 years. The Nigerian contracting entity is the Federal Government. |
| **Details of sponsor/ company** | Bi-Courtney Limited, a Nigerian firm, is the parent company of Bi-Courtney Aviation Services Limited. |
| **Financing and funding structure for the project** | The estimated cost of the project is US$200 million of investments in physical assets. The project was part-financed by a loan of US$150 million from a consortium of six banks – Oceanic Bank International PLC, Zenith Bank PLC, GT Bank PLC, First Bank PLC, First City Monument Bank PLC and Access Bank PLC. |

| | |
|---|---|
| **Other stakeholders** | n/a |
| **Review of the outcome of the project/VfM assessment** | MMA2 is the first major BOT infrastructure project completed successfully by a Nigerian company. While the airport has been in operation since 2007, the project has encountered various difficulties: |

- After being awarded the contract, Bi-Courtney faced significant challenges in securing financing and had to start construction without a long-term financing agreement in place. The company proceeded with the project with support from Oceanic Bank International PLC. It was only in March 2007 that it secured a US$150 million part-financing agreement from a consortium of six banks for the completion of the project.

- On the operations side, there has been considerable difficulty convincing the airlines to move from the old terminal, General Aviation Terminal (GAT), to the new terminal, making it difficult for Bi-Courtney to start recovering its investment. The major attraction of GAT, which is run by the Federal Airports Authority of Nigeria (FAAN), is the lower cargo charges FAAN imposes on the airlines.

**Key lessons learned**

- The MMA2 case highlights the importance of having long-term financing available on favourable terms and conditions. While Bi-Courtney did manage to obtain financial support from a local bank after winning the contract, its inability to lock in long-term financing until 2007 appears to have put pressure on the project at its early stages.

- The initial bidding process also points to the importance of managing politicians' expectations and setting realistic goals regarding timelines. The initial winner had its contract revoked within six months of signing, as the government was unhappy that no significant construction had taken place by then. Revoking the contract and re-awarding it to a different company not only delayed the project, but also caused the private participants to suspect that the changes were the result of political rather than economic considerations.

- The MMA2 case also shows the difficulty of enforcing contractual agreements in some developing countries. While the contract contains a clause that assures that all scheduled domestic flights in and out of FAAN's airports in Lagos will operate from the new terminal during the concession period, FAAN continues to operate the old domestic terminal. In addition, by charging lower cargo fees, it provides an incentive for the airlines to continue their operations at GAT. The conflict of interest faced by the government has put significant pressure on the ability of the private sponsor to recover its investments and has thus placed the financial viability of the project at risk. This reluctance to abide by the terms of the contract will also deter private companies from taking part in future PPP projects.

**Key references**

- Airport Technology, 'Murtala Muhammed International Airport, Lagos, Nigeria'. http://www.airport-technology.com/projects/mutalamohammad

- Murtala Muhammed Airport Two website. http://www.mma2lagos.com/about.asp

- *Punch*, 'MMA2: Giving Nigerian aviation a new face', 18 March 2009. http://www.punchontheweb.com/Articl.aspx?theartic=Art20090318302690

- *The Guardian*, 'MMA2 under severe threat from GAT', 27 March 2009. http://www.ngrguardiannews.com/travels/article01//indexn 2_html?pdate=270309&ptitle=MMA2%20under%20severe%20 threat%20from%20GAT

- This Day Online, 'FG Revokes Lagos Airport Terminal Contract', 16 November 2004. http://www.thisdayonline.com/archive/2002/05/28/20020528news05.html

- World Bank, 'Private Participation in Infrastructure Project Database'. http://ppi.worldbank.org/

# Panagarh-Palsit Highway Project, India

## Sector

| | | | |
|---|---|---|---|
| Transport | X | Energy | |
| Water and Sanitation | | Other | |
| Sub-sector: Roads | | | |

## Type of PPP

| | | | |
|---|---|---|---|
| Concession | | BOO | |
| BOT | X | Lease contract | |
| Management contract | | | |

## Status

| | | | |
|---|---|---|---|
| Financial close | | Construction | |
| Operations | X | Cancelled | |
| Distressed | | Other | |

| | |
|---|---|
| **Project concept** | The project involves the design, construction, operation and maintenance of a 63km four-lane carriageway between Panaragh and Palsit, which forms part of the Delhi-Kolkata section of the Golden Quadrilateral Project, a highway scheme linking the major cities of India. |
| **Procurement details** | Initially, the National Highways Authority of India (NHAI) shortlisted six bids from a mix of international and domestic companies – Larsen & Toubro, Kvaerner Construction, Road Builder, IJM Berhard Corp, Reliance Industries and Gamuda-WCT. The bid criterion was the lowest annuity amount that would be paid semi-annually by the NHAI to the private sponsor.[6] However, the NHAI found that the annuity amount quoted by the lowest bidder was too high and decided to call for fresh bids from all six parties in a second round of bidding. |
| | Only Larsen & Toubro, Road Builder and Gamuda-WCT participated in the second round. Gamuda-WCT emerged as the lowest bidder and won the contract. |
| | The contract was awarded for a period of 15 years, and the agreement between NHAI and Gamuda-WCT was signed in November 2001. |
| **Details of sponsor/ company** | Gamuda-WCT is a joint venture between Gamuda (70%) and WCT (30%), two Malaysian engineering and construction companies. |
| **Financing and funding** | The project's estimated cost is US$69 million. The financing package has a debt-equity ratio of 2:1. As the annuity payments are |

| | |
|---|---|
| **structure for project** | considered to be a secure and stable source of funding by the financial community, annuity-based models tend to be financed with higher debt-equity ratios than typical toll-based projects. |
| **Other stakeholders** | Infrastructure Development Finance Company (IDFC) acted as financial advisor to NHAI. IDFC was established in 1997 as a specialised financial intermediary to lead private capital to commercially viable infrastructure projects in India. |
| **Review of the outcome of the project/VfM assessment** | This was one of the first projects undertaken under the BOT-Annuity framework. The construction phase of the project was completed in June 2005, five months behind schedule. The delay was caused by land availability issues and finalisation of change of scope orders. |

In 2008 the Comptroller and Auditor General of India (CAG) published its report on the BOT road projects undertaken by the NHAI. Its findings relating to the Panagarh-Palsit section are as follows:

- Cracks and patch repairs were found to be less than 5 per cent, implying good maintenance.

- 132 locations were test-checked for roughness. One location's roughness was within the 'desirable' level and the rest were 'acceptable' under the terms of the concession agreement.

- Deflection values in 10 out of 12 test-checked sections were more than the 'acceptable' level stipulated in the agreement, which indicates that the selected sections of the road are structurally weak and require overlay.

- In two out of the five test-checked pits, the combined thickness of wet mix macadam and granular sub-base layers did not comply with the specifications.

**Key lessons learned**

- Private sector participants taking part in toll-based road PPPs normally need to bear significant revenue risks. These risks are due to factors such as the difficulty in charging the public for road usage in low-income countries and the scarcity of demand forecasting for roads. Revenue risks create significant uncertainty as to the private sector's ability to recover its investments and may discourage participation in toll-based road PPPs. Under the annuity scheme used in this case, the payments from the government to the private participant were fixed at the beginning of the contract. Thus the annuity method removes the revenue risks for the private sector and makes the deal more appealing to the private sponsor.

- On the downside, the annuity payments reflect a transfer of revenue risk from the private sector to the government. If the government encounters difficulties setting up toll charges, the annuity payments may put strain on its budget.

- Considerable attention needs to be given to the way in which the PPP agreement is structured in order to ensure that the private participant has sufficient incentives to deliver the project on time. In the Panagarh-Palsit case, the agreement did not stipulate target dates for individual project milestones and impose penalties for the non-achievement of milestones. That said, under the annuity scheme, the NHAI does not begin paying the annuity until the road is constructed, which gives the private operator an incentive to complete the project on time.

**Key references**

- Booth, Kathleen LS, 'New Approaches to PPP in the Roads Sector: India's Annuity Concessions', PPP Resources, Institute for Public–private Partnerships (August 2006).

- Comptroller and Auditor General of India, 'Commercial Report No. PA 16' (2008).

- International Finance Corporation, 'Summary of Project Information: IDFC II'. http://www.ifc.org/ifcext/spiwebsite1.nsf/1ca07340e47a35cd85256efb00700cee/00A9D050480B168D85256FDA007CD68F

- *The Hindu Business Line*, 'Panagarh-Palsit Highway Project – Six Cos Shortlisted', 12 August 2000. http://www.hindu.com/businessline/2000/08/12/stories/091240nh.htm

- *The Hindu Business Line*, 'Panagarh-Palsit Project – Potholes on Annuity Approach Road', 30 January 2001. http://www.hindu.com/businessline/2001/01/30/stories/093040ra.htm

- *The Hindu Business Line*, 'Gamuda-WCT Set to Bag First NH Annuity Project', 2 March 2001. http://www.hinduonnet.com/businessline/2001/03/02/stories/090240nh.htm

- *The Hindu Business Line*, 'NHAI to Take Panagarh-Palsit Project to its Board Again', 8 May 2001. http://www.hindu.com/businessline/2001/05/08/stories/090840nh.htm

- *The Hindu Business Line*, 'Pact for Panagarh-Palsit Annuity Project Signed', 23 November 2001. http://www.hinduonnet.com/businessline/logistic/2001/11/23/stories/0923b051.htm

# Cross-Harbour Tunnel, Hong Kong

**Sector**

| | | | |
|---|---|---|---|
| Transport | X | Energy | |
| Water and Sanitation | | Other | |
| Sub-sector: Tunnel | | | |

**Type of PPP**

| | | | |
|---|---|---|---|
| Concession | | BOO | |
| BOT | X | Lease contract | |
| Management contract | | | |

**Status**

| | | | |
|---|---|---|---|
| Financial close | | Construction | |
| Operations | X | Cancelled | |
| Distressed | | Other | |

| | |
|---|---|
| **Project concept** | The project involved the construction, maintenance and operation of a tunnel connecting Kowloon to Hong Kong Island. The 1.9km Cross-Harbour Tunnel (CHT) was Hong Kong's first underwater tunnel and formed the first road connection between the Island and Kowloon. |
| **Procurement details** | The procurement was done via reverse tender, where the bids were evaluated on the basis of the lowest public sector subsidy required. On the basis of this criterion, the Cross-Harbour Tunnel Company Limited was awarded the contract. |
| | The contract was awarded for a period of 30 years, commencing in 1969. |
| **Details of sponsor/ company** | The company is a Hong Kong-based investment holding company with emphasis on transport infrastructures, such as tunnel operation, tunnel management, operation of driver training centres and operation of electronic toll collection systems. |
| **Financing and funding structure for the project** | The financing package had a debt-equity ratio of 64:36. Royalty payments were 12.5 per cent of operating receipts. |
| **Other stakeholders** | n/a |
| **Review of the outcome of the project/ VfM assessment** | • Construction work commenced in September 1969 and the tunnel became operational ahead of schedule in August 1972. It successfully reached the end of its 30-year concession period and its control was transferred to the government in 1999. |

- CHT is the first BOT project that did not need to be renegotiated and is widely considered to be a success story.

- Despite facing competition from an effective and cheap ferry service, the tunnel proved to be very popular. It began to make a profit four years after opening, and had repaid all debt by 1977.

- At the time of its construction, CHT was at the forefront of tunnel engineering. The harbour's deep waters made a conventional underground tunnel impractical, so engineers devised an estuarine tube tunnel that would sit on the seabed. It was constructed on dry land in concrete segments, sealed at the ends and towed out to sea, where it was sunk into a pre-dredged trench, backfilled and the water pumped out. At the time, it was the longest immersed tube tunnel ever constructed.

- Two more cross-harbour tunnels have been built since CHT became operational, but CHT continues to be the most popular, with more than half cross-harbour traffic passing through it.

- The success of the project is due to a number of factors, including:

  - The private company had the necessary skills to undertake the project, as evidenced by the use of the innovative method used to build it.

  - It was the first cross-harbour tunnel, and hence occupied strategically the best location for harbour crossing.

  - The concession period coincided with Hong Kong's rapid economic development.

**Key lessons learned**

- The CHT case highlights the importance of having strong political support for the successful completion of a project. The tunnel project involved massive effort by the government through the planning and implementation stages. The government started undertaking feasibility studies in the mid-1950s, more than ten years before the contract was awarded to CHT.

- The project also shows the importance of structuring a PPP transaction in an appropriate way, in order to attract capable private sponsors. The construction phase of the CHT project entailed significant engineering challenges and required the use of innovative building techniques to overcome them. Hence, it was vital for the project's success to have capable private sponsors on board.

- In the CHT case, the government did not provide any guarantees to the private participant regarding revenue generation. The government was able to transfer much of the operating risk to the private company by choosing a central location for the tunnel and hence ensuring a steady flow of traffic. This shows that the government does not necessarily have to provide direct guarantees to sweeten the deal for the private sector, and that alternative incentives can be found that make the deal attractive to the private participant without increasing the risk incurred by the government.

**Key references**   • Asian Development Bank, 'First Workshop on Economic Cooperation in Central Asia – Challenges and Opportunities in Transportation', Conference Papers and Proceedings (1999).

• Asian Development Bank, 'Developing Best Practices for Promoting Private Sector Investment in Infrastructure – Roads' (2001).

• Mak, C and Mo, S, 'Some Aspects of the PPP Approach to Transport Infrastructure Development in Hong Kong', Proceedings of the Conference on Public Private Partnerships – Opportunities and Challenges, Hong Kong (February 2005).

• Hong Kong Transport Department, 'Tunnels and Bridges'. http:// www.td.gov.hk/transport_in_hong_kong/tunnels_and_bridges/ index.htm

• Walker, C and Smith, A, 'Privatized Infrastructure: The BOT Approach', Thomas Telford, London (1995).

# Meghnaghat Power Project, Bangladesh

| Sector | | | |
|---|---|---|---|
| Transport | | Energy | X |
| Water and sanitation | | Other | |
| Sub-sector: Electricity generation | | | |

| Type of PPP | | | |
|---|---|---|---|
| Concession | | BOO | X |
| BOT | | Lease contract | |
| Management contract | | | |

| Status | | | |
|---|---|---|---|
| Financial close | | Construction | |
| Operations | X | Cancelled | |
| Distressed | | Other | |

| | |
|---|---|
| Project concept | The project entails the construction and operation of a 450-mega-watt, combined-cycle, gas-fired power station. The private company is responsible for building and operating the power plant. The ownership of the plant is also in the hands of the private sector. The project is subject to a Power Purchase Agreement (PPA) whereby the Bangladesh Power Development Board (BPDB) will take or pay for all electricity generated up to a plant load factor of 85 per cent. |
| Procurement details | As a result of a competitive bidding process, the contract was awarded to AES Meghnaghat Limited for a period of 22 years; it reached financial closure in April 2001. |
| Details of sponsor/ company | AES Meghnaghat Limited is a subsidiary of AES Corporation, a US-based power company with worldwide generation and distribution businesses. |
| | In 2003, as a result of issues in its American operations, AES sold its equity interest in Meghnaghat to Globeleq Ltd. The new project sponsor is owned by CDC Group, which itself is a fund of funds that is 100 per cent owned by the UK government. |
| Financing and funding structure for the project | The estimated cost of the project is US$300 million. The amount will be spent on investments in physical assets. |
| | The financing package consists of 27 per cent equity (injected by the private sponsor), and 73 per cent debt (obtained from multilateral organisations and commercial banks). |
| | The Infrastructure Development Company Limited, a government-owned financial institution, provided a US$80 million loan, the largest loan ever made by a Bangladeshi financial institution. |

| | |
|---|---|
| **Other stakeholders** | ADB provided a US$50 million loan and made available its PRG scheme for the first time for a US$70 million loan from a syndicate of commercial banks. ADB also mobilised its Complementary Financing Scheme (CFS) for a US$20 million loan package from commercial banks. |
| **Review of the outcome of the project/VfM assessment** | The project is the first ever competitively-bid power project supported by the private sector in Bangladesh. In addition, it was the first project to benefit from ADB's PRG and to obtain funding from IDCOL. It was awarded the Asia Power Deal of the Year award by *Project Finance Magazine* in 2001. |
| | The plant commenced commercial operations in November 2002. In a country where just over 30 per cent of the population has access to electricity and those that do often suffer from power outages, the Meghnaghat project has increased power reliability at a reasonable cost and is regarded internationally as a success story. |

**Key lessons learned**

- For many investors, doing business in developing countries involves significant political risks. In case of commercial banks, these risks often lead them to refrain from, or charge excessively for, making loans for projects in these countries. For such countries, obtaining partial guarantees, via schemes such as ADB's PRG, is vital to securing affordable funding from commercial financial institutions. In the Meghnaghat project, the private sponsor was able to secure US$70 million of funding from commercial banks (almost a quarter of the total cost of the project) by making use of such guarantee schemes.

- The Meghnaghat project also illustrates the benefits of having an agreement that governs the interaction between the private sponsor and the government entity buying the project's output (in this case the PPA that stipulates that BPDB must take or pay for all electricity generated up to a particular plant load factor). Such an agreement makes the government's willingness to pay less of an issue and thus makes the project more attractive to the private sector.

- This case also shows the benefits of having a competitive bidding process that is deemed to be fair.

**Key references**

- Asian Development Bank, 'Bangladesh: AES Meghnaghat Limited'. http://www.adb.org/Documents/Profiles/Cofinancing/banmeghna.asp

- Asian Development Bank, 'BAN: Meghnaghat Power Project'. http://pid.adb.org:8040/pid/PsView.htm?projNo=31909&seqNo=01&typeCd=4

- *The Bangladesh Observer*, '230 kV transmission to help provide stabilized power supply in city', 14 December 2004. http://bangladesh-web.com/view.php?hidRecord=29396

- Corral, Violeta P, 'ADB-Funded Power Projects in Bangladesh', Public Services International Research Unit, University of Greenwich (September 2007).

- *Project Finance Magazine*, 'Asia Power Deal of the Year 2001 – Meghnaghat and Haripur' (February 2002).

- World Bank and PPIAF, 'Public–private Partnership Units: Lessons for their Design and Use in Infrastructure' (October 2007).

- World Bank, 'Private Participation in Infrastructure (PPI) Project Database'. http://ppi.worldbank.org/

# Tala Transmission Project, India

**Sector**

| | | |
|---|---|---|
| Transport | Energy | X |
| Water and sanitation | Other | |
| Sub-sector: Electricity transmission | | |

**Type of PPP**

| | | |
|---|---|---|
| Concession | | BOO |
| BOT | X | Lease contract |
| Management contract | | |

**Status**

| | | |
|---|---|---|
| Financial close | | Construction |
| Operations | X | Cancelled |
| Distressed | | Other |

| | |
|---|---|
| **Project concept** | The project is to build, operate and maintain five 400kV and one 220kV double circuit electricity transmission lines of approximately 1,200km, with a maximum load capacity of about 3,000MW. The new transmission system has been undertaken in order to transmit power from the Tala Hydro Project in Bhutan and to carry surplus electricity from north-eastern India to the power-deficient northern Indian belt. |
| **Procurement details** | As a result of an international competitive bidding process, Tata Power was awarded the contract. The only other pre-qualified bidder was National Grid of the UK. |
| | The contract was awarded for a period of 30 years and reached financial closure in April 2004. The Indian contracting entity was the Federal Government. |
| **Details of sponsor/ company** | The project is undertaken by Tala-Delhi Transmission Limited (TDTL), a joint venture between Tata Power (which owns 51 per cent of TDTL) and the Government of India's Power Grid Corporation of India Limited (PGCIL), which owns 49 per cent of TDTL. |
| | Tata Power's main business is the generation, transmission and distribution of electricity. It is the country's largest private power utility. |
| **Financing and funding structure for the project** | The estimated cost of the project is US$269 million. The amount will be spent on investments in physical assets. The financing package consists of 30 per cent equity and 70 per cent debt. The State Bank of India and IDFC provided term loans. |

| | |
|---|---|
| **Other stakeholders** | The project received support from the IFC in the form of a US$75 million loan. ADB also extended a US$62.24 million private sector loan to the project. |
| **Review of the outcome of the project/VfM assessment** | • The Tala transmission project is India's first interstate transmission project undertaken via PPP.<br><br>• It is also the first BOT electricity transmission line outside Latin America and the Caribbean region.<br><br>• The construction phase was completed within schedule and the project has been operating commercially since September 2006. In its first year of operation, the transmission line was able to ensure the exchange of about 3,500 million units of surplus energy from the eastern to the northern regions. |
| **Key lessons learned** | • The Tala case highlights the importance of structuring the PPP transaction in an appropriate way so as to make the project more attractive to the private sector. In this particular example, interest from private parties was initially limited, as the returns on the project were deemed too low due to the tariff structure adopted by PGCIL. As a result of a petition filed by National Grid, the Central Electricity Regulatory Commission (CERC) of India decided to allow private transmission players a 10 per cent mark-up on equity over that offered to PGCIL, which raised the internal rate of return for the private participants by 4.5 per cent on the Tala project.<br><br>• The Tala case also points to the importance of having risk mitigation measures in the PPP structure to secure private sector interest. More specifically, as state electricity boards in India have poor payment records, it was necessary for PGCIL to assure 100 per cent payment to the private sponsor for transmitting power to the state boards, making the project financially viable for the private sector.<br><br>• While the presence of a government-owned shareholder may make it easier to overcome bureaucratic hurdles, it may make private investors worry about potential balance of power issues. In the Tala case, such concerns were mitigated by both the shareholding structure, which gave the majority stake to the private participant, and the way management positions are nominated.[7] |
| **Key references** | • Asian Development Bank, 'IND: Tala-Delhi Power Transmission', Project Information Documents. http://pid.adb.org/pid/PsView.htm?projNo=36915&seqNo=01&typeCd=4 |

- Expressindia.com, 'Power companies seek tariff review for entering transmission', 13 October 2000. http://www.expressindia.com/news/fe/daily/20001013/fec13074.html

- Indianexpress.com, 'First private power transmission project inaugurated', 21 June 2007. http://www.indianexpress.com/story-print/60417/

- International Finance Corporation, 'Summary of Project Information'. http://www.ifc.org/ifcext/spiwebsite1.nsf/DocsByUNIDForPrint/962AAA682C245B9385256D3900822CF9?opendocument

- Smith, Anthony, 'What Does it Take for PPP Energy Projects? Case Study: Tala Transmission Project in India' (November 2008).

- *The Economic Times*, 'TPC Bags First Pvt Transmission Project', 5 December 2001.

- *The Financial Express*, 'Unravelling the Transmission Tangle', 21 April 2009. http://www.financialexpress.com/news/unravelling-the-transmission-tangle/449182

- *The Hindu Business Line*, 'Power Transmission: Govt May Allow Higher Returns', 14 October 2000. http://www.hindu.com/businessline/2000/10/14/stories/141456a1.htm

- *The Hindu Business Line*, '10 pc Pre-tax Mark up for Pvt Players in Power Transmission', 25 June 2001. http://www.hindu.com/businessline/2001/06/25/stories/14255612.htm

- *The Hindu Business Line*, 'Tala Transmission Project Achieves Financial Closure', 10 January 2004. http://www.blonnet.com/2004/01/10/stories/2004011001770200.htm

- *The Times of India*, 'Powerlinks Gets First Tranche of Rs 21.5 cr', 18 May 2004. http://timesofindia.indiatimes.com/articleshow/682354.cms

- World Bank, 'Private Participation in Infrastructure Project Database'. http://ppi.worldbank.org/

# National Referral Hospital, Lesotho

| Sector | | |
|---|---|---|
| Transport | Energy | |
| Water and sanitation | Other | X |
| Sub-sector: Health | | |

| Type of PPP | | |
|---|---|---|
| Concession | BOO | |
| BOT | X | Lease contract |
| Management contract | | |

| Status | | |
|---|---|---|
| Financial close | Construction | X |
| Operations | Cancelled | |
| Distressed | Other | |

| | |
|---|---|
| **Project concept** | The project involves the replacement of Lesotho's main hospital, Queen Elizabeth II, an ageing facility with derelict infrastructure. The private company is responsible for designing, building, partially financing, fully maintaining and operating the new 390-bed public hospital. The project also features the refurbishment, upgrading and operation of three urban filter clinics. |
| **Procurement details** | The Government of Lesotho undertook an internationally competitive bidding process for the project and selected Tsepong (Pty) Limited, a consortium led by Netcare, as its preferred bidder. The PPP agreement between the government and the consortium was signed in October 2008, and the contract was awarded for a period of 18 years. |
| **Details of sponsor/ company** | The private consortium is led by Netcare (40%), a leading private healthcare provider that has operations in South Africa and the UK, and is listed on the Johannesburg Stock Exchange. The consortium also included Excel Health (20%), an investment company for Lesotho-based specialists and general practitioners (GPs); Afri'nnai (20%), an investment company for Bloemfontein-based specialists and GPs; D10 Investments (10%), the investment arm of the Lesotho Chamber of Commerce; and WIC (10%), a Basotho women's investment company. |
| **Financing and funding structure of the project** | The project is expected to cost US$100 million. 80 per cent of the capital costs will be provided by the government and the remaining 20 per cent will come from the private sector. |

The capital structure (excluding the government grant portion) has a debt-to-equity ratio of 85:15. All debt is provided by the Development Bank of Southern Africa. 10 per cent of the equity is in the form of pure equity (40 per cent provided by Netcare and 60 per cent by the remaining consortium members). Ninety per cent is in the form of loans (40 per cent of which is a Netcare shareholder loan and 60 per cent mezzanine loan/bridge finance from DBSA).

**Other stakeholders**
The IFC acted as lead transaction advisor to the Government of Lesotho. In addition, the government has requested a PRG from the World Bank in order to provide the consortium, at its expense, with partial coverage against the government's failing to make the unitary payment. The World Bank will also provide support to the government in the form of contract management.

The GPOBA provided a grant of US$6.25 million, payable over the first five years of the project, to augment the unitary payment made by the government.

**Review of the outcome of the project/VfM assessment**
- This is a pioneering social sector PPP in Africa, which if successful will have strong positive demonstration effects for future transactions.
- The delivery of the project is still at an early stage. Construction started in March 2009 and is expected to be completed in March 2011. The hospital is expected to open in September 2011.

- The project was structured in such a way that the operating costs of the new facility will be roughly equivalent to those at the existing referral hospital; it will thus fit in the government's affordability envelope.

- Since the cost of the services remains the same, patients will not need to pay extra to benefit from the higher level of medical services at the new hospital.

- The project won the 2008 Africa-investor Social Infrastructure Deal of the Year award. The prize was awarded because of the pioneering nature of the deal and its potential for replication in other African countries, as well as its commitment to supporting local businesses and communities.

**Key lessons learned**
- This case study highlights the importance of robust political support for attracting competent bidders to the project. The strong support provided by the Government of Lesotho at the highest level is likely to have had a positive signalling effect for potential bidders. As a result, the government was able to obtain the services of a consortium led by a healthcare provider with international experience of hospital PPP schemes in South Africa and the UK.

- The Lesotho hospital example also points to the possibility of structuring a financially attractive deal for the private sector without increasing the charges imposed on users. In less developed countries such as Lesotho, increases in costs of public services are bound to have a negative impact on welfare and may turn into a political issue. Keeping the charges for the new hospital the same as those at its predecessor was essential in getting strong support from the community.

- As the Lesotho project shows, a financial deal can also be made more attractive to the private sector by securing risk guarantees from various institutions against the failure of payments from the government. This is likely to be particularly important in countries with lower credit profiles.

- There is substantial involvement of local and regional stakeholders in this project, as evidenced by the participation of Lesotho-based GPs and specialists, the local Chamber of Commerce and a Basotho women's investment company in the winning consortium.

**Key references**

- Bizcommunity, 'Landmark public–private partnership (PPP) healthcare agreement signed' (2008). http://medical.bizcommunity.com/Article/196/157/30714.html

- International Finance Corporation, 'IFC Supports Landmark Hospital Project in Lesotho' (October 2008). http://www.ifc.org/ifcext/media.nsf/content/SelectedPressRelease?OpenDocument&UNID=C74EB741366D3CF1852574F100541E26

- International Finance Corporation, 'IFC Wins Social Infrastructure Deal of the Year Award' (January 2009). http://www.ifc.org/ifcext/media.nsf/Content/Lesotho_Hospital_Award_Dec08

- Keshav, Divyash, 'COMESA RIA Conference – Public–private Partnerships', Netcare (May 2009).

- Ramatlapeng, MK, 'Public Private Partnership for Replacing the National Referral Hospital', Ministry of Health and Social Welfare (October 2007).

- World Bank, GPOBA and IFC, 'World Bank-administered GPOBA Supports Award-winning Hospital Project in Lesotho' (February 2009). http://www.gpoba.org/documents/Lesotho_health_Feb09.pdf

- World Bank, ICA and PPIAF, 'Attracting Investors to African Public–private Partnerships: A Project Preparation Guide' (2009).

# Notes

1. In Tanzania, fewer than 100,000 households have access to safe water (in a population of 3.5 million) – implying that water tariffs can be a very sensitive issue.

2. The project was encountering difficulties, but the latest public information suggests that the contract has been renegotiated and the project is once again operational.

3. This figure includes a quasi-equity product in the form of an IFC C-loan of US$10 million.

4. The PRG could only be triggered as a result of a termination due to a breach of the concession agreements by either government.

5. In the World Bank/PPIAF project database, this project is referred to as 'Murtala Muhammed Terminal One'.

6. Annuity schemes refer to models in which the private participant receives a fixed and periodical payment (an 'annuity') from the government rather than relying on toll charges to recover its investment.

7. There are ten management positions in total: Tata Power and PGCIL nominate four each, and two additional members are appointed by the lenders.

Public–Private Partnerships Policy and Practice

# ANNEX 6

# Technical glossary

**Affermage**  A form of lease arrangement where fees paid to the lessor vary according to the amount of revenue collected from the facility, rather than being set at fixed levels. This contract design feature enables greater sharing of commercial risk between the lessee and lessor.

**BOT, BOO, DBO and DBFO**  Build-operate-transfer arrangements refer to PPPs where the private partner builds and operates a facility over the duration of the contract, at the conclusion of which it transfers the assets to the public authority. Under build-own-operate arrangements, the private partner instead retains ownership of the assets at the end of the contract. Design-build-operate and design-build-finance-operate are similar greenfield PPP models which do not specify asset ownership at the end of the contract.

**Concession PPPs**  Arrangements where revenue is raised directly from members of the public as user charges (e.g. toll fees) rather than having the government as the buyer. These arrangements involve significant demand risk transfer to the private operator. Concession PPPs may involve substantial new investment. However, in franchise PPPs, a subset of concessions may involve the rehabilitation or extension of existing state-owned assets.

**EPC contract**  A fixed price construction subcontract, bundling engineering, procurement and construction to deliver a facility by a given date. These contracts are designed to transfer the risk of time or cost overruns from the project company to the construction subcontractor.

**Financial close**  A project development milestone achieved when all contracts and financing agreements have been signed and all conditions required before the initial drawing of debt have been fulfilled.

**Guarantees**  Guarantees are frequently used to transfer certain defined risks to creditworthy guarantors and insurers that can more easily bear the risk. These aid efficient risk allocation and can reduce the cost of debt and equity finance. Two examples are political risk guarantees and credit guarantees.

| | |
|---|---|
| **Internal rate of return** | The 'true' interest yield expected from an investment expressed as an annualised percentage. Calculated as the discount rate that sets the net present value of expected future cash flows to zero. |
| **Key performance indicators** | Quantification of elements of business or project performance along financial and non-financial lines. KPIs are used to monitor performance along dimensions that provide snapshot information regarding performance against various goals important to stakeholders. |
| **Lease contract** | A private operator leases government-owned assets for a fee over a fixed term. Operational risk is transferred to the private party, but it is not responsible for any significant capital investment. |
| **Management contract** | A short-to-medium term performance-contingent contract covering certain operational functions of a public facility and also some management functions. The private party contributes working capital, but will not necessarily be involved in any significant investment programme. Operational risk remains with the government. Management contracts may provide a segue to further private involvement. However, it is rare for management contracts to involve sufficient risk transfer for them to be considered as PPPs. |

# Index